DIRECTORS AND DIRECTIONS

Also by John Russell Taylor

The Angry Theatre: New British Drama
Cinema Eye, Cinema Ear: Some Key Film-makers of the Sixties
The Rise and Fall of the Well-Made Play
The Second Wave: British Drama for the Seventies

Directors and Directions

CINEMA FOR THE SEVENTIES

John Russell Taylor

HILL AND WANG · NEW YORK
A division of Farrar, Straus and Giroux

First printing, 1975
Printed in the United States of America
Designed by Paula Wiener

Library of Congress Cataloging in Publication Data

Taylor, John Russell.
Directors and directions.

Filmography: p.
Bibliography: p.
1. Moving-picture producers and directors. 2. Moving-picture plays—History and criticism. I. Title.
PN1998.A2T39 791.43'0233'0922 75-2129
ISBN 0-8090-3901-X
ISBN 0-8090-1375-4 pbk.

FOR NICOLAS

Contents

DIRECTORS AND DIRECTIONS

Introduction

It is always a little alarming to be categorized—one feels as though one has been found out. Recently a student at the University of Southern California introduced himself and announced that for a term paper for another professor he was supposed to research the writings and informing beliefs of the critic of his choice; he had, it seemed, chosen me. What he asked me was mainly practical and factual, but I remember one observation of his. "The unconnectedness of things," he said; "that's one of your recurrent themes, isn't it? It comes up in all your books. Is it the cornerstone of your critical theory?" How does one answer a question like that? Probably the only sensible answer is: "I don't know. Is it?" But once the question had been planted in my mind I found myself wondering. Yes, by and large I think I do tend to see things as separate, or at least I tend to see people as separate, artists as separate. I am wary of movements, successions, influences, anything that might compromise the individual integrity of the artist beyond the point that he may himself have been willing or forced to compromise it.

That is the main reason why this book is a series of separate studies of individual filmmakers rather than an attempt to chart trends and the like. Obviously the practicalities of any film artist's given situation must have some bearing on what he has to express and, more immediately important, on how he is able to express it. But I do believe that a degree of toughness is a prerequisite of any artist's career; few have it easy all the way, so to do what they want to do and go where they want to go, and preserve their own integrity, they must be ready to struggle. If they cannot do so, it may be unfortunate for them and for us, but that is the rule of the game, particularly for those working in an art that is also an industry. The one thing that all the varied filmmakers I discuss have in common is the toughness and obstinacy to keep plugging away at what they want to do. Some of them have chosen to do it outside the industry, on a level of virtual amateurism that confers its own freedoms as well as imposing its own limitations. Andy Warhol and his group are the most evident, and ultimately most spectacularly successful, examples of this approach; they could do without the industry until such time as the industry began to wonder if it could do without them.

At the other end of the scale comes a filmmaker like Kubrick, who has never attempted to function outside the industry since he first managed to fight his way in. He is an astonishing case of someone who has regularly succeeded in doing what he wanted (only one film, *Spartacus,* he dismisses as involving merely his technical know-how), making the studios pay for it, and making them pleased with what they got for their money. This happy state of affairs has been achieved mainly, I think, because Kubrick is that little bit ahead of the public and the industry, but not so far that he loses touch with the practicalities of communicating with a wide popular audience. *2001* has been called "the most expensive underground film ever made," but mistakenly, it seems to me, in that it is essentially the work of a popularizer, a communicator, rather than a hermetic work that has somehow, by a historical accident, come to be accepted by an audience far wider than was ever envisaged for it. If anyone is not surprised by *2001*'s popular success, I am sure it is Kubrick.

Between these two, Warhol and Kubrick (the two Americans in this book), come all the rest. Not all of them are at the esoteric, noncommercial end of the spectrum. Nor is there any reason why they should be. Some original artists following their own bent come up with obscure and unapproachable work, because it is their nature to do so. But communication and approachability are not necessarily things that have to be forced on artists at the cost of their integrity—some, temperamentally, have the common touch, and enjoy speaking to a lot of nonspecialists. Chabrol is a glowing example of a popular artist who has to make no accommodations to be so. Ray naturally tends to be conservative, as far as one can judge of such things within so alien a culture, and given that in India he is addressing of necessity a relatively cultivated linguistic minority.

Anderson, Pasolini, and Jancsó—now there is an unlikely trio to launch any generalization about—have all managed to tread a thin line between a very private utterance and mass appeal. Of course, the concepts of mass appeal governing the various situations in which they find themselves are very different—one would be tempted to say that Pasolini could not afford to make an *Agnus Dei,* except that *Porcile* might be read as a film of the same kind that happened to work, and for that matter one would probably say that Lindsay Anderson could not afford to make *If . . .* had he not done so and brought it off. Certainly none of them has compromised his vision in any obvious way by keeping at least one foot in the camp of commerce. Even when Pasolini makes unashamedly popular films like *Il Decamerone* and *The Canterbury Tales,* it seems to be because he genuinely wants to, because he has an inner compulsion to do so, rather than that he has determined to sell out for the time being, *reculer,* at least, *pour mieux sauter.*

But each one of these filmmakers is living at a particular time, in a particular place and a particular context, whether of national or of world cinema. Does that not make a lot of difference to them and the means of expression they find? Of course, it must make some difference; they all have to be, in one way or another, children of their time. But in general I think not—I see the artist's battle as being primarily to keep himself to himself, to ignore (and be allowed to ignore) what is going on around him, to explore his own personality and preoccupations with a minimum of outside interference. All the filmmakers in this book have achieved that goal, with more or less struggle, more or less opposition along the way. It is interesting to relate Jancsó, say, to Hungarian culture at large, to the Hungarian national character (if such a thing exists), to the other filmmakers working under roughly the same conditions. But he is of interest, finally, by the degree to which he transcends all these incidentals and accidentals, however important in some very practical ways they may be to him. He is not being studied, in other words, because he is more or less representative of anything, but because he has succeeded in being unmistakably and with total justification himself. At the university, when I was reading English literature, we used to have a regular question requiring us to date miscellaneous pieces of verse. The proper way to do this was to look for general characteristics localizing each to a particular century, a particular half century, a particular movement in letters. Having done that, one could then hazard a guess as to the author. Which is fine with minor poets speaking the language of the tribe. But either you recognize Milton because he is Milton or you don't. The same feeling exactly applies to Jancsó, and to everyone else in this book.

"The unconnectedness of things." Possibly, but if so, it is because this corresponds to a real response I feel. I am, in effect, presenting my selection of the *auteurs* of this decade, with full recognition that many readers may disagree with me. I could instead be writing about trends and movements in world cinema or new developments in this or that national cinema; that too can be useful. But it is a matter of history rather than criticism, and though the two are necessarily conjoined, my own inclinations are more to the side of criticism. I could point out likely growing points—there has been a succession of national cinemas emerging with greater or lesser éclat, some of it justified, some, one cannot help feeling when the excitement has died down a bit, more the result of the critic's urge to discover something than the actual pressure of new treasures ripe for discovery. And nearly always, when you come down to it, the reason for the excitement is one extraordinary individual rather than a homogeneous group. I suppose the Hungarian cinema in the 1960's came as near as any to a group identity, but finally it was Jancsó who led the way to international recognition and Jancsó who remains retrospectively the only major figure, however distinctive some of the lesser figures around him in those years. Makavejev occupies much the same position in the Yugoslav cinema, and it is dangerous to pretend otherwise, to confuse genius with talent.

And one can trace the same sort of pattern in emergent cinema everywhere. As I remark in my chapter on Ray, he was expected to herald a discovery of the Indian cinema, and obviously he did not; we would be foolish to expect any different from the Egyptian cinema on the strength of Shadi Abdelsalam or from the Iranian on the strength of Daryush Mehrjui. Nagisa Oshima, dubious though I am about many of his films, is a harbinger of nothing but himself in the young Japanese cinema; Glauber Rocha, hostile though I feel toward nearly all his films, has a quality, limited, strange, and obsessive, that no one else of the much-vaunted Cinema Novo in Brazil can claim; and can we really expect anything of general import to emerge following the discovery of such films as—to pick examples at random—Krzysztof Zanussi's *Family Life* from Poland or Mike Leigh's *Bleak Moments* from Britain or Tomás Gutiérrez Alea's *Memories of Underdevelopment* from Cuba? At most they might, perhaps, signify that things were easier, more open for exceptional new talents than before in their particular areas of the world (not that, except in Cuba, they did or do), but if so, a favorable climate does not necessarily, as we know all too well in the cinema, bring forth a rich crop. The wind bloweth where it listeth, and resistance may be the condition most favorable to the development of certain talents—Jean-Marie Straub, for instance, must thrive on it, since he seems almost to go out of his way to provoke it.

In other words, whatever my general political convictions or my personal social choices, in the arts I believe unashamedly and perhaps naïvely in the individual artist doing his own individual thing. That, really, is what this book is about: that is the connection of things apparently unconnected. The health of the cinema may depend on the quality of its general everyday output; the economic viability of a national industry depends on a constant flow of acceptable products to satisfy a regular (if increasingly patchy) market. But ultimately an art exists to produce great works of art, works that transcend their time and place to achieve some sort of universality. I believe that every one of the filmmakers treated in this book has produced such a work at least once—otherwise, why should any of us pay more than passing attention to any of them? Of course, only posterity, that old reliable menace, can prove me right or wrong; the best I can hope to offer is a provisional report from the front.

Claude Chabrol

OF ALL THE FILMMAKERS WHO EMERGED IN THE FIRST FLUSH OF the French *nouvelle vague* during the mid-1950's, none has remained more of a problem to critics than Claude Chabrol: mainly because there seems to be no problem. All the rest who belonged to the group of writers on film gathered around the intellectual magazine *Cahiers du Cinéma* and its inspirer and spiritual leader, André Bazin, were immediately recognizable as, in conventional critical terms, "serious" filmmakers. The works of Godard, Truffaut, Rivette, and Rohmer were evidently artistic, intellectually serious, the sort of films it seemed natural to discuss in terms of the ideas they contained, the technical and formal advances and ambitions of the films. But Chabrol, after what seemed like a decent if relatively conservative start in the same direction with *Le Beau Serge* and *Les Cousins,* drifted off into films that were taken as eccentric, baroque, marginal, camp, and then, horror of horrors, downright and unashamedly commercial. By 1967, almost ten years after *Le Beau Serge,* he had made fourteen features and three sketches, and had been almost universally written off as a failure, one who had sadly declined from the high ideals he had apparently had before him at the start of his career—or, as some saw it, he had revealed himself in his true light as a base commercialist after temporarily leading critical opinion astray with a couple of films that seemed to betoken something more.

Then came *Les Biches,* and a hasty reevaluation process began. A revival of talent was postulated, or a change of heart, or the triumph of Chabrol's better artistic nature over the temptations of commercial success, or a last, late chance to make something "worthwhile" bravely taken by Chabrol to release himself from the commercial grind which maybe (for we could have misjudged him) he had accepted only as a painful necessity preventing him from doing better things. Yet, if we look back over Chabrol's career to date, all these formulations seem simplistic, because the films he has made do not *feel* like that: of all the New Wave directors, Chabrol seems to have been the most consistent in his style, his choice of subject matter, his attitude toward his medium. None of these has been in itself fashionable, though from time to time they have lent themselves to the production of something that could fit in with fashionable prejudices of the moment. But faced with Chabrol's by now considerable body of work, it is difficult to believe that he has really cared whether he was fashionable or unfashionable, whether he seemed commercial or highbrow, whether (except for the most obvious requirement of being able to remain a functioning filmmaker) his films succeeded or failed at the box office. He, at least, has always been true to his own vision, regardless of whether or not it was acceptable to the public (which in his earliest films it generally was not), to the critics (which in his middle films it certainly was not), or to both (which in his latest films it most gratifyingly has been—gratifyingly no doubt more to us than to Chabrol).

To observe the lines of consistency in Chabrol's progress it is necessary—first and foremost—to see the films, and to see them with an open mind. There are few directors whose films are more difficult to explain or evoke on paper, if only because so much of the overall effect turns on Chabrol's sheer hedonistic relish for the medium. Obvious enjoyment of a craft or an art (or both) is one of the hardest things to convey in words, and one tends to fall back on a flat statement that it is there, hoping one's readers will accept this, or make allowances by referring written statements constantly back to their own experience of the work under discussion. It is difficult, though, to overstress the importance of this enjoyment factor in Chabrol: some of his films become almost private jokes, made to amuse himself in some way obvious (as in *La Route de Corinthe*) or obscure (as in *La Ligne de Démarcation*). The private element does not, let me say at once, make these films any better, though it may give them a certain snob appeal for those who can congratulate themselves on getting the joke where others don't. But even when the film is unsuccessful, uncommunicative, perverse on account of its private nature, there is something lovable about a director who can still, within the bosom of the commercial cinema, approach his medium in this grandly throwaway fashion.

And Chabrol is above all, I think, a lovable director; one who provokes a sort of personal loyalty or antagonism in spectators, according to how they react to his temperament as displayed in his films. "Lovable" may seem a strange word to apply to a filmmaker who has concentrated almost exclusively on crime and violent, often perverse passions in his films; who is consciously and unconsciously the most prominent and gifted cinematic disciple of that splendid old monster Hitchcock. And yet the quality immediately apparent in Chabrol's most ruthless films is a certain irrepressible jollity and good nature; his view of life is, I believe, essentially comic, even if sometimes bitingly, one might say cruelly, comic. Possibly this is at the root of accusations of light-mindedness leveled against him from time to time. But solemnity and seriousness are not the same thing; and within Chabrol's comic vision of things lurks an attitude just as serious as and decidedly more realistic than that of many whose seriousness is more obtrusively worn on their sleeve.

Chabrol's seriousness is, in any case, of a different kind: a kind that can perhaps best be gauged by reference to his major published writing, the critical volume *Hitchcock,* which he wrote in collaboration with Eric Rohmer and published in 1957, shortly before he began work on his first film. Chabrol was born in Paris in 1930, but of country stock (his father was a pharmacist), the family coming from the village of Sardent, in the department of Creuse, where *Le Beau Serge* was made. He studied (rather desultorily) law and pharmacy. From 1953 until 1957 he was a regular contributor to *Cahiers du Cinéma,* under his own name and a couple of pseudonyms (Charles Eitel, Jean-Yves Goute), but he never worked as a full-time professional critic and seems to have had his sights set on a career as filmmaker if anything even more firmly and exclusively than his contemporaries Truffaut, Godard, and Rohmer. The Hitchcock book, therefore, though intended primarily as a study of Hitchcock and his works, and a key work in the development of modern intellectual attitudes toward Hitchcock (whether defined by acceptance of or opposition to the ideas contained in it), reads much more convincingly as a statement of faith and purpose by Chabrol of his own attitudes and beliefs. (It is known that Chabrol himself wrote the sections on Hitchcock's British period and on *Notorious* and *Stage Fright,* but the book is presented as a joint work, so presumably Charbrol accepts and endorses the opinions expressed in those sections he had least to do with, and the whole book seems vitally relevant to his subsequent work in the cinema and quite peripheral to Rohmer's.)

The phenomenon is not unfamiliar in criticism. One would read, say, D. H. Lawrence's *Studies in Classic American Literature* less for the light it may throw on Melville, Hawthorne, etc., than for the light it throws on Lawrence. Creators, creators-to-be, or creators *manqués* are obviously unreliable as critics, simply because they tend to work out their own problems in terms of their ostensible subject rather than considering in a more detailed fashion the artistic necessities under which the subjects labored. Often implied is a statement on "How I would have written that novel or made that film" rather than an examination of what the artist wanted to do and how far he succeeded in it. This is true in some measure of Chabrol's views on Hitchcock. The book turns on the discovery of certain recurrent themes, such as the notion of "exchange" (transfer of guilt, changing of roles, schematic modifications of personality), which Chabrol and Rohmer trace with some show of reason to Hitchcock's Roman Catholic upbringing and education, with its emphasis on confession and absolution. They also find recurrent formal patterns in Hitchcock's work: a tendency to introduce mirror scenes of ironic or tragic reversal, coupled scenes, patterns of events through which Hitchcock works on his audience's unconscious.

What Chabrol and Rohmer are a little vague about in their examination of Hitchcock is how far (supposing what they find in his work is actually there—and sometimes it isn't—and has the value they place on it—which is often arguable) Hitchcock himself is aware of these things, how far they are the result of conscious thought, conscious artistry, and how far they are quite unconscious on his part. Not, perhaps, that this is particularly important; certainly it is impossible to get any clear answer out of Hitchcock himself, who remains impishly noncommittal about the odder theories of his wilder followers. It is no doubt safe to say, though, that when the same themes and formal procedures recur in Chabrol's work they are that much more likely to be conscious, and that insofar as Chabrol tended to find in Hitchcock's films the reflection of his own tastes and preoccupations, the analysis of these in terms of Hitchcock's career must have turned into a kind of self-analysis that clarified Chabrol to Chabrol.

Evidence of this can be found even in *Le Beau Serge,* Chabrol's first film, which he was preparing at the same time that he was working on *Hitchcock.* I say "even in *Le Beau Serge*" because superficially Chabrol's beginnings were not very characteristic. *Le Beau Serge* is in many ways a little gauche and awkward: shot entirely on location, it seems at times to be aiming for a rough, rather Italian air of neo-realism (no one would think this of a later film like *Le Boucher,* also shot largely on location but formally very *soigné* and glossy). And the drama is allowed to move in the direction of melodrama in a manner that seems accidental, the result of a pressure of not quite controlled feeling rather than, as in Chabrol's later films, a deliberate choice of melodrama as the best way of conveying what he wants to in the tone in which he wants to convey it. In relation to a film like *Que la Bête Meure,* "melodrama" is simply a descriptive term, a definition of genre; in relation to *Le Beau Serge,* it is, for the first and last time in Chabrol's work, clearly derogatory.

But *Le Beau Serge* nevertheless, when examined more closely, does demonstrate in rudimentary form most of Chabrol's characteristic preoccupations. And, formally speaking, Robin Wood has rather convincingly related its structure to that discovered within *Shadow of a Doubt* in the Hitchcock book: a "rhyming" of scenes, so that there are two church scenes, two garage scenes, two dinner-table scenes, two murder attempts and so on. A similar pairing of scenes is evident in *Le Beau Serge* (more evident than in *Shadow of a Doubt,* since the analysis there is sometimes rather strained), and it hardly seems possible that this could have been accidental on Chabrol's part, at precisely that time in his working life.

Le Beau Serge is also in some ways more directly personal than Chabrol's other films, while in the indirect ways which are so telling later on, it is decidedly less personal. For although it cannot be said that there is any character in the film who seems specifically to represent Chabrol, the location of the film's action in Chabrol's family village has some significance, and taken in conjunction with *Les Cousins,* his next film, which is in certain respects a companion piece, it does seem to reflect directly on a question that had some importance for the young Chabrol: the relationship between town and country in the life of a provincial bourgeois whose allegiances and sympathies are divided between Paris and the older but not necessarily simpler ways of life in the provinces.

The story of *Le Beau Serge* (a Chabrol original) concerns the return of François, a village boy (Jean-Claude Brialy), to his home after some years' absence during which, in the eyes of his old friends and relatives, he has made good—even though he is now very ill, perhaps dying, from tuberculosis. He finds that his childhood friend Serge (Gérard Blain) has become an alcoholic after his wife has given birth to a stillborn Mongoloid, and is now getting worse and having an affair with an old flame while his wife awaits the birth of another child. Through various complications François tries to reclaim Serge and in the end apparently succeeds by dragging him back through the snow to witness the birth of the child, who is completely normal. There is a faint suggestion that, in so doing, François may have sacrificed his own chance of recovery. If this sounds melodramatic and even sentimental, it is, but the effect of the film is considerably more complex than one would imagine it could be from such a bald summary.

For one thing, there is a typical Chabrol ambiguity in the distribution of our sympathies. The story is constructed in such a way that we are with François, seeing things through his eyes right from the beginning. This ensures that we initially assume him to be the good guy, the person in the right whose judgments we accept without question. But gradually

Chabrol slips in doubts, complicates and upsets our allegiances. For François's apparent altruism may be selfish, a form of compensation through interference in other people's lives. On the most reasonable level it may be doubted whether his final intervention in Serge's life makes that much difference: he would have learned anyway that his wife had given birth to a healthy child. And it is made clear that François's other interventions are not always for the best. The shame and sense of rivalry that his return engenders in Serge make his drinking worse; and the naïve misconstructions François puts on relations in the village as he sees them (between Serge and his wife, Yvonne; between Serge's mistress, Marie, and her supposed father) may be taken as destructive and leading to disaster or near disaster. We begin by seeing François as a hero of Christian self-sacrifice and end by wondering whether he has done any good at all, or merely succeeded in partially retrieving some of the harm he had done first.

These points are in fact rather important in considering what precisely Chabrol does believe in. If we choose to construe his films as social criticism, what is the position from which the criticism is launched? *Le Beau Serge* may be a key work here, in that it offers the only place in Chabrol's films which seems to embody a definite affirmation: the ending, which looks and sounds very Christian, and specifically very Catholic. Chabrol himself accepts this, remarking wryly that *Le Beau Serge* "de-Christianized" him by letting him get the vestiges of Catholicism out of his system once and for all. This appears to be true, though it is equally safe to say, as Chabrol and Rohmer say of Hitchcock, that no one brought up in that tradition ever throws it off entirely. And whether or not Chabrol is now a practicing Catholic, and though none of his films since *Le Beau Serge* has anything that could be read as an affirmation of faith, there are elements that clearly stem from a Christian view of things—in particular, I would say, Chabrol's preoccupation with evil, understood as such, not as the manifestation of some kind of psychological upset or the result of social and economic pressures. In Chabrol's world, evil is a reality, beyond pat explanation.

One cannot be so sure about good. Even François in *Le*

Beau Serge cannot be taken as an uncomplicatedly good person, let alone a good element in the lives of others. And it is hard in any of Chabrol's late films to find anyone who is clearly, heroically virtuous. Chabrol has indeed been tagged (like Hitchcock, again) as a cynic, turning his destructive gaze on the world at large and finding no positive values in it. While it is true that his view of the world contains some bleak spots and very few if any brighter-than-bright, he can best be regarded, from the standpoint of ideas, not as a destroyer but as a realistic critic, painting bourgeois society as he sees it, corrosively, and yet able to summon up a wide range of human sympathy. He enjoys even his monsters, and makes us sympathize with his less-than-monsters, his well-intentioned but humanly flawed characters. And yet, again like Hitchcock, he is a master at directing his audiences even more than he directs his films, making us sympathize with murderers by seeing things from their point of view, seeing how (but for the grace of God, I was about to write—significantly?) we could well find ourselves in their precise situation. One could say that Chabrol's world view is pessimistic, in that good seldom triumphs, innocence is contaminated, bad tends always to worse. But it does not come out like that in the films. One would not accuse him of anything as touchy as compassion; but whatever the horrors he observes, his good humor remains intact and indestructible.

Les Cousins (1958), his first mature film, brings all these points home. It is in a sense a reverse image of *Le Beau Serge,* featuring the same two actors in reverse roles: Gérard Blain as the serious, well-meaning innocent who comes to Paris to study, and Jean-Claude Brialy as the sophisticated, decadent cousin with whom he stays and whose life style, in a certain sense, he tries to influence and change. It is as though a sober Serge should come to town to redeem a loose-living François. But if we accepted this as the basic pattern of the film's intention, we would surely have to suppose also that Chabrol was deeply cynical in his attitude, for Charles's virtue is singularly unrewarded: not only does he fail his examinations, despite all his hard work, while his pleasure-loving cousin Paul passes, but he loses the girl he is attached to (and whom he ought by rights to be redeeming from sleeping around) to Paul, and in the end is accidentally killed by Paul. So much, we might say, for virtue. But Chabrol does not present things that way. Again we have a gradual shift of sympathy: we come little by little to see Charles as gauche, limited, priggish, and Paul, despite his often far from admirable behavior, as a more genuinely suffering human being, with a charm and gaiety and gift for human affection which Charles is far from sharing.

Also, Chabrol complicates the apparently simple situation. His screenplay (dialogue by Paul Gégauff, a college friend and his script collaborator on several of his early films) brings Paul and Charles into a sort of *huis clos* situation with Florence, the girl for whose affections they are competing: when Florence has moved in with Paul, Charles continues to live in the flat also, and what might be a competitive situation of black and white, bad and good, becomes a complex, richly ironical drama of enclosed human relationships. And then both Charles and Paul are provided with alter egos, or rather perhaps figures who carry their leading characteristics to extremes. For Charles it is an idealistic, scholarly bookseller who constantly urges him to work, seriousness, high moral purpose; for Paul it is Clovis, a satanic figure of pure unexplained evil who constantly leads him toward decadent excess and, as it were, stage-manages the relations of the cousins and their girl friend.

Chabrol the director goes several stages further than Chabrol the writer. It is he, above all, who sets the tone of the film, and that is very curious. The visual style is extremely glossy, tending toward *outré,* almost expressionistic effects of lighting. And Chabrol's editing technique, in sharp contrast to that which Godard and Truffaut were using in the films they made around that time, is deliberately smooth and traditional, along the lines of classic Hollywood theory: transitions are glided over as unnoticeably as possible, both from shot to shot and from sequence to sequence. There is, in fact, only one shock cut in the whole film, when we cut from a second, dizzying pan shot around Charles's room in the flat to the outside of the examination hall, where he learns that he has failed his examinations. (This picks up an earlier pan around the room which ends in a smooth change of shot as the camera goes out of focus and then comes into focus again on another part of the flat.) Elsewhere, everything is kept flowing, so that we have a sense of the continuous, inevitable evolution of a pattern toward its preordained conclusions. Even the obsessive neatness of the film's composition, its use of recurrent patterns of shots and successions of sequences, falls into place: Chabrol is a formalist in one sense—he is extremely aware of form and makes us aware of it—but all his formalizing is strictly functional, tending toward a greater, more complex expressiveness rather than toward sterile aestheticism.

The test of this is to be found in the strong emotional effect the film has, which is greater than anything that would be rationally applicable, and creeps up on one by slow, mystifying stages. Why, for instance, is Paul's big monologue near the end so affecting—a recitation in a Nazi uniform cap, to the strains of the Liebestod from Wagner's *Tristan und Isolde*—when it might well have seemed merely a baroque extravagance? Because we feel it to be the expression, for all its histrionic effect, of a genuine anguish, and because Chabrol has built up in Paul a complex of character indications—his fascination with the external trappings of Nazism (though Clovis is the actual Nazi), his love for the darkness rather than the light, his suppressed emotionalism (which it is permissible to think has something to do with a disguised homosexual feeling for Charles)—which have all come together in a sequence richly layered and textured with meanings, only a few of which are on the surface, and even fewer in the script skeleton that Chabrol has here given flesh.

Though there seems to me to be a clear line of consistency running through everything that Chabrol has done, it would be foolish to maintain that everything therefore has equal weight or equal importance in his work as a whole. *Les Cousins* was a success, critical and commercial, and for the next six films Chabrol has clearly engaged in activity common enough in the modern cinema: filling in the blank check. A combination of commercial success and critical fashionableness will often ensure a filmmaker relative freedom, on the strength of one film, to make several more very much as he wants, for various producers eager at the moment to sign him up for new projects. Of course it is a gamble whether they or the public will be pleased with what he does, but the situation might just be retrieved if one of the group achieves success enough to start the cycle over again. Chabrol would seem to have had his own way with his next six films, but none of them matched either the commercial or the critical success of *Les Cousins,* and this meant that after *Landru* (1962) he had to take whatever work was offered, thereby bringing upon himself (quite unjustifiably, if one looks at the films he made at this time) the accusation of having sold out, become a commercial hack, and so on. Then in 1968 came *Les Biches* and he was restored to favor.

Let us look first at the films he made while filling in the blank check. Some of them, like *Les Godelureaux* (1960) and *L'Oeil du Malin* (1962), I consider to be among his best; others, like *Les Bonnes Femmes* (1960), I do not care for greatly. Others, like *A Double Tour* (1959), the first film he made after *Les Cousins,* come betwixt and between, being quite deliberately much ado about nothing, but on their own level entertaining. Obviously, *A Double Tour* is intended, as much as anything, to be an essay in technical virtuosity, applied to the thinnest, most transparent fragment of a whodunit plot: the beautiful artist who lives next to a family of neurotics and eccentrics deep in the French countryside is murdered, and we are asked, with no great show of enthusiasm, to guess who was responsible. Was it one of the parents—the father whose mistress she was, or the hysterically bitter mother—or the mother-fixated son, or the father-fixated daughter, or even, conceivably, the daughter's slovenly, ill-mannered fiancé? In a household where everyone spies on everyone else all the time and tantrums around bed or dinner table are the normal small change of social intercourse, it could be anyone, and it hardly matters which. What matters is the sheer splendor of Henri Decae's color photography: the romantic ramble of father and artist through Pre-Raphaelite woods and a blazing field of poppies that would have delighted Renoir is unforgettable; and the mysterious, shadowy interiors of the artist's house, full of colored glass and tanks of exotic fish, are a setting that Chabrol obviously enjoys enormously and explores with a glee beyond its purely dramatic value.

But if *A Double Tour* is primarily a film of glamorous surfaces, it does nevertheless represent a number of unmistakably Chabrolian interests. The film is rigorously constructed on a symmetrical pattern all within one day (the observation of unity of time is firmly insisted on). There are two matching flashbacks, both to something that happened during the day under consideration, so that the film opens with an "objective" narrative, moves back over time, now seen subjectively through the eyes of the father as he describes the morning he has spent with his mistress, Léda; then the central sequence, around the dinner table (meal sequences are prominently featured in Chabrol films), at which the news of Léda's murder is broken; then the flashback to the son of the house explaining how he did it; then a final, "objective" episode in which he leaves to give himself up.

The story appears at first glance to be a whodunit, but the detective element in the audience's response is slight, and the puzzle is rapidly resolved. It matters little which member of the family murdered the beautiful outsider, Léda, because the whole film is angled so as to suggest their communal responsibility. It has been suggested that Léda herself represents a positive quality in the film's scheme of ideas, that she is the embodiment of a quality—freedom of spirit—which Chabrol finds, and wishes us to find, admirable. But this premise is difficult to maintain faced with the film itself, which seems too light in tone (I cannot find in it the harsh, despairing quality some critics see) and in any case uses the character of Léda, whom we hardly see objectively at all, as a catalyst to trigger a crisis within the family which seems to be Chabrol's central interest and concern. Much the same might be said of the other "outsider," the son's friend Laszlo (played by Jean-Paul Belmondo). He too is a free spirit, but he seems to be put into the film mainly in a mood of fun, a reflection of the sort of character he was playing in Godard's almost exactly contemporary *A Bout de Souffle* (on which Chabrol was formally credited as technical adviser), just as the choppy, hand-held way in which the character's arrival in the film is handled seems to be a reference to, or even a parody of, the New Wave procedures so far from Chabrol's own habitual practice. A joke, in fact, like so much in Chabrol's work over which critics have made heavy weather: if we discount the element of sheer fun in even Chabrol's most overtly serious films, we lose much of their essential quality and flavor.

What I do not like about *Les Bonnes Femmes,* I suspect, is its lack of this element of fun (by saying this, I realize, I am probably betraying my prejudice quite as much as those critics I have just been accusing of valuing the element of fun too little). It is the nearest Chabrol has come to soap opera, and the nearest to being pretentious, something from which he normally shies away like the plague. *Les Bonnes Femmes* tells the story of four girls working in the same shop in Paris, the main thing they have in common being their variously unsatisfactory relations with men: Jane, the most "animal" of them, the readiest for a bit of fun on the side, despite her engagement to a soldier; Rita, destined to marry an awful, stuffy, highly respectable shopkeeper's son; Ginette, whose aspirations lead her in the direction of show business and the pathetic fantasy revealed by her music-hall appearance disguised as a glamorous Italian singer; and Jacqueline, who aims highest and does worst, by thinking she has discovered true, idealistic romantic love in the arms of a motorcyclist, and finds violent death instead. The intention of the film is almost universally gloomy, and schematically so: the men in the girls' lives are hardly more than ciphers; the girls themselves are only elementarily characterized; and the alternation of episodes in which their individual histories are pursued with sequences (again symmetrically placed) in which we see them all together in the shop or, successively, in visits to a zoo and a swimming pool, becomes gratingly self-conscious. Sheer Chabrol devilment is reserved for the cashier, Mme Louise, with the *fétiche* she is asked to show, which proves to be a handkerchief soaked in the blood of an executed murderer. But, by and large, *Les Bonnes Femmes* is distressingly un-Chabrolian, solemn on matters that he usually treats with more depth by way of comic-ironic indirection. Possibly, as some critics aver, with this key Chabrol unlocks his heart. But, if so, the less Chabrol he.

His next film, *Les Godelureaux,* seems far more likely to provide a key to his heart, and his mind. Indeed, it and its successor, *L'Oeil du Malin,* are essential to the understanding of his later means and meanings, whereas *Les Bonnes Femmes* in the perspective of his subsequent films seems more and more of an aberration. If that film suffers from too much apparent "heart," *Les Godelureaux* suffered, in the eyes of the public and the critics of the time, from too little. It was widely accused of coldness and sterility, and Chabrol himself later, when asked to explain its lack of success, said: "Its subject was uselessness, and it failed because it became in itself too useless." All the same, *Les Godelureaux* has a hard, dry glitter that is appealing, a biting sense of the ridiculous which leaves none of the characters unscathed and gives us no one with whom we may readily or completely sympathize, but which seems to be a valid, if not very warming, way of looking at the world.

"The world," it should be said, is approached only by way of extreme formal abstraction. The film's world is almost totally enclosed; the subject and its treatment are reminiscent of Laclos's novel *Les Liaisons Dangereuses* or of the Bresson film *Les Dames du Bois de Boulogne,* to which direct reference is made in the dialogue, when Ronald (Jean-Claude Brialy) uses exactly the same line as Hélène (Maria Casarès) in the Bresson film: *"Je me vengerai."* Looked at another way, the film can be taken as a transposition of the subject of *Les Cousins* into another, less realistic mode, simplifying, concentrating, and purifying it to the limits of abstraction. Arthur, the young man on whom Ronald decides he must be avenged (for a schoolboy prank involving the moving of his car), is like Charles in *Les Cousins,* mild, solemn, innocent, while Ronald is like Paul (and is played by the same actor), though here a Paul whose unconscious destructiveness has become conscious, who has absorbed thoroughly the teachings of Clovis and made them his own. It is his idea to destroy Arthur by using a girl to lead him into romantic involvement and then let him down with a sharp shock (much the same as

Hélène's plan for her departing lover in *Les Dames du Bois de Boulogne*), whereas in *Les Cousins* the Charles/Florence situation may have been deliberately engineered by Clovis but seemed to be largely unconscious on Paul's part, he being manipulated by Clovis almost as much as Charles or Florence.

In *Les Godelureaux* nearly all the ambiguities of *Les Cousins* are ironed out, and the intrigue is unrolled in terms of a dry, rather inhuman *comédie grinçante*. And yet, somehow, Chabrol's great good humor comes through. A lot of Ronald's devices—like the terrible charity concert he organizes at the behest of his aunt and disrupts with a succession of increasingly outrageous turns, from a simple dance by some children, through a slinky, sexy dance by a professional, to a risqué song delivered with an outrageous barrage of nods and winks by a valiant and energetic old lady—are in fact very funny, though Chabrol nearly always continues them beyond the laugh just far enough to leave a bitter aftertaste. Cynical I would hardly say *Les Godelureaux* is; rather, it seems to mirror the anguish of someone whose view of the world is at once humorous and pessimistic, someone who has to laugh, if savagely, lest he cry. The overt emotionalism of some sections of *Les Bonnes Femmes* is irredeemably unmoving; the overt hardness and lack of emotion in *Les Godelureaux,* which forbid us to sympathize with the ineffectual Arthur, or even to feel some pang when Ronald's elaborate schemes for revenge at last go awry, somehow move and disturb.

Perhaps it has something to do with Chabrol's fascination with the virtually unmotivated evil of Ronald (for such it has become, in comparison with the half-formulated malice of Paul). Ronald is one of those beast characters, going back to Clovis in *Les Cousins,* through the motorcyclist in *Les Bonnes Femmes,* and on to the hit-and-run driver in *Que la Bête Meure* and beyond, whom Chabrol presents to us almost sympathetically, invites us to understand and even admire if not excuse. Obvious stalking horses in Hitchcock's work are Bruno in *Strangers on a Train* (far more interesting and appealing than the negative "hero") and the killer in *Frenzy,* through whose eyes we see much of the action and with whom we are pushed to side far more than with the surly and uninteresting innocent man victimized on his account. We, the audience, are led toward identification with these figures, and so toward a sort of understanding. Whether we like Ronald or not, we we find ourselves siding with him; and in *L'Oeil du Malin* the villain of the piece is clearly set up as the "hero"; we become the evil eye through which the good characters are surveyed. We assist at each stage in their destruction.

The action of *L'Oeil du Malin* is even more tightly enclosed than that of *Les Godelureaux:* in effect, it is a three-character piece. A failed writer of outward charm and angelic appearance (Jacques Charrier) is sent to Germany to write about a famous author. He finds in the author and his wife an apparently ideal, devoted couple, and at once begins to plot the downfall of their bliss. Motivation can be invented: there are elements of envy over Hartman's success, desire for his wife. But more than anything else it seems to be a spirit of pure destructiveness, evil if you like, which drives Albin to worry at any happy, settled situation until he finds some flaw in it that he can work on. In this case he convinces himself that there must be a worm in the bud of the Hartmans' marriage, and soon finds it—the wife, Hélène, has a lover in Munich. Albin follows her, photographs them, tries to blackmail her into going away with him on the strength of the photographs, then, failing there, gives them to Hartman. Hartman kills Hélène and then gives himself up to the police (like the son in *A Double Tour*). Albin is left desolate, not so much from a sense of guilt about what he has done to people who treated him with nothing but kindness, but rather because now, with nothing left to hate, he feels lost and alone, his life is without focus. He has played Iago, and now he needs another Othello, another Desdemona to make him feel truly alive.

The management of the plot is again very schematic, but not incompatible with a certain kind of realism, if only because everything in it is deliberately arranged by Albin, almost as a literary exercise (there are points of contact here between both *Les Godelureaux* and *L'Oeil du Malin* and Rohmer's far later *Le Genou de Claire*), and we see everything through the eyes of the malign schemer, who informs us directly in the opening narration that as a writer he now finds himself incapable of writing anything but this story. The only part of the action he does not control or arrange is the actual infidelity of Hélène, which seems therefore (especially in the context of the Hartmans' evident, and genuine, mutual devotion) too convenient and arbitrary. But even here the curse is taken off to some extent by the intensity of Albin's desire that it should be so; we feel that he has somehow made it come about, just as we feel in *Rear Window* that the observer is somehow responsible for what he observes, that he is also wishing it to be so. Otherwise, Albin is completely the *meneur du jeu,* and Chabrol's dramatic management of his character, so that we understand everything while nothing is explained, is one of his masterly coups in audience direction.

It is significant that *L'Oeil du Malin,* which can be regarded as the first film of Chabrol's maturity, is also the first feature since *Le Beau Serge* in which he did not have the script collaboration of Paul Gégauff. It establishes so clearly the pattern of Chabrol's later films, from *Les Biches* on, that it seems like a first sketch for them, or, considering its excellence, the first of a series thereafter interrupted and taken up again some six years later, when Chabrol was able once more to attain creative freedom. The film was almost a complete disaster at the time of its appearance, not widely distributed in France and hardly at all elsewhere. Using hindsight, one could say that its principal crime was being so obviously ahead of its time.

The two other films Chabrol made during this period can be rapidly disposed of. Neither *Ophélia* nor *Landru* looks much like a major work, though both have their intermittent charms. *Ophélia* is a modern variation on the Hamlet theme, and more than a little silly: a young man becomes obsessed with suspicions when his uncle marries his mother after the death of his father. And after passing a cinema where *Hamlet* is being shown, the young man determines to play out the Shakespearean drama in his own provincial French bourgeois setting. A film takes the place of a stage show and unleashes a series of dramatic crises ending in the suicide of the uncle. The hero, in the process, takes on something (though not enough) of the character of Albin in *L'Oeil du Malin,* thereby encouraging us to favor a Freudian interpretation of *Hamlet* in which Hamlet himself would become the unconscious creator of all his troubles, the designer of the action rather than its victim. This time, too, the pattern is unclear: Ophélia seems to be the "good," sane character, the representative of virtue, but she is too passive and colorless, even as one of Chabrol's trampled-on goodies.

Landru (written by Chabrol in collaboration with Françoise Sagan) is a jolly black comedy about the multiple murderer which toys in a fairly light way with some typical Chabrol themes: the inscrutability of human motivation, sympathetic identification with the monster's point of view. But *Landru* is not presented as a monster in the Chabrolian sense of the term, and we are not shown enough of him to identify with him or wonder at the inscrutability of his motivation or receive any complex challenge to our moral senses and susceptibilities. More, almost, than any other of Chabrol's films, *Landru* remains on the (admittedly handsome) surface of its subject—which is frustrating when one considers that *Landru* seems to be a subject with which Chabrol could and should do so much more.

After *Landru* came the days of Chabrol's commercial commissions, and his blackest period in the eyes of his critics. In a sense, of course, these critics were right in regarding it as a misfortune that Chabrol had to do what films he could get instead of what he wanted to do. *Ophélia* and *Landru* were apparently films Chabrol wanted to do, but they are not successful on any level. Perhaps he would not ever have chosen to make spy thrillers like *Le Tigre Aime la Chair Fraiche* (1965), *Marie-Chantal Contre le Docteur Kha* (1965), or *Le Tigre se Parfume à la Dynamite* (1965), but he shows a natural affinity for the genre, makes the films unpretentiously, with every appearance of enjoyment, and produces first-rate examples which put most of their grand and famous rivals to shame. A talented director, after all, should be able to turn his hand to almost anything (as Hitchcock has frequently proved), and we can judge only by the result of the labor, not by the grandeur of the intention. All three of the spy films defy reasonable synopsis, and anyway there would be little purpose in attempting it: more to the point is the observation that in them, particularly in *Marie-Chantal,* Chabrol seems to be having a lot of fun, and the fun is infectious. The spy and mock-spy films had become, in the days after the first Bond pictures, the most abstract of popular genres (an effect connected, no doubt, with the advent of television and the discontinuous way most people watch it, which, transferred to the cinema, resulted in a loss of concern for plot coherence and a more pressing desire for a succession of immediately diverting effects), and therefore it was by no means inappropriate that Chabrol, with his established tendencies toward abstraction, should naturally gravitate toward them as a commercially viable and yet not dishonorable way of continuing to exercise his craft, to make a living at least until something more to his taste came along.

And in the midst of them he contrived to make one of the most personal of all his films, the "Muette" sequence in *Paris Vu Par . . .* (1964). He had contributed sketches of no great importance to composite films before, but "La Muette" is a small masterpiece, a summing up of Chabrol's most lovable qualities. It tells briefly and ironically of a little boy's family situation with typical bourgeois parents—his mother the hypochondriac nagger, his father the ineffectual authoritarian, believer in capital punishment who flirts with the maid. Day after day the boy has to put up with their endless disputes over the dinner table (this is the *locus classicus* of Chabrol's dinner-table drama), until he discovers the merciful use of earplugs. These safeguard his sanity at the table. But when his mother falls downstairs and for once genuinely calls for help, he leaves her to die, sublimely unaware of her cries. Chabrol himself plays the father, with personal relish in the exposition of the father's greed and self-satisfaction, and Stéphane Audran, his real-life wife and the female star of most of his films from *Les Biches* on, and some earlier, plays the mother.

"La Muette" served as a useful reminder of Chabrol's continuing originality during the time of his commercial chores—more so, certainly, than *La Ligne de Démarcation* (1966), based on books by Colonel Remy. Much more than the *Tigre* films, this would seem to have been in Chabrol's mind an essay in a particular genre (the war drama with heroic-patriotic overtones), a technical challenge of no particular interest apart from the opportunity it gave to laugh up his sleeve at the effect it had on audiences because they persisted in taking all too seriously things he put in with deliberate mischief as exaggerations. All the same, such is Chabrol's skill that the thing works, on both levels: those who want to take it as a piece of patriotic nostalgia can; those who enjoy seeing a few private jokes and appreciate the Chabrolian naughtiness and fantasy of the two parody Gestapo men can also derive a lot of pleasure from it. Chabrol himself dismisses the film entirely; he is both right (from his point of view) and wrong (from ours) to do so.

The sixth of Chabrol's commercial chores, *La Route de Corinthe* (1967), is also of little significance. It is a complicated comedy thriller related in tone and style to the *Tigre* films, with Chabrol himself popping up in various disguises, and everyone involved extracting a lot of fun out of its nonsense. The only notable thing about it is Chabrol's vivid evocation of the Greek scene, at once dusty, squalid, and monumental, where menace stalks all the more sinister in the hard bright light of high noon. *Le Scandale* (or, in the English version, *The Champagne Murders*) (1967), which comes between *La Ligne de Démarcation* and *La Route de Corinthe,* is a different matter. At first glance it seems very Chabrolian, both in its subject matter and in its style. So much so that one critic has suggested it is like a parody of Chabrol, and a parody made with none too much sympathy. Thus the film may be regarded as Chabrol's only approach to artistic prostitution—a betrayal of his own kind of material to make it commercial instead of perfectly honest journeyman work in genres he would not necessarily have attempted of his own volition.

The judgment seems to me unfair. *Le Scandale* is a thoroughly enjoyable film which does not, obviously, achieve the subtlety or intensity of Chabrol's later thrillers in the same style and emotional territory, but its shortcomings, such as they are, seem to have less to do with any readiness to sell out than with an estimable but partially defeated attempt to make a film that is very much his own within the framework of an international co-production that proved resistant to it. The wonder is how much Chabrol survives, even in the English-language version, rather than how little. The plot is again an enclosed, familial drama of neurotic personal relations, with thriller/whodunit overtones that count for little more than those in *A Double Tour,* the earlier Chabrol film with which it is most immediately comparable. Paul (Maurice Ronet), a champagne heir recovering from extreme mental stress following a traumatic experience of violence, is living with and pretty well under the thumb of a couple of friends, Christine (Yvonne Furneaux) and Christopher Belling (Anthony Perkins). He wakes up on two occasions next to the corpses of strangled girls, whom he thinks he has unwittingly killed; Christine takes advantage of this to enforce her power over the champagne empire. But then she too is murdered, and the murderer turns out to be Jacqueline (Stéphane Audran), her secretary, who has been playing a double role throughout and is Christopher's mistress. The film ends with a battle of wills among Paul, Christopher, and Jacqueline/Lydia, the outcome of which is left uncertain.

It seems to imply, however, the same communal guilt as in *A Double Tour*—any one of the characters might have done the murders; they are all equally responsible. This time that simply is not true, at any rate on the basis of the evidence the screenplay offers us. Even though Paul is willing to accept the guilt for the murders which (reasonably enough) he does not remember committing, there is little reason why he should have done them (unless one counts the implications of his homosexual attachment for Christopher, which is inadequate as motivation for the strangling of miscellaneous ladies). And Christopher, though implicated, seems relatively innocent and even redeems himself toward the end by preventing Jacqueline/Lydia from shooting Paul. The ending therefore is both showy and arbitrary, lacking any connection with what has gone before, but tagged on as a *coup de cinéma*. It is this, above all, which vitiates the effect of the film, though earlier sequences contain moments of savage social comedy and intense pseudo-familial infighting in Chabrol's best manner, and even the unlikely international cast are somehow accommodated to one another in the film's oddly coherent private world.

With *Les Biches,* by general consent, we come back to vintage Chabrol, the beginning of his maturity. It is an elegantly perverse version of the triangle theme in which the arrival of an attractive man disturbs an apparently well-balanced, apparently Lesbian relationship. At the beginning of the film Frédérique (Stéphane Audran), a rich young woman, picks up a penniless young artist, Why (Jacqueline Sassard), and takes her to live in the South of France, along with a couple of licensed jesters, Robègue and Riais. The arrival of an attractive architect, Paul (Jean-Louis Trintignant), disrupts this situation. First, Why is attracted to him; then Frédérique, in the process of breaking up the affair, falls in love with him herself. The three of them continue to live together, with Why as the unhappy spectator of the other two's happiness (a situation similar to the triangle in *Les Cousins,* with Why playing the role of Charles). Robègue and Riais are eventually turned out, and Frédérique and Paul go to Paris to live. When Why arrives to join them, Frédérique tries to cast her off, whereupon Why stabs her and prepares to take her place with Paul.

Clearly, Chabrol is not interested in sex as sex so much as in sex seen as part of a power game: the film is cool, ironical, eminently civilized. Yet, after all, dark destructive passions lurk beneath the unruffled surface, and emerge in the strange and unpredictable climax. The only thing which for me keeps *Les Biches* from being not only absolute Chabrol but Chabrol at his best is a certain stylistic circumspection, an overobtrusive and insistent cool; for all his preoccupation with form and pattern, Chabrol is most enjoyable when he throws measure and discretion to the winds. *Les Biches* has been generally recognized as deliberate simplification of style, an abandonment of baroque elements and stylistic fireworks in favor of the more direct, unadorned style of later films. This is fine in principle, and finer still in practice by the time we get to *Que la Bête Meure* and *Le Boucher.* But in *Les Biches* I find a certain lowering of vitality, as though Chabrol is deliberately tying himself down when every now and then he longs to fly.

All the same, there is much to admire in the construction and realization of *Les Biches,* in relation to which this small doubt probably seems like straining at gnats. The ordering of the scenario shows an enormous increase of subtlety, economy, and precision over *Les Cousins.* All the possible permutations of relationships in the central triangle are explored, whereas in *Les Cousins* the hint of homosexual attraction between Paul and Charles remains only a hint. And the motivation of the characters remains far more interestingly ambiguous and mysterious. Frédérique, for example, seems to be the determiner of what will happen, but when her behavior is closely examined, this comes into doubt. She seduces Why, certainly, but what are her intentions concerning Why and Paul? Why has told her all and announced that she does not think she is in love with Paul; the visit to Paul seems as much in a spirit of concern for Why as an intended revenge; and Paul undoubtedly takes the lead in dismissing his night with Why and moving without more ado to Frédérique; in a very important sense she is seduced by him, not he by her. And in the later stages Why, through her dissatisfaction, gradually takes over the deciding role. In this triangle there are no heroes, no villains, no beasts, and no passive sufferers. The ironies are absorbed into the characterization of believable, if mysterious, people believably, if bizarrely, existing together.

Sometimes the mystery is a little too thick, particularly in what relates to Paul, whose reasons for what he does and does not do are hard to fathom. But the structure of the film is of a perfect formal simplicity and directness as the wheel turns and each new permutation is produced with unassailable logic from the last. Logic visual as well as intellectual—notice, for instance, Why's gradual transformation of herself into Frédérique, by making up like her, trying on her jewelry and clothes, and little by little assuming Frédérique's characteristic color, black, in her own wardrobe, until at the end she puts on the black fur coat we associate with Frédérique in the opening scenes. And the balance, though precarious, is kept right: we know enough about the characters to involve ourselves in what happens to them. The form, though sometimes overly elegant, cool, and distancing, never entirely overbalances the film's human content.

Les Biches represents first and foremost for Chabrol the

establishment of a style and approach, or its reestablishment if we remember *L'Oeil du Malin.* In the series of great films Chabrol has made since, he has triumphantly utilized the materials and techniques he established in *Les Biches,* with a corresponding stylistic sobriety but greater freedom and ease within that sobriety, and corresponding intensification of the passion within the form. Thus his next film, *La Femme Infidèle,* appears primarily as a triumph of storytelling, which is odd, considering that it has very little story and that plot as such had seldom been Chabrol's strong point in the past. But in this film he brings off what he attempted and did not quite achieve in *Les Biches:* a calm, classical piece of filmmaking in which the significance of the subject is distilled into a clear, simple story line, event following event with irresistible logic and inevitability.

The story is indicated by the title: it begins with a husband's first suspicions of his wife, follows his guilty and reluctant investigation, shows how he gets rid of the wife's lover, and how the increasing knowledge he gains of his wife, and his wife of him, actually revitalizes their marriage. Again, Chabrol shows himself fascinated by the balance of emotional power. Here, as in *L'Oeil du Malin* and *Les Biches,* there are three characters, the couple and the intruder who, one way or another, brings about a change in the balance. In *La Femme Infidèle* the intruder is hardly more than a cipher, a pawn in the complex emotional game husband and wife play with each other. The film pivots on the funny and unpredictable scene of the husband's interview with the lover, which begins when Charles, the husband, having found out through a private detective that there is a lover and where he lives, just turns up, introduces himself, and engages in a man-of-the-world conversation with the lover. The scene finally gets out of hand when Charles is unable to bear the progressive revelation of a Héléne far different from the woman he has known and, half accidentally, kills the man who presents him with this new knowledge.

The rest of the film, after he has disposed of the body and the evidence with the aplomb of a seasoned professional, concentrates on the deepening of mutual knowledge and love between Charles and Hélène as a result, direct and indirect, of the crime. He does not tell her he knows about her lover, let alone about the killing. She does not tell him when she finds a photograph and an address in his pocket which indicate what the truth must be. But they understand each other, and they present a united front when the police come, because they *are* united, more than ever before. When the police come a second time, presumably with more damning evidence against him, he gives himself up, like Hartman in *L'Oeil du Malin,* leaving Hélène with the words: "I love you madly." The film is, above all, a love story, taking up the situation of the Hartmans from *L'Oeil du Malin:* a devoted couple though the wife has (again, not very explicably) a lover. And since Charles is French instead of German, he kills the lover and loves his wife the more, rather than killing the wife as some sort of perverse proof of his love for her. It is a strange, beautiful, highly emotional film in which the emotion is kept under strict control without our ever doubting (as we may in *Les Biches*) that it is there.

And the central drama can retain its power over us without being artificially isolated from the world around it. Many of the most appealing moments in *La Femme Infidèle* come when the life around the couple breaks in. Sometimes in the past Chabrol's love of weird details, strange characters who amuse him, got a little out of hand, as with the jokesy Gestapo officers in *La Ligne de Démarcation.* But here the incidentals are perfectly managed. Charles's silly, impossibly provocative secretary forever tripping and dipping and curtsying cutely; the man in the bar from which Charles telephones, who repeats with a variety of individual inflection everything everyone says; the friend's wife who is never observed as anything but paralytically drunk—all these enliven the margins of the film without distracting from its main point and emotional center.

La Femme Infidèle is one of Chabrol's finest films; but the two which follow, *Que le Bête Meure* (1969) and *Le Boucher* (1970), seem to me, by any standard, masterpieces. All three films send us back willy-nilly to Chabrol's and Rohmer's Hitchcock work for their theoretical and philosophical basis. *La Femme Infidèle* turns on an exchange of culpability (Charles takes on the guilt of Hélène's illicit affair by keeping his knowledge of it to himself; Hélène likewise takes on the guilt of the murder by her silence) and the importance of confession, the "avowal," or lack of it. *Que la Bête Meure,* though not on an original subject, like its predecessor and its successor (it is closely based on a novel by Nicholas Blake), is a perfect example of Chabrol's Hitchcock leanings. It is a thriller about a man determined to avenge the death of his young son in a hit-and-run accident. As a thriller it works perfectly: the stages in his search for the culprit, his gradual insinuation of himself into the household of the guilty man, the elaborate cat-and-mouse game he plays with the man, or possibly that the man plays with him, the ironic conclusion—all these are recorded with the most unobtrusive skill. There is no show of "style," no evidence of a conscious determination to inflate the material, to elevate it into Art. Like Hitchcock, one would say. Chabrol has learned from him the secret of impeccably unpretentious professionalism. In other respects, *Que la Bête Meure* is more Hitchcock than Hitchcock himself—more in accord with the image of Hitchcock, so influential since, even on Hitchcock himself, which was first elaborated by Chabrol and Rohmer. All the fingerprints are there. The moral ambiguity in the position of the hero, who by the cold and calculating preparation of his own crime becomes, arguably, as culpable as the man he is tracking down—indeed, possibly more so. His intricate and puzzling relationship with the woman in the case, the monster's sister-in-law, who is at first merely the means to his end. The importance of the avowal—a confession substitute, of course—as when he pushes her to confess that she too has had relations with the man she, like all the rest of the family, detests. The exchange of culpability between the avenger and his victim's teenage son. The film is demonstrably, and deliberately, everything that Chabrol the critic found in the work of his idol Hitchcock.

Does all this make the film any better? No, of course not—not in itself. But it does give the film a density, a feeling that beneath its neat, classical surface—no advanced, New Wave technique here—impalpable presences are moving. It is a thriller; but it is also *un film sérieux,* one which makes the best of its genre without being limited by it. The character development, for instance, goes far beyond the norm of the thriller. The killer of the hero's son (as he is revealed to be), Paul, is perhaps the purest example of Chabrol's beast characters, a monster in all his personal and professional relations, loved only by his even more terrible old mother, who shows no response to anything except to cackle with senile glee at his more vicious dinner-table sallies. Yet even he is permitted his share of Chabrol's (and our) perverse sympathy: in the end, when he reveals that he knows Charles's designs on his life, and defies him to carry them out, he attains a stature and dignity, even in his unpleasantness, which are denied the vacillating and indecisive Charles. He is, unashamedly, himself, and does what he wants to, what he has to, without fear or compromise; it is Charles, the supposed hero whose viewpoint we share throughout the film, who loses sympathy and carries out his crime in a devious manner brought to light only by his final decision to inculpate himself in order to save Paul's son, who has confessed, so he says, in order to save him. Even then we do not feel altogether sure whether Charles did after all commit the murder or is just sacrificing himself in a somewhat Christian fashion (as François does for Serge in *Le Beau Serge*) for the sake of Philippe. (If this is what Chabrol intends, it is indeed a curious throwback.)

Not only that, but Chabrol's depiction of the horrors of family life has seldom been more vivid than in the scenes at the home Paul makes a misery for all its other occupants. Charles's role there, as the lover of Paul's sister-in-law (whom he has tracked down through the only coincidence in the whole ruthlessly logical plot), is touchy to begin with; but the meal-table scene is a perfect exposition of social and personal unease, the forces which bring a family together and those which hold them determinedly apart. Murder, it has been said, is in France always a family affair. *Que la Bête Meure* offers the clearest demonstration of just why this should be so.

Le Boucher is an even purer example of Chabrol's handling of the thriller form. Like *Que la Bête Meure,* it is only a thriller, if you care to put it that way. It is also the best possible argument for the thriller's right to serious consideration as such. Would one really need to argue that a film like *Le Bou-*

cher says something about social conditions in rural France, or makes a valid general point about the state of French primary education (the heroine is a schoolteacher), or something else of the sort, to feel comfortable in approving of it? Obviously not. Undeniably, *Le Boucher* is only a thriller, but it is such a superlative one that it can be seen again and again, and at each viewing new felicities come to light in it.

The form is classic. An unmarried teacher new to a small, closed rural community, meets the local butcher at a wedding breakfast. He is nice, friendly, by no means stupid, and there is clearly the possibility of a romantic involvement even though he seems conscious of a sort of social inferiority that keeps him from rushing things or taking liberties. So far, so good: the tone is light, almost comic. Or would be, were it not for the background, a series of brutal murders of young women, which make overcast and menacing what would otherwise be an idyl. The way Chabrol establishes his tone is masterly: the lead-in to the announcement of the first murder, with two police cars drawing up outside the schoolhouse in long-shot while in the foreground chickens peck around under the green and leafy trees, catches exactly the kind of cosmic unease required—the summer itself suddenly seems to be, in Harold Monro's phrase, "raging through the frantic countryside . . . great, large and terrible, like something doomed." And the discovery of the murdered girl's body, through blood dripping onto the bread of one of the children being taken on a country walk, is horrible and funny and worthy of Hitchcock himself.

Indeed, in this film particularly, one can never be unaware of the shadow of Hitchcock as interpreted by Chabrol. The inspiration of Chabrol's Hitchcock becomes, if anything, stronger as the film progresses. There is little or no obvious whodunit suspense. The butcher is the prime, in fact the only, suspect, and that suspicion rapidly becomes certainty: the thrills come, not from working out who did it, but from speculating what he will do next and how the heroine will react. (The most immediate parallel in Hitchcock is *Vertigo,* where the problem of the second Kim Novak's identity is immediately resolved, so that we can go on to something far more complex and interesting.) There is a favorite Hitchcock theme here: the exchange of guilt. The teacher in effect joins the butcher in his crimes, becomes emotionally as well as formally an accessory by not communicating her suspicions. And we too, by a familiar Hitchcock switch, come to take the murderer's side, to sympathize and hope against hope that he will get away with it.

Partly this is due to the inspired casting of Jean Yanne as the butcher—a likable, gentle man very different from the monster Paul he played in *Que la Bête Meure.* He and Stéphane Audran are perfectly matched, the emotional bond between them, and the strange, edgy balance of temperaments, coming over powerfully from the very beginning (in a virtuoso tracking shot as they walk right through the village talking a little, just a very little, tipsily after the wedding celebration) to the final, ill-fated drive to the hospital with its bleak conclusion. The film is a thriller, but moments like these have an explicable weight and density that make them deeply moving. And that even though the drive and Popaul's death come immediately after the most obviously thriller sequence in the film, when Hélène has become fully convinced of Popaul's guilt, he knows it and corners her in the empty schoolhouse, darkened, at night, and terrorizes her before turning his knife on himself. It is a measure of the distance Chabrol has traveled that he can pull off a set piece like this and still have us caring about the characters as human beings, make us feel the bleak emptiness of Hélène's riverside vigil after Popaul's death as near tragic in its intensity. Even the final impression of the song from the wedding breakfast at the beginning, "Capri, Petite Ile," which Chabrol explains as purely commercial, a device to send the audience out with a feeling that things aren't quite that bad after all, has a haunting quality that has nothing to do with commerce and everything to do with the unpredictable poetry of art.

Chabrol's next two films, *La Rupture* (1970) and *Juste Avant la Nuit* (1971), are not quite on the same level as *Que la Bête Meure* and *Le Boucher,* but they are part of the same cycle and each presents a new and valid variation on Chabrol's by now obsessive Hitchcock themes of murder and expiation, exchange of guilt and the efficacy (or, in Chabrol's case, the inefficacy) of confession. Of the two I prefer *Juste Avant la Nuit. La Rupture* is more arbitrary-seeming in its development than, say, *La Femme Infidèle.* It concerns a battle waged by a long-suffering mother and wife, Hélène, to keep her child despite the threats of her husband, Charles, and the schemes of Charles's father, who wants the child, and employs a poor man, Paul, to spy on Hélène in the hope of uncovering evidence against her which will give him custody of the child. The scheme goes awry, since it is Paul who kills Charles, not, as it might well be, Hélène, thereby himself assuming the guilt of something she may only have wished done, if that. The film is entertaining, but rather too littered with picturesque details that detract from the whole, like the other occupants of the boardinghouse where Hélène lives. There seems no reason for these to intrude on the integrity of the central drama, whereas in *La Femme Infidèle* similar incidentals serve to give it greater relief. Chabrol's rigid control of his materials (in the last few films, anyway) has here relaxed too far for comfort.

Juste Avant la Nuit, on the other hand, is vintage Chabrol. This time the subject is founded completely on the idea of confession and the inefficacy of absolution. Charles (of course he is called Charles) is married to Hélène (of course she is called Hélène) but seeks stranger pleasures in the bed of his best friend's wife. One day, carried away by their sexual games, he kills the lady. He panics and runs off, but he is even luckier than Charles in *La Femme Infidèle,* another accidental, amateur murderer, in that somehow no trace seems to be left which can lead the police to him; the bungled crime proves against all odds to be the perfect crime. But is Charles happy at his narrow escape? On the contrary, he feels an obsessive need, not only to confess the crime, but to be punished for it. He confesses to his wife, in two stages, first that he had a mistress, and second that he has killed her. She listens, understands, and forgives him. So then he confesses to his best friend, Michel, the sorrowing widower. And he also understands, forgives, and forgets. What Charles finds most unforgivable is all this forgiving: his need to pay for the murder will not let him rest. He announces to Hélène that he is going to give himself up, and she must understand his need for punishment. She argues that he will merely destroy his family, and when he takes no notice, administers a fatal dose of laudanum in the guise of a sleeping draft. The film ends with her sunning on the beach, talking about him and reflecting comfortably that the children are beginning to forget. Again the surface is cool, the irony cooler. *Juste Avant la Nuit* is in many respects a very funny film, much jollier than the others in the cycle commenced with *Les Biches,* because Chabrol obviously regards Charles's plight as absurd, and rapidly leads us to this conclusion too, though we start by being free to identify with Charles, whose viewpoint in the film is very much our own.

La Décade Prodigieuse (1972) is another variation of the whodunit/thriller formula, though compared with the romantic, emotional approach of the previous four films, it is very crisp and dry and alienating. The story comes from a novel by Ellery Queen, and has a lot of the traditional ingredients: a young sculptor who wakes up every so often with blood on his hands and a gap in his memory; an eccentric millionaire who has adopted him and lives in isolated splendor 1925-style because 1925 was his best year; the millionaire's attractive young wife, brought up with the son and of course secretly having an affair with him; blackmail; a series of strange and violent happenings that gradually reveal a pattern not recognized until too late to avoid a bloody conclusion (everything that occurs is eventually perceived to be a systematic breaking of the Ten Commandments, ending naturally with "Thou shalt not kill").

The film is abstract and geometrical, the style consciously applied, as though the millionaire's eccentric life style has been the governing factor in Chabrol's choice of the subject and he is using it more as a pretext for formal explorations than at its face value as a thriller. There are stylistic flourishes. A conversation between the millionaire (Orson Welles) and a stranger (Michel Piccoli) about the labyrinthine nature of human relationships is shot entirely from outside the window, with the camera moving about restlessly so that the window frame forms a shifting cage pattern imprisoning one or both of them. The flashback of the millionaire's wedding to his young bride, done in crane shot with the camera rising to reveal the couple's 1925-vintage car like some giant insect lying in wait behind the hedge as they leave the church, creates a feeling of menace with the most minimum means. But on the whole the film is made in a cool, formal way, as though to create a feeling of distancing: even the inserts in which various characters describe the past are staged at a distance, like *tableaux vivants,* to give an unsettling effect.

In this stylistic context the rather bizarre cast—Anthony Perkins as the son, Marlène Jobert as the wife, as well as Welles and Piccoli—also works, if not as an alienating device, at least to prevent too empathic an attitude in the audience. The previous films have the feeling of being all in the family (and not merely because we know Stéphane Audran is Chabrol's wife in private life). Here, though the principal characters are named Hélène, Paul, and Charles, the atmosphere and attitudes are completely different. Partly it may be that the film is made in English (*Ten Days' Wonder* is obviously the original version, and the French a not too well-dubbed substitute); but apart from that, it seems to be going off in a different direction from its predecessors, using the same kind of basic material to inaugurate a new phase.

Or perhaps not; only time will tell. Certainly Chabrol himself has said that he sees his subsequent film, *Les Noces Rouges* (1973), as marking in his own mind the end of a cycle, the last of the series of "family" thrillers dedicated to the proposition that murder is a private affair. In the case of *Les Noces Rouges* he ran into censorship problems because the story was based on an actual murder case still *sub judice* involving married lovers who conspired to kill their respective spouses. The story is treated by Chabrol in his most insolently black-comedy style: the meetings of the lovers, played by Stéphane Audran and Michel Piccoli, are observed from a rigorously objective standpoint, with no romantic aura whatever—they fling themselves upon each other with the uncomplicated frenzy of rutting beasts, and all the grunting and groaning becomes almost farcical. We recognize that theirs is a crime of passion, but we are never invited to participate vicariously in that passion, only to watch. All the same, as we would expect of Chabrol, we do sympathize with the murderers and hope that they will get away with it—not least because their victims really seem to be asking for it: Pierre's wet-rag, ailing wife, drifting glumly around the house; Lucienne's jolly, monstrous husband, Paul, a perfect example of a Chabrol beast along the lines of Paul in *Que la Bête Meure.* There are marvelous meal-table confrontations, some very good incidental jokes like the lovers' encounter on the margins of a conducted tour through the local stately home, the expected sharp observation of small-town life and intrigue, an ambiguous and sinister child (Lucienne's illegitimate daughter, who is, curiously enough, the Hélène of this particular drama, whatever that may signify), and a beautifully cool, ironic ending in which the guilty couple, finally apprehended through the misplaced zeal of Hélène, are asked why they didn't just go away instead of committing two murders, and they answer simply, flatly: "Oh no, we never thought of going away." Quintessential Chabrol; Chabrol at or very near the top of his bent.

Chabrol's next two ventures show a veering away in search of new materials, new areas to conquer. The first, a pair of fifty-two-minute adaptations of Henry James short stories—"The Bench of Desolation," the very last story he published, and "De Grey," one of the first—was designed for French television, and has not been screened at the time of writing. To judge from his own accounts, Chabrol was pleased by the melodramatic side of "De Grey," a slender tale of family curses and vampirism, and by the subtlety and complexity of "The Bench of Desolation," a virtually actionless story of a determined woman's mysterious waiting game for an unromantic man.

NADA is in every way a more substantial work. It looks on the surface like a political thriller with a topical subject of diplomatic kidnapping. But though the action scenes, like that in which the revolutionary group NADA actually carries off the American ambassador from a discreet brothel he attends every week, are brilliantly handled, the real purpose of the film seems to be to lay bare the shiftiness of authority, constantly divided against itself, intricately cynical and corrupt, with all the elaborate deals that have to be made, the games that have to be played in order to get results (and even then, what result? would not a dead, martyred ambassador serve someone's ends better than a live, aggrieved ambassador?), and to contrast this with the practical, downtrodden, unquestioning solidarity of the ragged and unimpressive group of none too competent revolutionaries. The NADA group may be a mixed bag of directionless disreputables, becoming increasingly aware as they go through the motions of the kidnapping that they are only playing the Establishment's game, but at least, without sentimentality, they achieve a sort of battered dignity as human beings that the side of authority never attains. The film is alive with details, some of them sharply funny (like the whole character of the madame, full of complaints because her expensive "protection" does not work) and some (like the first interview between minister and police inspector, with a large lampshade intervening) cunningly indicative of character and attitude. It is not what we would regard up to now as typical Chabrol, but it is difficult to imagine who but he could have done it so well.

Even today, it is hard to come to any cut-and-dried conclusion about Chabrol. Part of the problem is that he seems so easy to pin down. His world is so small and limited; he deals with the same situations over and over again, from slightly different angles; even the names of his characters recur—Hélène, Charles, and Paul forever locked in a triangle, forever reenacting the same drama, beginning with *Les Cousins,* which set the pattern and introduced us to the first Charles and the first Paul (*L'Oeil du Malin* gave us the first Hélène). Nearly all his films have a dinner-table scene; murder is involved at some point; detectives usually come in twos and Chabrol does not take them too seriously; most *femmes* are *infidèles;* and evil and its embodiments we can be sure exist.

Beyond that, one can see two distinct phases in his style, separated by his commercial period. The films from *Les Cousins* to *Landru* are visually ornate, baroque in their treatment of surface and texture, their penchant for extravagant effects of lighting and color. It was in the nature of the *Tigre* films that they be ornate, but maybe that necessity helped to exorcise the taste in Chabrol. At any rate, since *Les Biches* his films have been cool, limpid, simple in style almost to the point of self-denial. All these things are true of Chabrol. And yet the man himself, and the exact nature of his talent, remains elusive. Is he Christian or atheist, social critic or bourgeois conformist? Does he condemn his beasts implicitly, or is his obsession with them, his consistent attempts to get us to see their point of view, symptomatic of some deeper fascination: is it not for nothing that Robin Wood, in trepidation and fear of libel, has suggested that Landru comes closest of all Chabrol's characters to a self-portrait?

Chabrol is a puzzle, finally, because where others of his generation and background have devoted themselves assiduously and sometimes in a self-deflating way to art, Chabrol has given most of his attention to the elaboration of entertainment. Of all the French directors who emerged in the first New Wave—Godard, Truffaut, Rohmer, Rivette, and the rest of the ex-critics turned filmmakers—he has had perhaps the oddest career. Whereas the rest have behaved on screen as befits their intellectual background on magazines like *Cahiers du Cinéma,* alone of his generation he has been content, delighted even, to make unashamedly popular, commercial films, and let the art look after itself. And that is probably the best way to do it. What matters, in the end, is the film on the screen, not the frame of mind in which you set out to make it. Hitchcock provides an excellent example precisely because his mind is always on the end product and on how the audience will take it. He makes films that qualify on the highest level of art, not because he deliberately sets out to do so, but because he just can't help it. The same, I think, with Chabrol. His own tastes and interests are genuinely popular: if he sets out, as in his two *Tigre* thrillers, or *Marie-Chantal Contre le Docteur Kha,* to make a fast, funny action drama, he does so because that is what audiences want at that moment, and because he enjoys doing it, not with any lofty idea of enobling the genre and giving it intellectual respectability. It seems only right that the *Tigre* films have turned up in Britain and the United States in dubbed versions for double bills in suburban and provincial flea pits—though it is a pity that many have consequently missed them who would have enjoyed them—since they are in every way popular films, not foreign movies for highbrows only.

And yet, after all, though he can fit in with commerce and make, even at his most uncommercial, films that seem to present few surface difficulties to the spectator, no matter how complex the human truths they embody, his main concern outside the admitted potboilers is much more hermetic-seeming than that of most of his more evidently highbrow colleagues and contemporaries. His obsessions are thoroughly private and personal, and he has pursued them from film to film with a concentration and dedication seldom matched elsewhere in the modern cinema. Before *Les Biches,* a lot of people were inclined to write him off, feeling that by making shamelessly commercial films he was betraying the brilliant talent of *Les Cousins*. But now his films can be seen as all of a piece, diverse expressions of the same complex but appealing sensibility. When he wants to make a film just for fun, it is really amusing but none the less personal: he does not have to betray anything in order to do it. The tone, the sense of humor, the serious concerns are all the same. And when he wants to make a serious film, the popular aspects are not forgotten. For all their intelligence and sophistication, nearly all his films (except perhaps *Les Godelureaux*) work in terms which any audience can understand and respond to: often, of course, in terms of superficial adherence to the trappings of the thriller genre. Whether in commercial nonsense or in the subjects that we may suppose are closest to his heart, Chabrol has his own world of which he is complete master.

Pier Paolo Pasolini

IT IS NATURAL, SOMEHOW, TO DISTRUST THE ESTABLISHED LITERARY figure who enters the cinema—most of all, perhaps, if he happens to be a poet. Poetry in the cinema, especially if consciously worked for, is the most elusive and dangerous quality imaginable. And so much of so-called serious cinema in the past has been bedeviled by the application of literary standards of judgment that the very suggestion of literariness in the film leaves a nasty taste in the mouth. Accordingly, we should be highly mistrustful of Pier Paolo Pasolini, already a poet and novelist of fame and distinction when he made his first film, *Accattone,* in 1961, at the age of thirty-nine. And yet all such suspicions have turned out to be misplaced; if Pasolini's films fail, as some of them do, they fail as films, not as poetry or literature. It is almost as though, as seems to be the case also with Cocteau, he had been waiting, marshaling his many and varied talents until such time as he found his ideal medium, and that medium, the medium that could use them all and more, was the cinema.

Nor can it be said, in Pasolini's case, that he did not have a reasonable and realistic period of apprenticeship in the cinema: before shooting his own first film, he had worked on the scripts of no fewer than thirteen films by other directors, including Fellini (*Notti di Cabiria*), Bolognini, and Franco Rossi, as well as acting in a couple. He is philosophical now about what other directors did to his scripts, on the grounds that in the cinema the director is the artist and all the rest must accept the fact that their function is to provide the raw material. In any case, none of the scripts was wholly Pasolini's own work, though the script of *La Notte Brava* (Bolognini, 1959) is included in one of Pasolini's books, *Ali dagli Occhi Azzurri,* along with some of the *Cabiria* material and other scriptwriting of this period, and Pasolini says that he considers some of it, as writing, among the best he has done. Clearly, the desire to control the outcome of his own work, to move beyond writing for the cinema to expressing himself through the cinema, must have become increasingly imperative, and in 1961 Pasolini had two projects ready for himself: *La Commare Secca,* which he decided not to do (it was shot the next year by Bernardo Bertolucci), and *Accattone.*

To understand *Accattone,* it is necessary to do nothing but see the film; to understand the why and how of *Accattone,* one must look further into Pasolini's background, early life, and literary career—a career that is curious, to say the least. Pasolini was born in Bologna in 1922, of solid bourgeois parents, though his father, an army officer and a convinced Fascist, was of aristocratic origin. He began his literary career writing poems in the Friulian dialect, which as a literary language is remote and artificial, and anyway was not even his own dialect; he learned it as a child from the peasants around him and assumed it as a writing vehicle through a sort of defiant aestheticism. At the same time, an emotional attachment to and identification with the peasantry made him a natural Marxist before he knew anything about politics. At the university he began studying the history of art, but lost his thesis materials during the war and afterward decided instead to write a thesis on the poet Giovanni Pascoli, with whose subject matter, in its symbolic overtones and extreme artificiality, he felt a decided sympathy at that time.

Other factors that have been influential in Pasolini's career as a writer and as a filmmaker have been his attitude toward religion and his attitude toward the lower, particularly the criminal, classes. As an avowed Marxist (even if only temporarily a member of the Communist Party), Pasolini might well be supposed to be not only an anti-Catholic but an atheist as well. Pasolini himself, however, readily admits to a tangle of contradictory feelings on this score. He makes the point that, whatever an Italian's conscious beliefs, he can never escape the legacy of Catholicism, the fact that his ideas have been irrevocably shaped by the Church. Equally, he admits to a natural inclination to see things mystically or mythologically, in terms of redemption and revelation for his characters. This has caused some confusion in critical attitudes toward his work. On the one hand, critics were surprised and puzzled that a

Marxist could produce such a seemingly reverent work as *Il Vangelo Secondo Matteo* (*The Gospel According to St. Matthew*). On the other, he was arrested and imprisoned for the supposed blasphemous irreverence of "La Ricotta," his episode in the collective film *Rogopag*—mainly on account of his Marxist reputation, surely, for the point of the episode is, clearly, to criticize false, commercialized ideas of religion rather than religion itself. Pasolini at his trial firmly denied any intention of irreverence. In effect, he has come under fire from both extremes for his attitude toward religion. The orthodox Catholics consider him an atheist or a heretic, a menace, while the orthodox Communists denounce him as a shamefaced crypto-Fellinian.

Pasolini's views on the working class have been equally independent. He insists that he was a supporter of the Communist Party before he studied Marxism, because emotionally he sides with and identifies with the peasants. This purely emotional response is still a strong motivating force. Pasolini's attitude toward the working class is in some respects one of old-fashioned romantic idealization rather than a more correctly Marxist appreciation of the workers' central role in the revolutionary struggle. Moreover, he is not a supporter and admirer of the solid, responsible, serious working-class hero: he has tended in his writings and his films to identify, rather, with the outcast, the criminal, the sub-working class. A case could be made out, of course, for seeing this as an expression of Marxism: crime being the inevitable response of the oppressed to an impossible social and economic situation. But perhaps we should more properly interpret it in psychosexual terms as a sort of *nostalgie de la boue*. Pasolini himself readily admits to being most at home with people of the roughest class, and many of his closest friends and associates, the most frequent actors in his films and members of his film units, are drawn from this class. Not for nothing was he employed in his script-writing days primarily as a low-life expert, able to provide firsthand details on the language and behavior of thieves, pimps, and prostitutes. And in fact his paradoxical, teasing attitude toward the social classes can perhaps best be summed up by his well-known comment on the battles between police and students in 1968: that he sympathized with the police, because they were working-class, whereas the student revolutionaries were all bourgeois—and, anyway, the policemen were a lot more attractive.

These complex and apparently contradictory attitudes might be deduced from a viewing of *Accattone*. Despite his brief involvement with Fellini after Fellini had finished with his neo-realistic phase, Pasolini as a scriptwriter had seemed primarily an ally of the second-generation neo-realists, and might perhaps have been expected to continue this allegiance in his first film as a director. And from a broad plot outline one might suppose he had done so. Accattone is a pimp, separated from his wife and son and living off the earnings of a prostitute. When she is arrested, so is Accattone, who spends some time in jail. Set free, he finds himself without a livelihood and tries to entice another girl into prostitution, but in the end softens toward her and does not make her go through with it. This faint taste of bourgeois ideals sets him to dreaming of a settled life again. But the only way he can think of bringing this about is through theft—a silly, small theft of a ham and some sausages, rather incompetently carried out. While eluding pursuit on a motorcycle, he crashes and is killed.

All this is quite conceivable in terms of the neo-realism practiced by De Sica in *Bicycle Thieves*. But Pasolini's approach to his material is very different: from the start he demonstrates that he is a filmmaker first and foremost, not a writer who merely transposes his screenplay to the screen. In *Accattone,* tone and atmosphere are everything, the literary basis very little. The visual style is extremely simple: Pasolini explains that it had to be, because technically he knew nothing and was feeling his way from shot to shot. But it comes across as the sophisticated simplicity of rejection and selection, rather than the awkward, enforced simplicity of the primitive. In most respects *Accattone* is a highly sophisticated piece of filmmaking, giving its simple and picturesquely squalid subject matter a new and puzzling dimension. For the first word I would apply to *Accattone* is mysterious; and the second, mystical.

Crucial in the establishment of tone is Pasolini's use of music

—a selection from Bach which seems, on the surface, unrelated or even contradictory to what is happening before our eyes, but imposes itself by sheer conviction of its own rightness, and from the beginning influences us to see Accattone's progress in a transcendental light, as a pilgrimage toward grace (the religious terminology is tendentious but inescapable). And the visual style, carefully considered, reinforces this impression. It will be remembered that Pasolini was once a student of art history and had a well-tuned eye in the visual arts. So it was natural that in deciding on a simple visual style as the only one at that time within his technical capacities he should have looked for some model or parallel in painting. The model he chose, he tells us, was Masaccio, and Masaccio's lofty simplicity, his monumental clarity and repose, seem to have rubbed off, transmuting a picturesque story of low life, acted by nonprofessionals on the streets where it might actually have happened, into a rarefied, hermetic experience.

And to make doubly sure that he would not be mistaken for a neo-realistic anecdotalist, Pasolini inserts at a crucial point in the narrative a dream sequence in which Accattone dreams his own death and seems to equate death with paradise, therefore accepting death as the inevitable end and consummation of his ambitions. That is not, of course, a very Marxist way of seeing things, and it helped to create serious doubts among the Communist critics in Italy and France about Pasolini as a Marxist thinker and artist. These Pasolini could explain away to some extent by saying that "atavistic, pagan, superstitious Catholicism" is proper to the character of Accattone, not to him; it seems to apply to him only because the film is made in the first person. What this does not explain, though, is the romantic aura that surrounds Accattone and the then nonprofessional who plays him, Franco Citti. In *Accattone* Pasolini comes close to idealizing this rogue member of the working class with his crypto-bourgeois aspirations, though, intellectually considered, the character should be the reverse of all that a good Marxist would consider admirable. If Pasolini can slip out of the charge of cleverly disguised religious conformity, he will not so easily elude that of (damaging to fellow Marxists, at least) formalistic aestheticism and inverted romanticism. And this would not be the last time that Pasolini the filmmaker would appear to be closer to Cocteau than to Communism.

Whatever the critical success of *Accattone* (and with critics between the two doctrinaire extremes of Catholicism and Communism it was great), Pasolini's second film, *Mamma Roma* (1962), has generally been regarded as a failure. Pasolini agrees, and points out three reasons for its failure: an ingenuous tendency to repeat himself from his first film while pursuing his technical education in cinema; the casting of Anna Magnani as a proletarian almost completely assimilated into the petite bourgeoisie, although she is not naturally like that and he himself usually casts people according to their natures rather than their acting ability; and the impossibility of acclimatizing a story of petit-bourgeois aspirations to the "mythic" style of *Accattone* and all his better films. Be that as it may, the film does seem patchy and inconsistent, partly because the story of a respectable prostitute and her son who is shattered when he learns the truth about his mother, and dies in prison after attempting a life of crime in reaction, is not inherently so interesting as that of *Accattone* and, evidently, does not engage Pasolini's sympathies to the same degree. Partly, too, Magnani seems altogether too powerful for the role, too histrionic, too much the star, and at every appearance tears the fabric of the film asunder. On the other hand, the son, played by Ettore Garofalo, a waiter Pasolini discovered who reminded him of a figure out of Caravaggio, does at times achieve the same sort of mythic status as Accattone, and at certain moments when the film concentrates on him, the choice of Vivaldi music is as natural, even inevitable, as is the Bach in *Accattone*.

With his next film, the "Ricotta" section of *Rogopag,* Pasolini achieved notoriety and got into a lot of trouble. Neither seems justified, since "La Ricotta" is both relatively harmless and not very good. It is a fantasy about a tempestuous director making a film on the life of Christ, setting the subject against the drab, materialistic life of the extras, the tantrums and bad taste of the filmmaking establishment, and the heartlessness of a situation in which an actor fictionally crucified could actually be left to die from sheer negligence and forgetfulness.

Stylistically the film is interesting, if again not very successful, in its juxtaposition of Pasolini's Masaccio style in the black-and-white framework with a much more mannered style drawn from the Florentine painters Il Rosso Fiorentino and Pontormo for the colored extracts from the film which is being shot. It is also curious to note the casting of Orson Welles as the director—cast, that is, for his natural characteristics as a man rather than his ability as an actor, in true Pasolini fashion.

"La Ricotta" points the way to Pasolini's next major film, in many ways his most controversial, *Il Vangelo Secondo Matteo* (1964). It is just what the title announces: a retelling of the Gospel story according to St. Matthew. Certainly it is the most serious, sober, and—despite doubts widely expressed during the shooting on account of Pasolini's much-publicized Marxism—deeply reverent film about Christ the cinema has given us. And yet, in a way, these are negative qualities: their presence does not necessarily mean that the director has come to terms with the central problems of his subject. It is not frivolous to say that the story has no suspense (everyone knows how it turns out); this is a problem in any dramatic representation of the life of Christ—the more so since it is all too easy to rely exclusively on the emotions that inevitably color it in the spectators' minds, instead of trying to make some positive contribution. It would not be fair to say that Pasolini has done this, but the film sometimes looks perilously like it. He approaches the story in strict literalness, with the dialogue straight from the Bible text, and deliberately strips the film of anything savoring of self-conscious "style." Unfortunately, it looks as if, instead of refining and disciplining, he has merely subtracted. The film is at times pictorially beautiful, and the nonprofessional players act with striking restraint: it is all quite distinguished, in a wan sort of way, but also, truth to tell, more than a little dull.

At least so it seems to me, though for many it is one of Pasolini's finest achievements. The reasons that brought Pasolini to make this film are strange, and not totally explicable, or at least not up to now totally explained. Pasolini has stressed that, though he is not a Catholic and did not even have a Catholic upbringing (his father was a nonbeliever who went to church just for show), he has always accepted the idea that the Christian heritage is inescapable for a Westerner, as well as the fact that his films are essentially religious in style and approach, even if the religion is a nondenominational one of his own invention. What seems to have intrigued him above all about the life of Christ is its closeness, as a story, to his own preoccupations. Christ, for example, is the proletarian hero elevated to the status of myth, and a literal rendering of the events in his life as given in the Gospel would almost inevitably take on the epic, mythic qualities Pasolini tends to see in all things. Also, as he points out, the Bible is not read in Catholic countries as much as elsewhere, and therefore characteristics of Christ which are familiar to Protestants from reading the Gospels produce controversy and contestation in Italian audiences: the film was a sort of journey of discovery for Pasolini and his audiences alike.

This may explain why Pasolini tends to see more novelty and ambiguity in the characterization of Christ than we see—in his violence, his revolutionary message, everything that made orthodox Italian Catholics feel that this Christ was shown as bad, upsetting, and was being used by Pasolini as the Devil's Advocate against the Church itself. Pasolini disclaims any conscious intention to present a new interpretation of Christ. At most, he wanted to produce an effect similar to that exerted by the Gospel story, with all its contradictions, and to tell the story straight with no attempt at a historically accurate reconstruction, modifying the original story simply by the way his viewpoint must differ from that of St. Matthew as a result of two thousand years of elaboration and interpretation. This, of course, places the film in a context for Italians, and for Pasolini himself, quite different from that for foreigners of non-Catholic background. It may even help to explain why for some it seems flat and conventional, even platitudinous. For all that, the film does show some change and advance in Pasolini's style as a filmmaker. He began the film in what he calls his habitual "reverential" style, but rapidly found that a reverential style for a subject already sanctified in the popular imagination was useless and destructive duplication, so after a crisis in which he thought of abandoning the film altogether, he began to shoot in a much freer, less formalized way, verging at times on *cinéma vérité*. The film became almost willfully a mélange of styles and approaches, and though this effect is not repeated elsewhere in Pasolini's films, the process obviously had a loosening and liberating effect on him. If *Il Vangelo Secondo Matteo* is not completely a success in its own terms, it is in many ways a necessary steppingstone to other, better things.

Between "La Ricotta" and *Il Vangelo* Pasolini made two documentaries (three, if you count *Sopraluoghi in Palestina per "Il Vangelo Secondo Matteo,"* a film about his abortive attempts to scout locations in the Holy Land—which at most he vaguely supervised and improvised a commentary for). I have not been able to see the second, *Comizi d'Amore* (1964), a filmed inquiry into views on sex, love, and marriage in Italy which was little shown there and not at all anywhere else. The first, *La Rabbia* (1963), was also suppressed, and even more completely, because it was coupled with an episode by Giovanni Guareschi, author of the *Don Camillo* books, which was adjudged racist. Pasolini's portion is entirely an editing job, from already filmed material concerning society in the late 1950's, put together as a critique from a fairly conventional Marxist point of view and commented on in verse. Pasolini dismisses the film as worthless, apart from a section on the death of Marilyn Monroe, and though *La Rabbia* is of interest to a student of Pasolini's development, it is hard to disagree strongly with his judgment.

After *Il Vangelo* comes an extreme change of pace, to produce one of Pasolini's most fascinating films, *Uccellacci e Uccellini* (1966), together with two episodes starring the same actors, Toto and Ninetto Davoli, which were intended as part of a complete feature but were instead integrated into two unrelated composite films: "La Terra Vista dalla Luna," in *Le Streghe,* and "Che Cosa Sono le Nuvole?" in *Capriccio all' Italiana* (both 1966). *Uccellacci e Uccellini* (called in America *Hawks and Sparrows*) is a wayward, fanciful sort of politico-social allegory—or so Pasolini explains it. But then, Pasolini has an explanation for everything, many of his explanations confected with almost perverse ingenuity. It is not so much that any of them are specifically true or not true, but it is part of the way his mind works that he will embark on an explanation in general Marxist or Christian or whatever terms and then regard it as an intellectual challenge to fit every detail into the general pattern, maybe just for the hell of it. So we may take note of Pasolini's statements that in *Uccellacci e Uccellini* Toto and Ninetto represent humanity on its journey toward and beyond Marxist consciousness, without following him too deeply or seriously into his systematic definition of every stage in their journey according to this program.

At the start of the film, as at the end, Toto and Ninetto, father and son, are walking along a dusty road. Where are they going? Though they are asked the question several times, they never offer a satisfactory answer. They appear to be a fairly normal bourgeois pair, going through life politically unaware, making decisions pragmatically from moment to moment. A number of minor incidents happen to or around them (notably, a double suicide). Then, while walking along a road under construction, they meet a talking crow. The crow (accompanied by Russian music at his first appearance) announces that he comes from the country of Ideology and that his parents are Doubt and Conscience. (Later a title coolly observes that, for anyone still in doubt, the crow is a leftist intellectual before the death of Togliatti; Pasolini has also said that the crow's role is entirely autobiographical.) Ninetto replies that he is Simplicity, Innocence, and Grace—a very religious definition, says the crow. The crow then tells a long story in which Toto and Ninetto reappear as medieval friars charged by St. Francis with evangelizing the birds. After a series of comical adventures while they search for a means of communication with the birds, they succeed in getting through to the hawks and the sparrows and converting them. The only trouble is that while the hawks as hawks and the sparrows as sparrows profess love of God, the natural tendency for hawks to prey on sparrows continues unabated. St. Francis is not nonplused, though: he sends the friars back to make the birds understand, predicting that one day a man with blue eyes will come to preach that struggles between classes must cease and the class system must die away.

Back in the present (or maybe the year 2000, which is mentioned at one point), Toto and Ninetto decide to relieve themselves on the property of a peasant farmer, who promptly drives them away with big guns. Immediately after this, Toto, as landlord, harasses an impoverished family of peasant tenants who are trying to live off cooked birds' nests. Then Toto and Ninetto (and the crow) meet a group of traveling players, who put on a show called "How Rome Ruined the World," interrupted when the leading lady, heavily pregnant, suddenly gives birth. In the following episode Toto and Ninetto visit a property owner, who proceeds to pressure Toto for money owed, so that we see Toto, recently preying upon the poorer and weaker, being himself preyed upon. At this point, actual film of Togliatti's funeral is inserted (Pasolini regards this as the turning point in the definition of Italian Communism). Then, after a brief interlude with a sexy young woman at the roadside (she represents vitality, says Pasolini), Toto and Ninetto turn on the crow and eat him, which seems only fair, since the crow has just observed that "professors should be eaten with *salsa piccante,* but those who eat them become a bit of a professor themselves."

Ergo, says Pasolini, the consumption of the crow shows that Toto and Ninetto, our typical unconscious Italians, have absorbed the crow's Marxist message by a quasi-Christian process of communion-like cannibalism, and thereby have achieved a new level of political consciousness. This may or may not be true. It would be difficult from the film itself to isolate any evidence of progression, or even of change, in their characters and attitudes. Rather, what we get is a picaresque fable, with a lot of humor and oddity; a play with ideas rather than a play of ideas. Certainly the film can be interpreted the way Pasolini suggests; but equally it can be interpreted in other ways, or in no way at all. Its tone is whimsical and teasing, showing Pasolini in an unusually relaxed and playful mood. Pasolini himself feels that the ideology weighs heavy on it, and that was one reason why he was eager to make the two episodes with Toto which followed. They are brief, eccentric, peripheral—indeed, Pasolini admits that "Che Cosa Sono le

Nuvole?" which is about a group of puppets (played by humans) performing *Othello* for a popular audience, is so short it probably makes no sense except in the imaginary context of the unmade episode film with Toto. "La Terra Vista dalla Luna" exploits further the Toto-Ninetto rapport of *Uccellacci e Uccellini,* on a more obviously fantasticated, fabulous level. It is a surrealistic film, even though all the places in the film—the cheap seaside resort, the Colosseum (where Silvana Mangano's fake fall takes place), the pink villa—are real. It is a puzzling fantasy of miraculous transformations, finding the surreal, the mysterious, the magical, in the heart of the real and the ordinary—the surrealism, Pasolini says, of Kafka rather than of Dali, deriving from a decadent symbolist tradition. Pasolini considers "La Terra Vista dalla Luna" one of the most successful things he has ever done.

All these Toto films are, in their various ways, triumphs of Pasolini's mythmaking faculties in the cinema. When he takes his myths ready-made, as in *Il Vangelo Secondo Matteo* and in his next film, *Edipo Re,* the effect is somehow less compelling. *Oedipus* has a splendid opening sequence in prewar Italy, which implies a whole Oedipal situation. But the body of the film, set in primitive Morocco and following Sophocles fairly closely, comes over as much more decked out than felt: one chafes at Pasolini's insistence on telling the story as though we had never heard it before, instead of taking some knowledge of it for granted and going on from there. Maybe Pasolini is assuming in us something of his own obsessive interest in the Oedipus myth. He has often spoken of his own Oedipal situation within his family, his obsessive love of his mother and hatred for his father, which much later on he discovered was a form of love also. The prologue to *Edipo Re* is thus, literally, autobiographical: the army officer father, the loving bourgeois mother, the child torn between them ("You are stealing your mother's love from me," says the father to the child at one point), and the period, beautifully, lyrically evoked, all correspond to Pasolini's own experience. But though the main body of the film may well have been intended, as Pasolini says, to be a mythicized autobiography, it becomes merely a familiar myth with vague autobiographical overtones too faint and rarefied to be caught by the normal ear.

It is difficult to feel that in *Edipo Re*—except in the prologue and the brief coda that shows Oedipus walking through the streets of modern Bologna—Pasolini has done much more than take the myth, and Sophocles' telling of it, for granted, instead of rethinking it or reexperiencing it. And, given this feeling, the unlikely trappings he has found for the Sophoclean past seem far more arbitrary and dandyish than integral to his conception of the story. One can appreciate the *idea* of recreating a primitive society (ancient Greece) in terms of a different but comparable primitive society (modern Morocco), but the inevitability of the identification somehow does not come across. The same with the choice of music, which is mostly Rumanian folk music augmented by a little Japanese music. The Rumanian music was selected by Pasolini for its cultural ambiguity, situated between West and East, Mediterranean and Slav, so that the unknowing listener would have difficulty guessing its source. The force of the intellectual notion—insisting on the universality of the myth by situating it outside history, beyond any specific cultural framework—can be appreciated intellectually, but it is not sufficiently felt, and the film remains, the prologue and coda apart, a clever but empty exercise in style.

Not so the other, contrasting (yet also closely related) film Pasolini made the next year, *Teorema*. This I believe to be Pasolini's masterpiece, the single work that triumphantly brings together all his talents at their highest, all his preoccupations at their most intense. Here he is back with myths of his own devising, and in that field he is incomparable; like the Ancient Mariner, he holds us with his glittering eye, and even if we resist or positively resent the story he is telling us, we still have to sit there enthralled and hear it out. *Teorema* is the sort of film that makes one think what a nuisance it is that, in the cause of intellectually respectable criticism, one must pretend to be interested in what films *mean*. That is not true, of course: part of the fascination of this extraordinary, intricate, and teasing film is to work out exactly what Pasolini thinks he means by it. But the first thing that strikes one is its mastery as a piece of storytelling, the way it keeps its audience agog to know what will happen next. It is far and away Pasolini's most entertaining film to date.

In it we meet an ordinary prosperous bourgeois Italian family—father, mother, teenage son and daughter, maid of all work—going about their everyday lives in black and white. A telegram comes, saying simply, "I arrive tomorrow." "I" is a beautiful young man (Terence Stamp), and with his arrival everything takes on color. His presence (completely unexplained, by the way: we never know who he is or why he is there) arouses everyone in the house, sexually and emotionally, and perhaps—though here we drift into interpretation—spiritually. Eventually he leaves, as mysteriously as he came, and the rest of the film follows the lives of those he leaves behind. The father gives away his factory and ends up stripping naked in a railway station. The mother (played, not altogether coincidentally, by Silvana Mangano, who played Jocasta in *Edipo Re*) drives around picking up strange young men. The daughter sinks into a cataleptic trance. The son goes off alone to become an artist. The maid goes home and starts levitating and performing miracles.

Now all this is fascinating simply as a story. We do not have to read it as a sort of allegory in order to enjoy and be gripped by it. Admittedly, part of the film's appeal does lie in its mysterious atmosphere, the feeling it gives of meaning more than it says, having an effect greater than or of a different kind from what we can logically explain. In a way it is best to leave it at that, to accept the idea that significances may hover around the heads of characters like a cloud of witnesses but resolutely refuse to be pinned down or analyzed. But narrative media do pose problems of their own: we would not ask what a still-life painting *means,* unless some allegorical detail is thrust upon our attention, but something which works, at least in part, through words seems somehow to call for explanation in words. The more so in this case, since the film was a center of controversy, as winner of the Catholic Office prize at Venice in 1965 and occasion of a court action on the grounds of obscenity and/or blasphemy thereafter. This would seem to presuppose that a number of people believed it had a paraphrasable significance, even if they disagreed violently about what it was.

On the whole it seems more useful, however, and more relevant to Pasolini's intentions, to think in terms of vague associations that color our responses to the story. For example, whether or not we identify the Terence Stamp character with Christ, we can hardly be unaware of a Christ-like aura about him: he is a redeemer, if not the Redeemer, bringing tidings of great joy which change those who hear them forever. Pasolini seems to share with Tennessee Williams in *The Milk Train Doesn't Stop Here Any More* a vision of the redeemer as a magnetically attractive young man and the notion that his new covenant has something to do with sex. (Pasolini has stated that he first conceived the character as a sort of visitant fertility god, and though he dropped the idea, something of it remains in the finished film.) Whether the sex is real or symbolic, or both, is another matter. I take it that it is both real (everyone in the household has sexual relations with the young man) and a symbol for mystical experience: understood in that light, the film makes sense as a religious document. No doubt, it is that anyway. We would not need *Il Vangelo Secondo Matteo,* which makes matters explicit, to understand that Pasolini's whole *oeuvre* is religious—whatever his expressed political convictions may be. The atmosphere of *Teorema,* as of *Uccellacci e Uccellini* and of *Accattone,* is that of religious parable, all the more vivid for its defiance of objective analysis. Pasolini's greatest gift in these films, the one that gives life and meaning to all the other gifts, is that of a modern mythmaker.

This is especially so since the myth is so evidently polyvalent. I have suggested that the Terence Stamp character is a sort of redeemer, and it seems to me that most of the overtones in his presence unmistakably imply this. But this is partly due to something Pasolini may not be consciously aware of, or might even deny: that a vital strand in the film is specifically one of homosexual eroticism. The sensuous quality of Terence Stamp's person, his touchability, is constantly emphasized, and even in the scenes in which he does not appear, such as the mother's first sexual encounter in a grubby hotel room, the camera dwells lovingly on male underwear, the gleaming white underpants cast off onto the floor. There is in the film, as far as I can see, no unmistakable eroticism directly connected with women at all. This obviously affects the balance of our responses, and our reading of the intellectual structure. Without it, one could maintain that the Stamp character is entirely negative in his effect, that his intervention destroys every member of the bourgeois family completely. But, with it, we are driven to see the change he brings about as positive, life-giving: the earlier security and order of the family was built on sterility and death; the chaos into which they are thrown is the way toward a new life. It is a revolution of destruction and creation, though some, particularly the daughter, may not be able to move beyond the first phase.

Formally, at any rate, *Teorema* shows a new and complete mastery of means on Pasolini's part. The style is pure, simple, and direct, in Pasolini's familiar "reverential" manner. There are no fireworks, and sometimes, as in the episode of the maid's levitation, or in her eventual self-sacrificial act of burying herself alive, the effect is deliberately analogous to that of primitive painting, the filmmaker withdrawing into an apparent naïve literalness that leaves us to supply our own comment, should we feel any comment is necessary. *Teorema* is Pasolini's first dramatic foray into the middle classes—something he had always avoided before, because of his ingrained dislike of the bourgeois and his unwillingness to spend any time with them, even on the set of a film. But the bourgeois background is simplified and stylized, with no attempt at realistic detailing: their world is hermetically sealed off from the world around them. Pasolini has been accused of being uncharacteristically charitable toward his bourgeois personages here—to which he retorts, reasonably enough, that they are not realistic bourgeois anyway, and that the film mirrors a change in the situation of the bourgeoisie, resulting from the gradual conversion of the whole world into bourgeois (a point implied earlier, in the aspirations of Accattone and Mamma Roma). If there is to be a revolution, says Pasolini, it cannot be simply against the bourgeoisie, it has to be within the bourgeoisie. This no doubt accounts for the otherwise confusing scene in which the father tries to hand his factory over to the proletariat and gets only a mixed, ambiguous answer: now it is not bourgeoisie and proletariat; they are all bourgeois.

But then—whether Pasolini himself would consider this a triumph or a disaster—one does not really worry too much about any confusion in this scene, or about what *Teorema* as a whole is finally supposed to mean. In the years since *Accattone,* Pasolini had gained in sureness with each film, and by the time he arrived at *Teorema* the significance, whatever one may decide it to be, is so completely expressed in non-literary terms, through the form of the film itself, that it leaves spectators affected, stimulated by an experience but with no irritating need to find a key, to puzzle out a symbolic or allegorical pattern beyond and beneath the story itself.

Porcile, the film which immediately followed *Teorema,* carries the technique further. It has two stories, interwoven with an apparent casualness which clearly conceals extreme care and calculation. Explicitly they are not in any way connected. In the first, set in a vaguely Renaissance period, a desperate bandit driven into a desert waste decides to resort to cannibalism in order to survive. He is joined by others, is finally trapped and condemned to death, but dies repeating, "I have killed my father, I have eaten human flesh, and I tremble with joy." In the second, the son of a rich German industrialist behaves mysteriously, evading attempts to get him engaged, to involve him in protest action, and generally to mix him with his kind; he even (like the daughter in *Teorema*) goes into a catatonic trance for some months. Finally, in the cause of a power game, a rival industrialist reveals the son's secret to the father: he has an overwhelming sexual passion for pigs. In the end the pigs eat him.

These two strange tales are held in delicate balance, each moving step by step to its climax. Visually the film is of extraordinary splendor; it is beautifully photographed in color which makes the most of the alternation between the bare volcanic uplands of the first story (like the wasteland in which the father in *Teorema* ends his journey) and the glittering baroque palace where the family in the second story lives. The slow revelations of horror and bestiality in both are impeccably filmed and synchronized. And the structure of the film as a whole is built with the inevitability of a piece of great music, a pattern that is completed with perfect emotional logic by the last "say nothing" gesture of the winning industrialist when he has satisfied himself that the aberrant son has been consumed, hair and hide, down to the last button.

The internal logic and emotional coherence of the film are so perfect that the last thing one wants to do is to look for meanings, to search for symbols and equivalences that, put together, could provide a clear, noncinematic statement on the human condition. Of course, there are references to other Pasolini films which we are probably meant to catch—the desert and the trance from *Teorema;* and the boy (Ninetto Davoli), who is the only character to appear, if only as a detached observer, in both stories, and who in Pasolini's films nearly always seems to stand for (dare one say?) holy innocence and unquestioning simple joy in life. That at least is what he seems to represent as the jigging telegram boy in *Teorema* and the dancing carrier of flowers in "La Fiore di Campo," the episode Pasolini made for *Amore e Rabbia* immediately before *Teorema.* Also there are touches which suggest a politico-social interpretation, particularly the situation of the industrialist family and the incidental reflections on the *haute bourgeoisie.*

If we really must find a formula for interpreting the film, the most useful is to see it in terms of an argument for the necessity of extreme solutions, of following through one's own logic to the end without flinching. The bandit is reduced to a state where the only way he can survive is to prey on his fellows, so why not follow this through to the extreme of actually eating them, and if he does, why should he be superstitiously ashamed? The industrialist's son lives in a world of human pigs—his parents are frequently compared to pigs, and the world around him is represented as a pigsty—so why shouldn't he follow this through to the extreme of literally living like a pig? In both cases, the central characters achieve a heroic integrity that the others lack: they are the only ones who manage really to live, by piercing through the outworn conventions and subterfuges of a society ripe for destruction.

All of this, even if true—and at least it is not untrue—does not make the film any easier to label: as Marxist, for instance, since we know Pasolini is a Marxist, or, as a Roman Catholic friend of mine remarked at once on seeing it, "Very Catholic." But then the great advantage of the film is that we do not have to label it, and probably do not want to label it. As private myth made public, it is sublimely self-sufficient, and stands alongside *Teorema* as one of Pasolini's most magisterial cinematic statements; these two films, above all the others, entitle him beyond argument to a leading and unique place in the contemporary cinema.

After this climax of intensity and mastery, there was, perhaps inevitably, some relaxation. As Pasolini himself has wrily remarked, he seemed to start with no sense of humor, then bit by bit acquired one, as part of the natural maturing process. Consequently, it would seem that, after *Teorema* and *Porcile* (which are themselves by no means devoid of humor, sometimes of a decidedly black kind), he passed into a comic phase. Before embarking on it, however, he was involved with two films that seem to be parentheses in his career. The first, *Medea* (1969), is a retelling of classical myth along almost exactly the same lines as *Edipo Re,* except that no explicit modern parallel is drawn. Again, the story of Jason and Medea is set against a background of exotic primitive societies of today, as an analogy to ancient Greece and Colchis. And, again, the whole process, though intellectually defensible, seems in practice disturbingly arbitrary, and one cannot help suspecting that the film was devised mainly as a vehicle for the opera star Maria Callas's dramatic debut, rather than from any deep artistic necessity. On the other hand, Pasolini's ostensible lack of personal involvement in the story may have made him more conscious of the need to dramatize, to interpret (if not radically reinterpret) in order to make a valid modern film, and *Medea* is certainly, on a fairly low level (for Pasolini), gripping and well done.

In this way, with its picturesqueness and relative lack of

intensity and internal complexity, it seems to look forward to the cycle of entertainment films based on medieval stories —*Il Decamerone* (1971), *The Canterbury Tales* (1972), and *The Arabian Nights* (1974). Before them, though, there is a film, *Ostia,* which seems to constitute an unmistakable backward glance. It was written, produced, and technically and artistically supervised by Pasolini, and features many of his usual actors, such as Franco Citti and Ninetto Davoli, but was directed by Sergio Citti, Franco's brother and for a long time Pasolini's first assistant. The overall effect is decidedly agreeable—more so, for instance, than that of *Medea*—but it does confirm that the *auteur* theory is essentially right: the film is so near to Pasolini and yet in the last analysis unbridgeably far from the films he has directed himself. But at least in its own terms, which are essentially those of early Pasolini, the Pasolini of *Accattone* with a dash of *Uccellacci e Uccellini,* it is gripping and entertaining. Franco Citti and Laurent Terzieff are brothers, ineffectual criminals who get involved with a strange girl whose presence finally separates them. But the routine-sounding story has little to do with the film as made, which is full of dreams and fantasies, often very funny—particularly when dealing with the Church and the anarchists (the brothers are anarchists but also devout)—and it is a very pretty film indeed. The episode of the boys' childhood, in which their father kills their pet ram and eats it in parody of the Last Supper, after which they calmly kill him, has its curious overtones in relation to Pasolini's often-mentioned hatred of his own father and his concentration on the patricide theme rather than the incest theme in *Edipo Re.* The final death scene on the beach at night, with one brother sitting by the other's body till morning, is haunting and poetic. The film would undoubtedly have been stronger and more compelling if Pasolini himself had directed it, but presumably it is the sort of subject which, though frequently used by him in the days of *Accattone* and *Mamma Roma,* he no longer finds exciting. However, like *Fortunella,* which occupies a similar position in Fellini's work (Fellini wrote it and cast it, but it was actually directed by a man of very different temperament, Eduardo di Filippo, presumably because Fellini was afraid of getting stale turning out vehicles for his wife, Giulietta Masina), it is fascinating for the light it throws on the art of the master himself, and it is an unusually pleasing piece of work on its own, necessarily less exalted level.

In *Il Decamerone* the air of joyful relaxation and good humor is complete: it is the loosest, most warmly human of all Pasolini's films, and also, obviously, the most commercial, a consideration which may or may not be coincidental. The film gathers about ten of Boccaccio's stories into a loosely organized panorama of medieval life. In the first half the continuity is preserved by the character of Franco Citti, weaving in and out of the action as a grand but decadent pederastic crook who at the end of the first section decides, for some reason known only to himself, to make a good death by frantically and heartbrokenly confessing to only the most minor transgressions of his sin-filled life, and is consequently treated as a saint and martyr after death. Incidental to his progress are the stories of Ninetto Davoli as a lusty young man who is dropped into a latrine in a scheme to rob him but retrieves matters by thrashing some tomb robbers and then robbing the tomb himself; of a young man who literally plays dumb in order to satisfy the lust of a conventful of nuns, but eventually finds it too much for him; and of a pair of young lovers caught together in bed by the girl's father but then blessed when he realizes what an advantageous match the young man is after all.

The second half introduces a new device for maintaining continuity, in the shape of Pasolini himself as Giotto, in the process of painting one of his most famous frescoes. While he broods and dreams, hesitates and then works madly, a succession of further stories is unrolled for us. A girl's lover is murdered by her brother, but she keeps his head in a pot of basil (the story used by Keats in "Isabella"); two brothers make a pact providing that the one who dies first will return to tell the other what the afterlife is like; a priest takes advantage of an avaricious simpleton's wife by pretending that he can turn her into an ass at will by having intercourse with her; a cheating wife, on the unexpected arrival of her husband, hides her lover in a large pot and then, when he is discovered, pretends he has come to buy it. The stories in the first half are on the whole more interesting, and certainly more energetically done, though the death of Franco Citti is a trifle perplexing in such a lighthearted context. Those in the second are less interesting, or more summarily managed (the pot-of-basil story in particular is cut off arbitrarily, as though Pasolini has suddenly lost interest). But the audience carries away from the second part an unforgettable image of Pasolini as the artist—gruff, awkward, absorbed in his own private world, seeking the dream and when it comes (a naïvely literal vision of judgment, surmounted by Silvana Mangano as the Virgin Mary) frenzied to capture it in permanence before it fades. The characterization is funny, and perhaps not so far wide of the mark as a self-portrait—a portrait of the artist as a middle-aged man, still driven, but able to relax and enjoy himself when the opportunity offers, as perhaps it offered itself to Pasolini in *Il Decamerone*.

In *The Canterbury Tales,* Pasolini again appears, again as the artist, Chaucer. But it can hardly be said that he gives himself any chance for characterization, any hint of personal identification. In fact, it is impossible to make any sense of Chaucer's role except as an arbitrary linking device, dropped in between tales (sometimes but not always) to be nagged by his wife, interrupted at his writing, giggling over a copy of *The Decameron*. Indeed, in the version of the film that has been publicly shown it is hard to make much sense of anything —it appears to have been assembled by a total stranger from a mass of possibly incoherent material shot by Pasolini. The version shown in Berlin (allegedly on a promise that it would win the main prize, which it did) was scarcely more than a rough-cut, lacking the prologue, and Pasolini afterward subjected it to a lengthy recutting. Now the prologue is there, more or less, but having taken the trouble to establish the idea of a pilgrimage to Canterbury and the proposal by the host that each pilgrim shall tell a story, the film blithely dismisses the whole notion. At one point Chaucer scribbles "notes" for a Cook's Tale (which Chaucer himself left unfinished), but this leads into a quite un-Chaucerian series of farcical episodes involving Ninetto Davoli disguised as a sort of medieval

Chaplin figure, hat, cane, and all, getting into various scrapes in his search for work and committing a number of more or less innocuous frauds, in two cases leading to the speeded-up ducking of his adversaries in the river.

Otherwise we can see odd remnants of Chaucer's stories, and even a hint or two of the "debate" involving the Miller's Tale against the Reve matched by the Reve's against the Miller. The Wife of Bath also recurs, in an episode from her autobiography, though we would have to be quick to spot her as the same lady who appears briefly in the prologue. There is a remarkable amount of nudity, mostly incidental, and inevitably the two stories involving farting, the Miller's Tale and the Summoner's Tale, are both included. Less inevitably, the lead-in to the Friar's Tale—a summoner's pact with the devil—involves two explicit cases of sodomy, the rich sodomite getting off and the poor one being gruesomely burned to death on a griddle. The Pardoner's Tale is reduced to the interlude of the three young men who go looking for Death and find him with some money under a tree, but it is elaborated with an introductory tour of a whorehouse and some urination on the heads of the assembled guests. The Merchant's Tale of the marriage of January and May, which is attributed to no particular narrator, is at least told fairly straight, perhaps because it comes early, before things had started to get out of hand, as in all the later stories. It is hard to imagine what Pasolini had in mind when he began the film, but whatever it was it clearly has not come through in the released film. Hardly any of it is funny, and the English dialogue is, even by usual Italian standards, poorly spoken and execrably dubbed. If Pasolini wanted to abandon the pilgrimage framework and concentrate on Chaucer as the storyteller, that would be fine, but then why has he made some ineffectual gestures toward putting in the pilgrimage anyway? Without knowing the inside story (if there is an inside story to know) we cannot begin to guess, and from the fragments that remain it is hard to care very much.

At least the third section of the medieval storybook trilogy *Il Fiore delle Mille e Una Notte* (*The Arabian Nights*) suggests more overall control than *The Canterbury Tales.* It uses some ten stories slipped into a framework derived from the tale of Mur-el-Din and his search for his lost slave-girl love, Zumurrud. Stories are constantly interrupted by other stories in a complex succession of exchanges and cappings of one narrative by another. Most of the stories chosen are, as one would expect, both exotic and erotic; the first aspect enables Pasolini to rehearse again his fascination with primitive communities as shown earlier in *Edipo Re* and *Medea,* with visits to some of the same places—the Yemen, Iran, Eritrea, and Nepal, among others. The second aspect helps give the film a broad popular appeal—a lot of attractive people, male and female, are laid alluringly bare in the course of the film, and there are enough sex variations, homo- and hetero-, to satisfy the most jaded audiences. A number of Pasolini's old standbys appear, sometimes a little incongruously, among the actors, including Ninetto Davoli and Franco Citti. Visually the film is the most handsome of the three, and completes (as we may suppose) this phase of Pasolini's career in fine style. Certainly it seems that though Pasolini is still drawn to the episodic and anecdotal material with a strong erotic slant from which these three films have been derived—at least to the extent of writing and supervising two more, *Storie Scellerate* and *The 120 Days of Sodom,* directed by his long-time associate and assistant Sergio Citti—he apparently has no desire to direct any more such anthologies himself.

There are perhaps a number of reasons why Pasolini made these three films. Maybe he just wanted to relax a little and have fun, after the intensity of his previous works; it is, after all, not unknown for maturity to be mellow and good-humored. Or maybe, as a professed populist and sympathizer with the working classes, he wanted to see if he could actually communicate with them, attract a large general audience (though the argument against that is that the audience these films attract will surely be largely bourgeois in search of a respectably naughty thrill). Maybe he just wanted to have a few moneymakers to strengthen his commercial position so that later he may choose to make less popular subjects nearer his own heart. Who knows? Possibly not even Pasolini for sure. But while the interest of *Il Decamerone* at least is not negligible, it is hardly surprising if we choose to continue thinking of Pasolini as the fascinating combination of intellect and instinct revealed in *Teorema* and *Porcile,* the ingenious re-creator of ancient myth in *Edipo Re* and *Medea,* the discoverer of the mystical in the heart of the ordinary in *Accattone,* and the whimsical fabulist of *Uccellacci e Uccellini.* If his later films are far less distinguished, that can hardly be more than a temporary accident of fate and film politics, bound sooner or later to be put unerringly right with a new masterpiece from one of the most extraordinary filmmakers in the world today.

Lindsay Anderson

Among the directors at present working in the British cinema, Lindsay Anderson is the only one, of any generation, who is truly an international figure, who can without apology or special pleading be considered in the same frame of reference as Pasolini or Jancsó or Ray—who is, in short, undoubtedly and unarguably an *auteur.* Of the older generation, Michael Powell, once the subject of some of Anderson's harshest criticism in his early writing for *Sequence,* was a filmmaker with style, flair, and a highly personal way of looking at things, consistent even in his extravagant and perverse taste. Among the newer directors Ken Russell (heaven help us) has turned out a body of work difficult to like but with its own crazy consistency and certainly impossible to ignore, however tempted one may be to try. Single films by other directors suggest interesting talents—Albert Finney's *Charlie Bubbles,* Ken Loach's *Kes,* Mike Leigh's *Bleak Moments*—which may confirm themselves with more exercise in a larger context. But from all these, and from his colleagues in the Free Cinema movement, which was so influential as a focus of activity in the mid-1950's—Karel Reisz, Tony Richardson—Anderson remains distinct. He has considerable technical abilities, he has a large body of work to his credit, especially if one bears in mind his closely related work in the theater, and above all he has the complex temperament, the burning necessity to express himself in film, and the consistent originality that makes any of his films immediately recognizable not only by the way it is made but also by what it says (and by the fact that the two are, in any case, indistinguishable)—qualities that mark him off as one of the world's relatively few true film creators.

Despite these attributes, or perhaps because of them, it is easier to assert the consistency of Anderson's vision than readily to capsulate it. Much in Anderson's work, as no doubt in his private personality, is built on contradictions, and the beginning of his career as a critic with a clearly held body of opinion and principle as to what the film ought and ought not to be is not so much help to one's assessment as might naïvely be supposed. A cynical humanitarian, a toughly practical idealist, a classical romantic, a realist fantasist, an intensely committed political man whose characteristic subject matter is intensely private—the more contradictions we pile up, the further we seem from a clear formulation of any sort. But the consistency of a personal vision is something, after all, which one feels rather than formulates—if we do not exactly murder to dissect, our analysis, at the very least, is likely to end up with many component parts which make sense and take on significance only when they have been synthesized by the creator in the course of creation. So it is good to take Lindsay Anderson's own writings—most of which, after all, appeared nearly twenty years ago—with, if not exactly a pinch of salt, at least a realization that they can never be regarded as a complete indication of his attitudes at the time, let alone as a program he had set for himself for the future.

In that light, however, it is still interesting and sometimes illuminating to look at *Sequence* and Anderson's own contributions to it, as well as his other writings on film. Anderson, like his associates on the magazine, was never hesitant to appear opinionated, balancing bitter denunciations of the commercial norm, *Kitsch,* virtually anything emanating from the (at that time) irredeemably bourgeois British cinema with generous enthusiasm for favored filmmakers and ideals of filmmaking. At the time *Sequence* was founded, in 1946, Anderson was twenty-three, an undergraduate at Oxford, where he had returned after a period in the Army (the time at which, in a famous phrase from a later article, he and other junior officers "nailed a red flag to the roof of the mess at the foot of Annan Parbat" in order to celebrate the election of a Labour government in 1945) to read English. His background, as he has always readily admitted, was impeccably middle-class: his father was a general, and he went to prep school and public school (Cheltenham College). He had graduated in a once familiar fashion from an uncritical, film-fan devotion to the cinema in all its generally accessible forms to a more critical and specialized interest on first contact with foreign-language cinema at Oxford, where he had also been an amateur actor and become interested (to a lesser extent than in films) in live theater.

He was therefore a young man of very decided ideas and something of proselytizing zeal. He was eager, like the nearly contemporary (though seemingly unconnected) group of young French filmmakers involved with *Cahiers du Cinéma,* to express his appreciation of certain films and filmmakers (John Ford, Humphrey Jennings) whom he felt to be unappreciated, or insufficiently appreciated, by conventional film critics with conventional ideas of what did and did not constitute art. This appreciation therefore inevitably involved a series of reevaluations, an upsetting of traditional, accepted priorities in film criticism, and so an attack on the critical establishment and the playing-it-safe "tradition of quality," as *Cahiers du Cinéma* was to dub it. The principal grounds of attack, on critics and films alike, were these: that the attitudes and material were entirely bourgeois, conformist, middle-class, and metropolitan, or at any rate southern English; that the approach to the cinema was still almost exclusively literary; and that British cinema took itself seriously neither as art nor as entertainment. What was advocated in place of the effete British cinema then on display was something that would be personal, with the possibility at least of individual creation rather than so many expressions of the famous British team spirit, that would acknowledge the existence of a Britain which was not middle-class, southern, and "nicely spoken," and that would have the density and complexity of a poem, instead of being, as most of British production was felt at that time to be, limited by the literary value of its script, respectable rather than revelatory.

Inherent in this criticism, of course, was the understandable desire of all young revolutionaries to take over the functions and prerogatives of the establishment. Those who wished to remain critics wanted, naturally, to be critics of national influence and importance; but most of the group regarded themselves as critics only for the time being, propagandizing for the type of cinema that they not only wanted to see but wanted themselves to create. The first issue of *Sequence,* to which Anderson contributed an article on contemporary French cinema, came out in December 1946 (he became an editor with the second issue, in winter 1947). But before the magazine finally expired in 1952, even before Gavin Lambert and other *Sequence* staff members staged a successful coup at the British Film Institute to take over the highly conservative, respectable quarterly *Sight and Sound* and make it over into a forward-looking critical monthly at the end of 1949, Anderson was involved in filmmaking—small-scale filmmaking, to be sure, but sponsored and from the first unmistakably professional. In 1947 he had met a film-society enthusiast who was married to the managing director of a Yorkshire conveyor-belt factory. The next year he was commissioned to make a film that would not just demonstrate what Richard Sutcliffe manufactured and how, but would also convey something of the firm's human context, how it fitted into its northern community, and what the special flavor of the firm and its workers was. The result was *Meet the Pioneers,* the first of three documentaries Anderson made for the firm on minimal budgets over the next four years.

The full range of Anderson's talents is not, of course, demonstrated in these first three films, but given the circumstances in which they were made, with Anderson teaching himself the rudiments of filmmaking as he went along, it is remarkable how much comes through. Particularly in the first, which is long (thirty-three minutes) and rather shapeless, but obviously has a subject and approach congenial to Anderson, and even more notably in the episode inspired by the factory lunch break showing the workmen eating and relaxing in various ways, something of the real quality of Anderson's work (its gentler side, anyway) is clearly visible—specifically the enjoyment of unpretentious people in their natural surroundings, the strong feeling for people as part of a whole context of life going on around them, which Anderson may have learned, or merely recognized as congenial, in the films of Humphrey Jennings. The other two films, *Idlers That Work* (1949) and *Three Installations* (1952), are less human in their orientation, more frankly instructional, dealing respectively with a component of conveyor belts and three different types of installation in which the belts are used, but they do show an expected progression in technical skill and professionalism.

With *Wakefield Express* (1952) we come to the first fully recognizable, characteristic Anderson film. Assigned to him as a result of his work on the three films for the Sutcliffes, the film commemorates the centenary of the local newspaper in nearby Wakefield. Again the subject centers on the relations of the individual to a community—we find out in the course of the film, which runs thirty-three minutes, something about the processes of printing and publishing a newspaper, but the essential is a demonstration of how the newspaper mirrors the community it serves. The film starts with a series of interviews between a reporter and various local people with odd hobbies, opinions on current local issues, or plans for local events—a typical cross section of local newspaper stories, in fact. The next section takes us behind the scenes to meet the staff of the paper, then back to a variety of events—sports (a Rugby League football club—shades of *This Sporting Life*), a carnival, a children's concert party, a ceremony at a war memorial, the triumphal return of a Channel swimmer. Back with the paper, we see a new edition going to press, climaxing in a condensed summary of what has gone before, the stories that have gone into the paper, and a quick finale as the paper goes into distribution and the reporter of the opening sequence starts his rounds again for the next issue.

The material is familiar enough from many British documentaries, but the only close comparison possible is with Jennings. The quality Anderson and Jennings have in common can best be described as a feeling for the texture of British life. The picture of the ordinary people of Wakefield and its vicinity is warm, sympathetic, entirely uncondescending, with full enjoyment of their idiosyncrasies and full acceptance of their qualities as individuals, not merely examples of something or other. Many of the people we meet for a moment are at once vivid—the budgerigar-breeding bus driver who is helping to organize the local Coronation pageant (we might recall Jennings's involvement with the Mass Observation survey of the 1937 Coronation), the woman seen in the war-memorial sequence, the bored child on the Pontefract carnival float. The style is easy, fluid, the whole film beautifully designed and proportioned, the vision of the people and the community romantic and idealistic certainly, but salted, as always in Anderson, with moments of tough reality.

It was in 1953 that Lindsay Anderson's reputation and abilities as a filmmaker became known to more than the limited, specialized audiences of sponsored films, when he co-directed *Thursday's Children* with Guy Brenton. It concerns the work of the Royal School for the Deaf in Margate and how they go about teaching children deaf from birth to speak. Though it is difficult to assess the role played by Anderson in the making of this film (Guy Brenton has since made several more admirably unsentimental films about those suffering from various diseases), at least we may be sure that the film contains nothing contrary to his wishes and inclinations. And the most notable characteristic which emerges from this film, as compared with the earlier ones, is a tough-mindedness that will never be absent from Anderson's later work. It might be possible on the basis of *Wakefield Express* to imagine Anderson as a soft-hearted liberal, a sentimental kind of humanist who rather uncritically loves people, the quainter the better. But the humanity of *Thursday's Children* is something altogether tougher, harder won. It would be stretching a point, but not too far, to see a comparison with Buñuel, particularly his *Los Olvidados:* the answer to these children's problem is communication, the breaking down of the barrier to their private world that deafness creates. The children are closely observed; they are attractive but not excessively cute, and we see them hard at work—sometimes agonizingly so—learning the look of sound they cannot hear, the feel of it as vibration on a balloon held close to the speaker's mouth, and gradually, painfully, how to create a similar effect by similar means, even if the sound making involved is, for the moment, an incidental side effect. Though the information conveyed by the film is by no means uncomplicatedly optimistic—only a third of the children, we learn, can ever hope to achieve true speech—*Thursday's Children* comes across as a hymn to man's potential, a study not so much of suffering as of triumph over suffering.

The film's sureness of touch, its absolute certainty of rhythm, its selection of detail in relation to the wished-for effect of the whole, were so remarkable that it received an American Oscar (not, of course, that that is necessarily any guarantee of artistic respectability) and on the strength of that a commercial showing in Britain—more, certainly, than most twenty-minute documentaries could expect. Anderson's next film was not specifically intended for a public or any other kind of showing, but, for the first time, was made just to please Anderson himself, to express something he felt a burning need to express. When *O Dreamland* (1953) finally put in an appearance as part of the first series of Free Cinema programs at the National Film Theatre in 1956, along with a selection of other independently made films by young filmmakers from Britain and France, it was revelatory—though perhaps what precisely it revealed was less clear at that time. If *Thursday's Children* showed a new tough-mindedness in Anderson's work, *O Dreamland* moved further into something very like savagery —*Los Huerdes* rather than *Los Olvidados.*

It was conceived when Anderson, while working on *Thursday's Children* in Margate, visited the famous Dreamland amusement park there. The film that arose from this experience can be read in various ways, but, strangely enough for a work assumed at the outset to be directly propagandist, it defies easy and precise definition. In fact, it is the first film that brings us face to face with the contradictions and paradoxes of Anderson's nature and the explosive effects that may be expected from them. The film has no commentary—we are left to reach our own conclusions. During the film's twelve minutes' running time we are presented with a picture of the English working class taking their pleasures glumly. In Dreamland we cut in impressionistic fashion between the apathetic spectators and the tawdry, cheap, often naïvely sensational sideshows. The film begins with a short sequence of shots setting the scene and getting us, and the people, into the amusement park. Then, to the sound of harsh recorded laughter (it belongs to a sinisterly nodding dummy in one of the sideshows), we see some of the cheerful entertainments offered—tableaux showing "the death of a thousand cuts," an electrocution, "torture through the ages," and so on. The people shown are hardly more attractive—the caged animals are more worthy of our sympathy than the gullible, overweight, phlegmatic spectators who trudge around to the ironic strains of Frankie Laine singing "I Believe."

But already interpretation creeps in. In the context of the rather simple-minded left-wing idealism in vogue in the later 1950's, the era of protest, *Look Back in Anger,* the Aldermaston marches, and later Arnold Wesker's Centre 42, advocating folk festivals and the general elevation of debased popular entertainments, the film could superficially be read as a denunciation of the exploitation of the working classes in a consumer society where rubbish such as we see for ourselves was all that was offered as cheap popular entertainment. But the film does not feel like that. Despite the opening shots of a chauffeur polishing a Bentley, it is hard to feel that the film-maker's attitude toward the people he shows is entirely compassionate; often it is hard to see it as compassionate at all. Maybe they are victims, but it hardly seems in Anderson's nature to feel or enjoin much sympathy for victims so passive, so ready to accept their lot. After all, it is one of the effects of cross-cutting as a technique that it can be taken either way: when the film brings together the hideous dummies of the side-shows and the unresponsive visitors gazing at them in a cross-cutting sequence that enforces comparison, we can see at once that the equation implied is hardly flattering to the human elements of the sequence, who are almost necessarily reduced to the status of dummies themselves, and scarcely if at all more appealing. Why, after all, are they there? They have free will, they can choose not to accept exploitation in this way; and if they do not, if they have been completely brainwashed, they do not deserve our sympathy. On the contrary, we may well come away from the film feeling they have got no better than they deserve, blaming them for doing nothing to help themselves. Humane, in a true, critical, unsentimental sense, the film may be, but anger replaces the conventional gesture of condescending sympathy. "Only connect" is the film's message, and anger at those who refuse even to try, who remain passively stuck in their tawdry amusement-park world, is the only humanly possible reaction.

The film has suffered a little with the passage of time, and some of its observations and devices became hackneyed in the next few years, when a visit to a seaside amusement park, screaming visitors, nodding dummies, and all, was standard procedure in virtually every manifestation of the British film-making new wave. Also, a shift in sensibility has transformed some of the popular entertainments the film so enthusiastically denounces into the appreciated raw material of the Pop Art vogue. But the film continues to work as powerfully as ever in most respects, because it has the richness and complexity of a poem, and a highly personal poem at that, transcending its immediate occasion and its period through sheer force of the creator's conviction. And it does contain in microcosm much of the later Anderson—his humanity and his savagery, his pity and his anger, and the impossibility of pinning him down to any simple formula. *O Dreamland* is immediately recognizable as a work from the same hand as *If . . .*

The rest of Anderson's short shorts call for fewer comments: another film sponsored by Sutcliffe, *Trunk Conveyor* (1954); a group of four five-minute films made for the National Society for the Prevention of Cruelty to Children in 1955—*Green and Pleasant Land* (note the Blakean title, with its Jennings-like overtones), *Henry,* a miniature drama about a runaway child of quarreling parents who wanders the West End of London at night, *The Children Upstairs,* and *A Hundred Thousand Children;* some other bits and pieces; and, perhaps most interesting, *Foot and Mouth* (1955), a powerful and alarming depiction of foot-and-mouth disease made for the Ministry of Agriculture, intended as a warning and an explanation of what happens during an outbreak of this cattle disease. Fortunately the film had to show everything by suggestion since no actual outbreak was available for filming at the time. At about this time Anderson also had his first direct experience with the most commercial side of filmmaking: the making of filmed commercials for such products as Kellogg's Corn Flakes, Lux Toilet Soap, Cracker-Barrel cheese. Also in

1955–56 he made five half-hour episodes for the popular filmed television series *The Adventures of Robin Hood,* an experience (his first filmmaking with professional actors) which he seems to have found, if not an important challenge to his creative abilities, at least educative and by and large enjoyable.

But 1956 was most important as the year of Free Cinema. Important, though, in what way? Despite the flurry of publicity at the time, the importance of the moment is more symbolic than actual. It seems that the season at the National Film Theatre was a passing idea of Karel Reisz, then program director of the theater, using as keynote a phrase coined by Anderson in *Sequence.* The idea was to show a selection of independently made films from various countries—the six programs included, as well as the new films by new British directors, films by Truffaut, Chabrol, Georges Franju, Roman Polanski, and Lionel Rogosin—with no well-defined common program, though most of them were of that awkward medium length between twenty minutes and an hour. In all, eleven British films were shown, the best-remembered being *Momma Don't Allow,* a study of a teenage dance by Karel Reisz and Tony Richardson, *We Are the Lambeth Boys* by Karel Reisz, and the three films Anderson was directly connected with, *O Dreamland, Every Day Except Christmas,* both of which he directed, and *Together,* directed by Lorenza Mazzetti, on which Anderson was supervising editor and did some extra shooting. The makers of these films were united by friendship, several of them worked on and off for the British Film Institute, and the technicians also worked on various other films in the series. The impression created is of a tightly knit group, but not necessarily one which had any kind of ideological uniformity.

Nevertheless, the films did have certain things in common. Most obviously there was their acceptance of classes other than the middle classes as worthy to be taken seriously in films. Of course, the emotional journalistic statements suggesting that before Free Cinema the working class had never been seen on film were as overstated as some of the exaggerated claims made for the post-Osborne British drama. All the same, there is something new in *Momma Don't Allow* and *We Are the Lam-*

beth Boys—a ready, unquestioning acceptance of the working-class boys from South London as people in their own right, with no need to place them socially before establishing them as worthy of sociological study. (Possibly this has something to do with the presence of an outside eye, that of Czech Karel Reisz, who may be supposed to have come to the cinema without all the social hangups an English contemporary might evidence in dealing with the same kind of subject matter.) Lindsay Anderson's contribution, *Every Day Except Christmas,* comes in a rather different category. If the two Karel Reisz films have a refreshing objectivity about them, Anderson's film, though made on the same sort of basic assumption and co-produced by Karel Reisz, has a very different flavor. Though the surface is realistic enough, the overall tendency is toward mythologizing. Again we are driven for comparison to Humphrey Jennings—the film is (this time) mostly gentle (like Jennings), and is informed throughout by an almost mystical feeling (like Jennings) for the fabric of British life, an unashamed patriotism and enjoyment of the Englishness of England (curious in Anderson, who is largely Scottish and claims to be in temperament much more Scottish than English), a liberal regard (which could easily be mistaken for a conservative right-wing regard) for all classes and groups as part of the whole pattern of life, a vivid recognition of the interrelation between people and place.

Every Day Except Christmas (1957) is a forty-minute documentary about the Covent Garden fruit and flower market and those who work there. It takes us, in a simple, easy, but tightly plotted progression through the entire daily cycle, from the setting out of a load of mushrooms from Sussex to the last of the sales in mid-morning to the West End flower ladies. The picture presented of the market workers is, if not too idealized, at least decidedly idealistic. No apparent connection between these people and the apathetic denizens of Dreamland. Possibly Anderson might justify this by maintaining that the market workers represented the uncorrupted working class, retaining their original class integrity, as opposed to the corrupted workers of *O Dreamland.* More probably he would say that they could be precisely the same people, at work and at play, but that he has the right as a creator to select, and on this occasion he has chosen to select the heroic aspects, to give a positive image, which is neither more nor less true than the negative view of *O Dreamland.*

Whatever the explanation—and no explanation is necessary—*Every Day Except Christmas* is an extremely *soigné,* effective, romantic documentary of a rather old-fashioned kind. The opening sequence sets the tone, with the truck setting out from Sussex as the Light Programme on the radio closes down with the National Anthem, shamelessly used to give a proud lift to the film as it moves into an evocation of the other vehicles converging on Covent Garden through the night from the orchards and farms of the Home Counties, the ports of the West. Next we see the deserted market gradually filling with workers, and the tempo quickens as the market itself is set up, the trucks are unloaded, and the whole scene is built into a complex pattern of sights and sounds. After the intensification, a relaxation—the tea break around four-thirty in the morning (comparable to the lunch break in Anderson's first film, *Meet the Pioneers*). This episode is perhaps the most personal of all; it captures to perfection the easy comradeship, the strange mixture of people in the café—workers, derelicts, and the mysterious collection of people, who knows what or from where, who drift in out of the dark for half an hour or so and vanish as quietly as they came. Again, the attitude is romantic, relishing, but tinged with curiosity and a feeling for the bizarre which prevents the film from becoming too sentimental and cloying. After this middle section the tempo of the film picks up again, as shot after shot of massed flowers leads us into the concluding morning sequences, with the old, reminiscent flower women coming to collect their barrows full of flowers, and the final succession of smiling faces suggesting the satisfactions of a good job well done, the uncomplicated friendliness of the unspectacularly heroic workers.

If that sounds sentimental—and it does—the charge cannot be altogether denied. Most of *Every Day Except Christmas,* for all its technical skill, its cunning assemblage of vivid, vivifying detail, is just that little bit too bland and rosy to be altogether true. It is rosy realism which does not quite come across as a genuine feeling. The act of selection and the nature of the selection are fair enough—obviously some sort of selection is inevitable and any selection must at least imply the criteria by which it is made—but I have the impression that the darker, tougher sides of Anderson's observation are being deliberately suppressed, that his tribute to the spirit of Jennings (and Ford) is a little too self-conscious, so that it comes across as a mask deliberately (and willingly) assumed rather than the creator's true face. The only place where we are allowed any real freedom and ambiguity of response is in the tea-break sequence, when all in the garden is not lovely, where derelicts and examples of the undeserving poor drift into the picture, and the prevailing conspiracy of jolly Cockney bonhomie is momentarily muddied with the intrusion of something less responsible, less easily categorized. No doubt about it, *Every Day Except Christmas* is a distinguished piece of filmmaking, but an anachronism—not a bad thing in itself, if the creator were himself an anachronism, but Lindsay Anderson is anything but—and the film cannot but seem profoundly irrelevant to the fast-developing talents of the man who, only six years later, was to make, as his next major film, *This Sporting Life*.

It is possible, of course, that Anderson himself underwent some radical changes during this time, but on the strength of *O Dreamland* one would not suppose so. Between 1957 and 1963 he worked on only one film, the anonymous, collective documentary *March to Aldermaston* (1958), chronicling that year's march by anti-nuclear demonstrators to Britain's main nuclear experimental station, on which he was one of some half-dozen directors, overall supervising editor, and mainly responsible for the commentary. But, much more importantly, he developed a busy career in a different field of directorial activity, the theater. In 1957 he accepted an invitation to direct a Sunday-night production at the Royal Court Theatre, center of the "New Drama," and in subsequent years he directed several productions there, the most notable in terms of popular success Willis Hall's *The Long and the Short and the Tall* (1959), and the most challenging John Arden's *Serjeant Musgrave's Dance* (1959). In 1960 he directed his first West End production, *Billy Liar,* with Albert Finney, and in 1963 he adapted, with Richard Harris, Gogol's *Diary of a Madman* as a monodrama starring Richard Harris, and directed it at the Royal Court.

The significance of this work in the theater is threefold. It added another string to his bow as a filmmaker, by habituating him to working with actors at all stages of production (the casting of the *Robin Hood* episodes was governed by the overall pattern of the series, and of course most of the actors' characterization and performance were set already by what had gone before). It made him more of a name to be reckoned with—though, as he has wrily remarked, not sufficiently to get him offered direction of the film of his big stage hit *The Long and the Short and the Tall.* And, quite apart from what effect it may have had on his career in films, it has its own independent significance and value. Though Anderson's first allegiance has been, and I suppose still is, to the cinema, and he was passionately involved with films at a time when he disliked and distrusted the atmosphere and attitudes of the theater, he has come to be one of the most brilliant stage directors in Britain, bringing to his theatrical productions a mastery of tempo and shaping, an extraordinarily close grasp on his actors, not only as individuals but also as functioning parts of an exquisitely orchestrated whole, and—what is most unusual in the British theater—the impress of his personality to the extent that, without underestimating the contribution of dramatists such as David Storey, with whom he has been associated on several occasions (*In Celebration, The Contractor, Home, The Changing Room*), or his dedication to the precise realization of their texts, one can still appreciate the final result as part of Anderson's own *oeuvre,* the expression of that rare creature, an *auteur* theater director.

Anderson's first feature film, *This Sporting Life* (1963), initiated two collaborations that were to be important in Anderson's working life, with the actor Richard Harris and, longer and more fruitful, with the writer David Storey. The film is based on Storey's first novel, published in 1960. Anderson had read it and been interested in it when it first appeared; the producers who eventually acquired the rights to the book approached Karel Reisz to direct the film—on the strength of his first feature, *Saturday Night and Sunday Morning,* and a supposed affinity of theme and background. He did not want to, but suggested that he should produce and Lindsay Anderson direct. They decided that the only person who could adequately write the script for the subject was Storey himself, though he had never before written anything in dramatic form. The script evolved from the book in close collaboration between Storey and Anderson and Reisz, and later Richard Harris. And obviously, in Storey, Anderson found a writer whose point of view on human and social matters was very close to his own. In a program note for the first production of Storey's play *The Restoration of Arnold Middleton* (1967), Anderson has described himself at the time of his first meeting with Storey:

> At that time I still believed, or wanted to believe, that things (society) could become "better." David, whose father had not been some sort of General, and who had managed to fill out his State School Scholarship by battering and being battered, every Saturday during the Season as a forward in the Leeds Rugby League "A" team, was not under this misapprehension. Also he was not interested in surface, but in essence; not in what was representative, but in what was exceptional. This made him, and makes him, a very exceptional kind of English writer. A lot of glib generalisation has been made about the "Northern" writers who appeared in the late 'fifties and early 'sixties. In fact a certain kind of honesty, a certain kind of vitality is all they had in common. David Storey's unique quality—and it is one I personally value above all others—seems to me a sort of elemental poetry, a passionate reaching-out, an ambition of concept that carries him beyond neatness, completeness, civilised equilibrium. He seeks to penetrate the soul; yet he never forgets the relevance of the social world in which souls meet, conflict and struggle. He labours, often desperately, to balance the ambiguities of our nature, our situation: male and female, tenderness and violence, isolation and love.

We can no doubt take Anderson literally when he suggests that at the time of preparing *This Sporting Life* for filming he was still socially committed in a rather naïve way, a believer in social amelioration and the potential of the film for helping to bring it about. By comparison Storey was not so much disillusioned as realistic—he had experienced at first hand what

Anderson, with his bourgeois background, was conscious of having only studied from a distance, and his progression had been what a near-contemporary dramatist called in the title of one of his plays "the birth of a private man." Whatever Storey's political and social convictions, they are not vitally relevant to his work as a writer: one might guess at them, but he is an observer of how human beings are rather than a prescriber of how they ought to be; he is not a propagandist for any particular set of attitudes, however admirable. As Anderson correctly observes, he is most interested in soul-states, and what in *This Sporting Life* is still given the semblance of a realistic story of life in the North (hence the implied comparison with Alan Sillitoe's *Saturday Night and Sunday Morning*) emerges in his later novels, particularly *Radcliffe,* as a symbolic drama in which the surface of reality is re-created only in order to be pierced in search of something deeper and stranger, the essence. In this, of course, it is unlikely that he brought any great new revelation to Anderson, but rather that his literary practice matched a shift in Anderson's own nature and interests in a direction already indicated by *O Dreamland* and some of his theatrical productions, notably John Arden's violent and ambiguous *Serjeant Musgrave's Dance*—away from direct social propaganda, away from too ready categorization and capsulation, toward the more elusive, mysterious essence of human nature.

The film that resulted from this collaboration was at the time of its appearance unique in the British cinema, and if there is anything to compare it with since, it is only the work of Anderson himself. The film's most immediately striking quality is its unashamed emotionalism. Here is no stiff-upper-lip understatement of emotion; when the characters suppress or repress their emotions, it only produces an even more powerful charge of violence—every scene in the film is charged with the passion of what is not said and done, as well as what is. It now seems incomprehensible that *This Sporting Life* tended to be judged (or misjudged) on its first appearance as another generally realistic, semi-documentary picture of life in the North, like *Saturday Night and Sunday Morning* or *A Kind of Loving*. It would be more to the point to compare it with *Wuthering Heights,* a book Anderson and Harris planned to film immediately afterward—the same elemental drama of souls in conflict, the same titanic emotions, the same kind of obsessive passion which racks the superficially unlikely pair of principals, footballer Frank Machin and his dowdy middle-aged landlady, Mrs. Hammond. Though real enough and believable enough, this kind of *amour fou* is remote indeed from what the staid middle-class British cinema would generally regard as realism.

No need now, anyway, to rehearse the errors of the past. Despite initial misunderstandings, the film has established itself as a classic of modern cinema, its true nature well understood in the light of Anderson's subsequent films and out of the misleading context of British cinema in which it first appeared. It is constructed on a grand scale, and begins with—I am tempted to call it a flourish, except that it is entirely practical and functional, a gesture which at once unmistakably establishes the style and approach. The film is in effect, like the book, a first-person narrative—we tend to see things from Machin's point of view, if not literally through his eyes. At the opening it is established that he is a professional football player (of that strange Northern variety called Rugby League), he is fouled during a game, smashed in the mouth, and has to have his broken front teeth extracted under anaesthesia. While this is happening we are given a shuffled pattern of flashbacks which continues after he has come out of the anaesthesia and while he goes to a Christmas Eve party at the home of his patron (or ex-patron, as it turns out); the use of flashback, and the interrelation of the two time levels, past and present, is established with the "excuse" of the administering of the anaesthetic gas (which the conventional-minded among the audience will at once recognize as the expected lead-in to a flashback—an interesting example of Anderson's considerable practicality when it comes to clear communication with his audience: he is no ivory-tower theorist who does not care whether or not he gets his points across), but as soon as it is clearly established and thus is of no further use, the convention is unobtrusively dropped.

The flashbacks themselves introduce us to Machin's private

life and emotional history, which, in all conscience, is bizarre enough. As a football star, even of this small-time, local variety, he is a hero in the neighborhood—a status insisted upon by the devotion of the team hanger-on, Johnson (an ambiguous figure whose emotional and covertly sexual devotion to Machin is left, like the complex sado-masochistic attitude of the patron, Weaver, meaningfully undefined). He could more or less have his pick of the local girls, not to mention their willing seniors, such as Mrs. Weaver. But he, with a kind of built-in, inescapable perversity, chooses to love his landlady, a severe, puritanical, obviously repressed middle-aged widow, Mrs. Hammond. In the course of the flashbacks we see Machin as a new boarder in the house, his beginnings as a footballer of some stature, after a tryout and a once-over look by the team managers. We also see his gradual ascent, as far as he does ascend—the £1,000 contract, the status-symbol white car—and the equally slow development of his relationship with Mrs. Hammond, taking her and her children for a ride in the country, maneuvering her to the point where she will accept his lovemaking but without response. We also see something, though not very much, about how the team is run, the sponsorship of the local rich, and in Machin's case the special interest the wife of one of the local rich, Mrs. Weaver, takes in his career, though she does not succeed in seducing him.

At the Weavers' Christmas party the two strands come together, and from then on we follow the further history of the relationship between Machin and Mrs. Hammond directly. The relationship is doomed, if not necessarily to tragedy, at least to frustration on both sides. Machin is determined to break her down, to make her react in some way, to show some tenderness, and she is determined at all costs not to. The only tenderness she shows is toward her dead husband's boots, kept always cleaned and ready in the hearth. An appearance of softening when Machin comes home on Christmas Eve is only temporary; she is hard, stiff-necked, obstinate to a degree which takes all joy out of their sexual encounters, making them begrudging to the point that he virtually has to behave like a rapist each time. And indeed his attitude toward her is in general somewhat that of a rapist—as in his game, so in his life, he plays hard and dirty; he is aroused by her willful indifference, her refusal to be affected, and his passion for her expresses itself in inarticulate violence, as the structure of the film, bringing together the game and the private life, makes very clear. If she gives nothing of herself, he gives nothing essential of himself either.

A key to the film's method comes near the end, in which a terrible, nightmarish football match, shot in slow motion as the players wrestle in the mud like prehistoric animals (an effect repeated in the last battle sequence of Welles's *Chimes at Midnight*), leads into the sequence of Mrs. Hammond's death, in which he returns to the house to find her missing, carried off to the hospital with a stroke that seems almost like her last, definitive line of defense against him, follows her there, and arrives in time to see her die. Again, everything is done in a ruthlessly exterior way—the bare hospital room, the trickle of blood from a corner of Mrs. Hammond's mouth, and a violent resolution of emotion which cannot be expressed when Machin smashes a spider on the clinically white wall with his fist. From here, back to the football field, with Machin running away from the camera to join a remote game at the far end of the field, vanishing as it were into the scenery, fading from our view as he begins what we presume to be his downward course as a football pro, out of every one's sight and back, maybe, to the coal mine where we saw him start. The structure of this sequence is symptomatic: the boldly symbolic use of the detail of the football games, the sandwiching of the crucial scenes of Machin's private relationship between two football scenes, the crystallization of emotion not in words but in the action of killing the spider. The whole film works by similar juxtapositions, conveying emotion and attitude by a complex net of references and implied equations or substitutions. Anderson is never afraid of the big effect, the bold and sometimes the crashingly obvious—the killing of the spider is powerfully effective, giving exactly the needed emotional release, but subtle it is not.

For the novel's more introspective style of first-person narrative, often commenting on and explaining emotions, the film substitutes happenings, external, observable happenings from which we can draw our own conclusions. The syntax is entirely functional—the exact ordering of scenes and actions is very important to the significance of the whole, and the beginning in anaesthetized recollection and the concluding slide into nightmare establish the feverish emotional temperature of the film without need for further explanation. Not that the other side of Storey's (or Anderson's) talent in the clear-eyed observation of realistic detail is let go by default—if the interest of both in this story is in the essential, the conflict of souls, we are never allowed to lose sight of the fact that these souls dwell in particular, expressive bodies (notably those of Richard Harris and Rachel Roberts), and their conflict is not only cosmic but localized in time and place, situated within a believable context of life. If appearances are to be penetrated so that we may glimpse the essence, at least the appearances have to be recognized first. Some of the film's best moments come from the relaxed observation of people and milieux, as in the pub scene with its bouncy, confident, incompetent entertainers and the funny, vulnerable image of a Machin, for once all violence put aside, singing with slightly sheepish seriousness "Here Is My Heart." The flavor of life in Mrs. Hammond's house, all spotless with mean-minded, finicky attention to the details of drudgery, and the contrasting vulgarity of the nouveau riche Weavers, are captured with believable accuracy.

Only in one instance, I think, does the method go astray—the scene in which Machin takes a resentful and resistant Mrs. Hammond to a posh restaurant in order to impress her and show her off, and then behaves with such obtrusive boorishness, putting his feet up on the table and so forth, that she leaves. One can see what the scene is intended to do, precipitating into symbolic action Machin's sudden resentment of the world he can enter only on suffrance, and at the same time dramatizing one of his frontal attacks on Mrs. Hammond's mind and emotions. But on the realistic level the scene comes rather out of focus—we feel that the symbolism is being stretched to make a point, at the expense of believability. But for a film of such boldness in conception and complexity in execution the errors are amazingly few—the film remains true to David Storey's conception, but at the same time takes on the quality of an *auteur* work, the unmistakable expression of Lindsay Anderson's own tender, violent temperament in images of unshakable power.

In his next film, *The White Bus* (1966), the tenderness is uppermost. It is a forty-six-minute-long short story shot mostly in black-and-white, with occasional brief excursions into color. It was intended originally to be part of a three-episode feature which went through various transformations at the planning stage and finally emerged as *Red White and Zero,* with other episodes directed by Tony Richardson and Peter Brook (or rather, did not emerge, since to my knowledge the episodes have only been shown separately). *The White Bus* is based on a script by Shelagh Delaney, which is obviously semi-autobiographical, depicting as it does the return of a young girl to her native town in the North (Manchester being used as the location). From the start it establishes the right mood of light-hearted yet slightly barbed fantasy when among the ordinary, realistic shots of the girl working late in a London office is inserted one shot of her hanging from the ceiling while the cleaners go about their work taking no notice. This surrealistic touch carries us at once into another, more magical realm than *This Sporting Life,* where even the boldest symbolic touches never break wholly with reality. And the whole of *The White Bus* has the quality of a fairy tale for grown-ups, funny and sad and sharp, using the girl as a focus for our attention, so that we see the town as she sees it, with a level, interested, unflinching, unalarmed gaze.

On her arrival in the North, the girl joins a conducted bus tour, in the white bus. Nearly all the film from then on consists of a series of little incidents and encounters on the tour. The group includes a whimsically assembled party of foreigners—a Japanese lady in a kimono, a Nigerian man—and a scarcely less foreign traditional Englishman in a bowler, plus the mayor with his mace bearer and mace in attendance. The conductress rattles off facts and figures like a machine, the mayor orates in resounding generalities, and the visitors trot patiently around factory and school, park and playground, library and art gallery, with little more positive response to their surroundings than the apathetic denizens of Dreamland. All, that is, except the girl, who fantasizes intermittently, placing herself among the choir at her old school or seeing the people in the park, in a burst of color, arranged in tableaux from Fragonard, Manet, and Goya (the effect of this sequence is curiously reminiscent of James Broughton's fanciful 1952 short, *The Pleasure Garden,* which Anderson produced and acted in). It is no doubt because she alone is not totally at the mercy of the tour guides that, near the end, she is the only one who remains alive and responsive when all the rest turn into stuffed dummies at a civil-defense demonstration which is supposed to be the spectacular highlight of the tour. At the end she is solitary again, as at the opening, roaming the streets at night, watching other people going about their own lives inside the lighted windows, and finally making no contact with a young man in a fish-and-chip shop who chatters on endlessly about his routine as he stacks up the chairs for the night.

The White Bus is deliberately light and slight, but it is, beneath its deceptively whimsical exterior, already an exercise in the freer, even less realistic form of cinema Anderson was to move on to in *If . . .* Except that it does not seem as arid as calling it an exercise in anything might imply; fantasy and documentary reality meet, mingle, and are interfused inextricably in a film that moves with the unpredictable, unanalyzable certainty of a poem. Though not at all "poetic" in the vague, impressionist sense of the term—everything in it is absolutely sharp and precise—it yet uses the procedures of poetry to transfigure its prosaic materials into something rich and strange.

So does *Raz Dwa Trzy* (*The Singing Lesson*), a short Anderson made in Poland in 1967 while he was directing a Polish production of John Osborne's *Inadmissible Evidence.* The starting point seems to be documentary—the framework of the film is a series of six contrasted songs sung by members of a singing class at the Warsaw Dramatic Academy in the course of twenty minutes. But a title at the outset of the film tells us that it is conceived as "a sketchbook or a poem," and the thread of the songs is used to string together a series of glimpses of the world around, evoked by the songs themselves, sometimes reinforcing, sometimes contradicting or in ironic counterpoint. Anderson's pleasure in people is no less marked here than in his early documentaries (evidently he responds with particular enthusiasm to the enthusiasm of the students), but here the rosy realism of *Every Day Except Christmas* has given way to something altogether tougher. The travelers who are linked with the first song, the listless shoppers in the third, are no less critically examined than the day-trippers in *O Dreamland:* a beat number is at once matched and counterpointed with images of a rainy day in Warsaw, the last number dissolves into a rush-hour scene, and only in one number do we never leave the classroom. It is all light and charming, like *The White Bus,* and also, like *The White Bus,* rather black beneath the surface and curiously disturbing.

Distinguished as *This Sporting Life, The White Bus,* and *The Singing Lesson* are in their various ways, in the light of *If . . .* they all look rather like practice runs. In *If . . .* the covert preoccupation of the last three films, the style Anderson has been striving toward and secretively perfecting, clearly emerge once and for all. It is an extraordinary film, a film that virtually defies ordinary verbal description because it works as only the cinema can, on the indistinct border between fantasy which has the solidity of tangible experience and reality which seems as remote and elusive as a dream. One cannot even fall back on comfortable formulas to describe what it is "about." It is about, to use the fashionable word of the time, a confrontation, but of whom precisely, and on what grounds, it would be impossible to specify without misrepresenting the film's richly suggestive ambiguity. The action of the original screenplay by David Sherwin (and Lindsay Anderson) takes place in a fictional public school. During the first half we observe the progression of three natural rebels through the school term, with its absurd rituals, its intricate hierarchy, its desultory learning and passionately serious intrigue. This part is entirely believable, and gives a truer, less sentimentalized picture of boarding-school life than any I can remember, in any medium. Even that old stumbling block, adolescent sex, is handled with a clear-eyed precision that does not prevent the film at moments from being quite touching.

However, that is not all there is to it. Little by little it edges over into fantasy, or rather fantasy penetrates more and more deeply into the film's reality.The boys dream of revolt, and gradually the thought is embodied in action: the chaplain shot, a store of ammunition found in the cellars, a final desperate battle with parents and faculty mowed down by the young revolutionaries from the school roof. What are they for? What are they against? Where do we stand? Impossible to say —deliberately impossible. The film is a rich, complex, obscure metaphor of the way we live now, the tone of the times. To give some idea of how this works, it is necessary to go in more detail into the structure of the film, the way that reality and fantasy are related. The quickest answer to that, if not the easiest, in that it immediately involves one in a string of further questions, is that they are not related, since they are never really distinguished. With one small exception—the surrealistic scene in which the shot chaplain is resurrected from a drawer in the headmaster's study—there is nothing in the film that could not be real, and nothing that absolutely has to be. The depiction of the school itself, with its intricate rituals, is lovingly detailed and believable—and "lovingly" is meant literally, since one senses that by one of those contradictions we have observed elsewhere in Anderson's work he at once disapproves of the public-school system and has a great nostalgic attachment to it, or at least to his own experience of it. A lot of what happens in the earlier sequences of the film, within the bounds of the school, could be fantasy, and yet we are willing enough to accept them as fact; a lot that happens nearer the end will be willingly accepted by most audiences as fantasy, and yet it could perfectly well be fact—as Anderson himself, when questioned on the subject, said, for him "it's all real."

For all practical purposes, though, the film may be said to exist in some ambiguous territory betwixt and between, owing rather more to the overtly surrealistic *Zéro de Conduite* (directed by Jean Vigo) than the suspectly pseudo-realistic *Goodbye Mr. Chips.* The film is divided into eight chapters—a "Brechtian" distancing device, consciously so used, as is the seemingly arbitrary alternation of black-and-white and color in the film, which firmly resists all attempts to line up the sequences in question along a fantasy/reality divide. In the first chapter, "College House," we meet the principal characters, notably the three rebels-to-be, Mick, Johnny, and Wallace, observe the reassembly of school, and the reestablishment of this strange private world's stranger rituals, which, when we come to think of it, are a microcosm of the larger, stranger world outside. In Chapter Two, "College," lessons start, and we begin to get a clearer idea of the staff—the prim, slightly sadistic chaplain, the self-consciously liberal headmaster. In Chapter Three, "Term Time," various strands of plot are laid down; we meet Philips, an attractive, rather effeminate junior boy who is given by one of the prefects to another, as a sort of test and temptation; we see the rebels drinking vodka and talking of independence and adulthood. Chapter Four, "Ritual and Romance," contains three major incidents: the eye contact effected, very romantically, between Wallace and Philips in the gym; the real (though slight) wounding of Mick in a practice fencing match; and the scene in a café in which Mick, after running off with a motor bike, meets the waitress and in a rapid transition is seen rolling naked with her on the floor, making love like a great fierce cat.

Chapter Five, "Discipline," shows the punishment of the rebels by the prefects, a ritual caning not for any particular offense but just for general insubordination and objectionableness. This provokes Chapter Six, "Resistance," in which the idea of rebellion is mooted in Mick's comment: "One man can change the world—with a bullet in the right place," and which concludes with the calm before the storm, a series of idyllic shots of a quiet night, a teacher singing while his wife accompanies him on the recorder, matron dreaming, Phillips sleeping in Wallace's arms. Chapter Seven, "Forth to War," involves the first actual bloodshed, when the chaplain is shot dead in the middle of a cadet exercise just after the teacher's wife has walked naked through the deserted dorms. He is not permanently dead, though; he pops up alive and well while the headmaster makes a magnanimous speech about fully understanding youth's urge to rebellion and sets the rebels to cleaning out the space under the stage of the school hall as a punishment. Here, joined by Philips and the girl, they find a number of more or less significant objects, notably the pickled fetus of a baby in a glass jar, and then come upon a stock of guns, ammunition, and grenades. The rebellion is on, with love as part of it (clearly, since Philips and the girl are also involved)—Anderson has capsulated it as "something which is the opposite of death, which is life, violence and sex."

And so to the final chapter, "Crusaders" (which was originally intended as the title of the whole film). During a ludicrous prize-giving ceremony, replete with platitudes addressed to parents and children, attended by symbolic figures in fancy dress, smoke begins to rise from beneath the stage. As those inside the hall begin to pour out in panic, the rebel "crusaders" open from the roof. The girl shoots the headmaster in the middle of the forehead, and confusion reigns. But then the forces of the establishment rally, and the rebels are left fighting desperately what must surely be a losing battle.

The technical means employed to put this on the screen are very simple, even, as Anderson would have it, somewhat old-fashioned. Little or no virtuoso camera work—the fast moving-camera shots during Mick's fugue with Johnny on the "borrowed" motor bike are a liberating exception—and even the fantasy (if fantasy it be) handled very simply, prosaically almost. Is Mrs. Kemp's nude promenade through the school fantasy? It need not be—it is shot in black-and-white with almost documentary matter-of-factness. Are the matron's torchlit VD examination of the newly returned boys' privates and the romantic shot of Wallace and Philips in bed together fantastic or actual? No matter—they are all treated in the same "realistic" way. *If . . .* carries even further the characteristic technique we have observed in *This Sporting Life* and *The White Bus* of creating strangeness, ambiguity, and magic by juxtaposing things in unexpected ways, so that all the pieces, each perfectly credible in itself, do not quite fit into an immediately credible whole. There is a disturbing sense of a gap in the system somewhere, which always keeps us on our toes, ready to use our intelligence as well as react through our instincts. The equal but not exactly matching realities of the various sequences are combined in a way suggestive of Buñuel's practice in such of his late films as *The Discreet Charm of the Bourgeoisie,* which exhibits surrealism of the spirit rather than the surface.

The inspiration of *If . . .* , as of much of Buñuel, is anarchic in the strict philosophical sense of the term—it confronts rival notions of reality, of responsibility, rather than merely opposing order with chaos. And in detail the film is richly, meaningfully contradictory. As Anderson notes in his introduction to the published script, it is the rebels who are the real traditionalists, the true patriots: they use phrases like "England Awake" and "Some love England and her honour yet," while the headmaster is the image of the new bureaucracy spawned by the technological society. Tradition is both loved and criticized: rebellion is romantic, backward-looking, and practically doomed. Anyone looking for a simple left-wing liberal tract, condemning the public-school system, disapproving of violence, advocating sweet reasonableness as the best way toward making things "better," will find naught for his comfort in *If . . .* Like all major works of art, it defies definition, it refuses paraphrase. It is more than the sum of its analyzable parts, and finally exists in its own right as a self-sufficient work of art, sublimely careless of how we choose to read it. It is just monumentally there, and that, after all, is the main thing.

The effect of *O Lucky Man!* (1973), Anderson's follow-up to *If . . .* , is much more diffused. Its script was also written by David Sherwin, based on an idea by Malcolm McDowell, and it can be regarded as a sort of sequel, taking the character played by McDowell in *If . . .* , Mick Travis, out into the world. Though the name is the same, the character is not quite—as Anderson points out, he starts out much more naïve than the character in *If . . .* and ends up far wiser; also, he seems to come from a more humble background, and though at one point he is asked if he thinks his headmaster was right to expel him from school, it is difficult to imagine that school as the school in *If . . .* Still, the general continuity between the two films is evident. The course of *O Lucky Man!* is deliberately much wider: as against the compactness of *If . . .* the narrative here is picaresque—the progress of a more knowing Candide through a fantastic and sometimes nightmarish landscape of the world as it might be and certainly ought not to be.

The beginning has been taken as realistic in intention, blossoming little by little into overt fantasy, but I cannot really understand this view. The very start of the film is a sort of burlesque small-screen black-and-white left-wing documentary of the 1920's or 1930's showing the exploitation of the poor workers on a Latin American coffee plantation—the principal sufferer being played by Malcolm McDowell in a black wig and false Zapata mustache. From this we move on, after a credits sequence woven around a song sung by Alan Price in a recording studio, with Lindsay Anderson in attendance ("If you've found a reason to live and not to die—You are a lucky man!"), to a sequence showing Mick Travis ending his period of training as a salesman in the factory of Imperial Coffee. Though the factory background seems real enough, the tone of slightly fantasticated burlesque already hinted at in the opening is clearly in evidence, and even if the whole of the following sequences, in which by a giant step in promotion Mick becomes chief salesman for the Northeast, is based on Malcolm McDowell's own experience in a similar salesman's job, it would be a very simple spectator who could suppose himself to be in for a realistic drama.

One of Lindsay Anderson's greatest gifts, after all, is his ability to establish with complete conviction the tone of something and integrate everything with that tone—the acting, the camera work, the pacing. In these opening scenes, in the factory and on the road in the Northeast, there is something indefinably fabulous about the atmosphere (reminiscent of *The White Bus*—a resemblance intensified by the appearance of Arthur Lowe in two roles, the factory manager and the hotel manager, and of Patricia Healey at the hotel); character hovers on the brink of caricature, the job is fantasized, the episode in which Mick first really encounters Them—the policemen who warn him against proffering evidence in a road accident—already has a dreamlike feeling about it, with the strange (though not totally inconceivable) appearance and disappearance of the mist, and Ralph Richardson as the neighboring lodger in the boarding house where Mick's predecessor mysteriously disappeared, is presented, without explanation, like a visitant from another world, bearing his curious gift of a suit shot with gold thread. The sex club in which Mick is entertained by one of his clients also takes on a nightmarish quality, not so much from what happens in it—the elementary stag film, the innocuous sex show—as by the audience watching, in which lecherous councillors and businessmen mingle with groups of respectable-looking ladies in churchgoing hats.

In other words, the scene is subtly set for fantasy before we plunge into it with Mick's arrival, after a midnight phone call, to sell coffee to the catering manager of a secret military establishment, his arrest and torture in order to extort a confession from him, and his escape when the whole place blows up. Here again, the horror is created not so much directly as by the absolutely cool, matter-of-fact way in which the great British tea lady goes on unflappably serving tea from a trolley while Mick is tortured before her eyes. After a magical interlude in which the exhausted Mick is suckled at a young matron's breast in a church decorated for a Harvest Festival, we are back with horrors when he signs on (to make some money) at a medical research center, to find out almost too late that terrible operations are performed there, like something from the Island of Doctor Moreau. Escaping from there, he runs in to Alan Price and his group, who here enter the story for a while instead of merely commenting on it from the outside. His contact with a girl who has tagged along with them brings him to her father (Ralph Richardson again) and the world of big business—specifically a large deal with the dictatorial government of a fictional Third World state in which revolutionaries are to be put down by the use of a napalm-like new weapon, supplied of course through Sir James. But when the law catches up it is Mick who gets the blame and is sentenced to five years' hard labor.

Out of prison, he is directed toward the East End to make a fresh start, but things go from bad to worse. An encounter with derelicts around a mobile canteen gets him beaten up when he tries to address them as "brothers," and the iron appears to have entered his soul when by chance he is solicited to try his luck at what turns out to be a casting session, presided over by Lindsay Anderson. He is singled out from among hundreds of young men, and photographed holding books, then holding a gun, aggressively (as though in trial images for *If . . .* rather than *O Lucky Man!*). Then he is told to smile. Why? he wants to know. The director tells him just to do it, but he insists there is nothing to smile about. The director considers for a moment, then quite arbitrarily hits him. He begins to smile. (Significantly, earlier in the film there was heard a radio talk on Zen, and presumably this Zen confrontation leads to understanding or obedience or both.) The finale is a party in which most of the people from earlier in the film are seen dancing joyously together to the music of Alan Price, now visible again among them. By a journey through fantasy, illusion, and nightmare Mick has come to understanding and reality only in the world which is fantasy embodied, the world of the film, as indicated by the casting session and the clapper board for *O Lucky Man!* itself, briefly glimpsed on screen in front of his face.

What does it all mean? Hard to say, and quite unnecessary. Obviously it is a fable suggesting a journey from innocence to experience through a fantastic dream vision of modern Britain. Many things about it suggest the dream—the constantly dissolving scenes, the transforming recurrence of actors (many of them familiar from other Anderson films, particularly *If . . .*), so that we see Arthur Lowe as the manager of the coffee factory and almost at once as the hotel manager/mayor in the North, and then, most alarmingly, in blackface as Dr. Munda, premier of the state of Zingara, or Mona Washbourne as a shopkeeper, a nurse in the experimental clinic, and an usher in the law courts, doubling as a flagellator for the judge in his off moments. It is the sort of film which invites—indeed, compels—one to suspend intellectual judgment till one has seen it through, accepting each stage in Mick's journey as one would a dream of one's own, and wait for illumination to burst afterward. It works on this level only as a whole, and finally works on one as the slap does on Mick—it explodes into meaning all at once, in a nonrational way. As soon ask the significance of any particular detail in the film, like the gold suit or the suckling by the vicar's wife (for so the published screenplay identifies her) as ask why *If . . .* goes from black-and-white to color and back again in the eccentric but completely unquestionable way it does. If you ask the question the film is failing in its effect on you—it should move, and move you, with the certainty of a sleepwalker. Lindsay Anderson's most extraordinary quality as a filmmaker—and in this he comes closest perhaps to Pasolini—is his ability to keep his instincts uncontaminated by his intellect, his intellect unmuddled by his instincts. His films are about ideas, but defy paraphrase. At a press conference after *O Lucky Man!* one unfortunate critic began a question with "What were you trying to say in that scene where . . ." Anderson curtly replied: "I wasn't *trying* to say anything. What I *said* was . . ." I don't think I could better that as a summation of his films' quality. They do not fumble, they do not need explanation. They speak to our eyes and our ears; the medium, triumphantly, is the message.

Stanley Kubrick

In general the 1950's seemed like a good period for the American cinema. A period of change, of course: the decade began with Hollywood facing the challenge of television and fighting back with some gimmicks of its own, like 3-D, CinemaScope, and the other wide-screen processes, and it was the time, as gradually became clear, of the erosion of the old studio-factory system, with its stables of contract artists and its systematic star building, by the proliferation of independent production—the last contract stars built up in the old way were Marilyn Monroe and James Dean, and James Dean's death in 1955 seemed like the end of an era. But not all the change was for the worse. The new structure of innumerable independent producers releasing their films through the old studios, now mainly distributing organizations, put more power than ever before into the hands of directors, and if they did not always use it wisely, at any rate they had the chance to do so. And the menace, television, was also to prove productive in terms of new talent fed into the making of movies for theatrical release. Some of these were a direct spin-off of television, like the group of films based on Paddy Chayevsky scripts; more interesting and significant was the proportion of the new generation of movie directors who served their apprenticeship on television drama series—people like Arthur Penn, John Frankenheimer, Sidney Lumet, Robert Mulligan, Delbert Mann, and many others.

There were, however, exceptions. Some directors, like Roger Corman, still managed to make their careers entirely within the cinema by way of B features and learning their craft from the ground up; by the end of the decade the proliferating underground cinema was beginning to feed talent into the commercial cinema—people like John Cassavetes, whose first feature, *Shadows,* appeared in 1961. And, at the beginning of the 1950's, there was Stanley Kubrick. Kubrick was a good, old-fashioned example of the movie-struck kid who was determined to get into the industry as quickly as possible, by hook or by crook, and did. He was born in the Bronx in 1928, became involved with still photography as a hobby in his early teens, and after failing to get into college sold some of his photographs to various magazines; he was taken on by *Look* as a staff photographer at the age of sixteen and stayed on for five years. During this period he was an obsessive filmgoer and dutifully read all the books on filmmaking he could lay his hands on (Pudovkin's *Film Technique* was apparently the one he found most useful). In 1950 he decided to make a short film of his own, inspired by discovering that *The March of Time* spent $40,000 on a one-reel documentary, and believing that he could do something comparable for $1,000. In this he proved too optimistic. *Day of the Fight,* a sixteen-minute documentary on the prizefighter Walter Cartier suggested by a photo series he had done for *Look,* cost $3,800 of his own money, but he sold it to RKO-Pathé for $4,000 and found himself in business as a professional filmmaker. He followed it up with another, shorter film, *Flying Padre* (nine minutes), about a Catholic priest who served a far-flung New Mexican parish of four hundred square miles, also sold to RKO-Pathé for a sum that just covered its costs. The stage was set for his first feature film, *Fear and Desire* (1953).

Such were the simple beginnings in the cinema of one of the most remarkable figures in films today—or should I say the maker of some of the most remarkable films of the last decade? There is, perhaps, a difference. The difference, which we have been taught to regard as crucial, between the *auteur* and the mere craftsman-filmmaker, however brilliant. The point may seem to be academic—if the films are good, why worry about the connecting links, the informing personality? My own answer to that would have to be: I don't know, but I do worry. And evidently the worry is not just an eccentric private preoccupation of my own. Norman Kagan, in his book *The Cinema of Stanley Kubrick,* goes to great lengths to define Kubrick's creative personality in terms of recurrent ideas from film to film—"imaginary worlds," "the distrust of emotions, errors of intelligence," "the journey to freedom," "triumph of the obsessional, dedicated hero," and "suicide-homicides." He even makes out a fair case for the constant appearance of these themes, though the exercise does perhaps sometimes savor a little of intellectual jigsaw-puzzle playing—it is possible, after all, to find some elements of continuity in virtually any random collection of films, if one really wants to. But since the evidence is only occasionally a trifle forced to fit the case, and since as we know Kubrick has selected his material and had a hand in the scripting of all his films except *Spartacus* (on which he calls himself a "hired hand"), we could reasonably accept all this as evidence that Kubrick's is a unified, coherent *oeuvre,* in the best *auteur* tradition. And yet, for myself I find there is always something in Kubrick's films, brilliant though most of them are, that seems to stop short of the total creative involvement of the true *auteur.* Is it perhaps that he is keeping back something vital of himself, that the films seem in a way like so many masks assumed by their maker rather than various aspects of his own face? Possibly. Anyway, a sense of slight disquiet persists. I find it easier to bring the films in focus one by one, as isolated phenomena, than to get a unified picture of them all together.

All the same, Kubrick's distinction is not for a moment in question. Any director who could make *Paths of Glory, A Clockwork Orange, Lolita,* and (with all reservations) *2001* has to be taken very seriously indeed. In his finest films his ambition is matched only by his achievement; and there is not one of the nine features he has made in the last twenty years which does not have some strong virtues and some critics to expound them enthusiastically. Even his very first, slightest, most inexperienced work, *Fear and Desire,* for all its gaucheness and pretentiousness, could hardly mark the appearance of any but a very unusual and (to say the least) extremely promising filmmaker. Especially considering the circumstances in which it was made, on a minimal budget ($9,000 for the actual shooting; another $30,000 to post-synchronize, owing to a number of misfortunes arising out of inexperience) and with no previous experience in directing actors, making a feature film, or indeed selling it when it was finished. The film was made totally independently, more as a gesture of faith by the young filmmaker than anything else, and should no doubt be regarded indulgently now—more so, anyway, than does Kubrick himself, who called it "very inept and pretentious." In any case, looked at in its original context, as a low-budget B war movie, it does not need too much indulgence, comparing more than favorably with others of its kind by far more seasoned professionals.

Though made almost entirely in the open air, the film is in fact a closely knit chamber drama, based on an original screenplay written for Kubrick by Howard Sackler, a poet-playwright and school friend of his. It has in effect only four characters, the key to understanding them being given in a poem on the soundtrack at the outset of the film:

. . . the enemies that struggle here do not exist
Unless we call them into being . . .
These soldiers that you see keep our language and our time,
But have no other country but the mind.

We are being directly asked to see the characters as symbols, and accordingly the four principals are shown as stereotypes rather than individuals: the lieutenant, Corby, is the intellectual of the outfit, given to tiresome intellectual chatter about great abstractions; Mac is the opposite, all raw violence, physical, instinctive; Fletcher is the mild, slow-spoken, world-weary Southerner; Sidney, the callow youth, hysterical to the verge of insanity. On their journey from nowhere to nowhere, they talk a lot, circle an enemy command post (complete with a general), build a raft, and attack a shanty in the woods, killing two enemy soldiers and incidentally capturing a girl. Each of them slips deeper into his own obsession—Mac raves on about the enemy general, and when Corby arranges a reconnoitering party, Sidney, left in charge of the tied-up girl, makes muddled attempts to charm her and rape her, releases her, and then shoots her before rushing off jibbering into the forest. Meanwhile the raft is ready, and Mac, still obsessed with killing the general, argues Corby and Fletcher into actually doing the job while he stages a diversion from the raft. The plan works: Corby and Fletcher kill the general and his aide (played by the same two actors—they are killing themselves, or enemies which exist only in their own imagination) and escape in a captured plane, while Mac is rejoined by the crazed Sidney. By the river at an Allied military landing strip Corby and Fletcher watch and wait, until out of the fog drifts the raft, with Sidney crooning crazily and Mac unconscious or dead.

Kubrick is of course right to see this farrago now as pretentious and naïve. But despite its rather childish ideas of what constitutes intellectual conversation, its straining against the limitations of realism which it never decisively throws aside, so that there are moments more than a trifle ludicrous as the characters fall heavily between the twin stools of symbol and actuality, the film still has a surprising confidence and panache. Technically it leaves little to be desired: Kubrick's own camera work has considerable polish and a good professional finish spiced here and there with touches which suggest that his hours at the Museum of Modern Art were not ill spent —in particular the evocation of the dreamlike forest landscape in a way which suggests some Japanese films, specifically Kurosawa's *Rashomon* for the sunlight flashing through the leaves; but also perhaps his *Tora-No-O* for the placing of the soldiery within this landscape. Occasionally Kubrick goes a little overboard with flashy camera effects, as with the subjective camera work when the two enemy soldiers in the forest shack are stabbed with trench knives jabbing straight into the camera, but, considering his youth and inexperience, the film has surprising coherence—even its lurches into melodrama are interesting and indicative, pointing the way (without the application of too much hindsight) to the mature Kubrick who has shown in *Dr. Strangelove* and *A Clockwork Orange* a unique gift for playing drama on and over the edge of melodrama into the sort of black farce which sometimes seems implicit in *Fear and Desire* if only he would or could let himself go.

The film received some showing, though not enough, apparently, to pay back its investors their very modest outlay. Nevertheless, Kubrick was able to raise enough money to make another independently financed B feature, *Killer's Kiss* (1955). This film shows a considerable advance, though to a certain extent by taking a step back into an altogether more modest conception. *Killer's Kiss,* based on an original screenplay by

Kubrick, his only original, was obviously suggested by his first documentary, *Day of the Fight,* putting a rather vaguely plotted and again somewhat melodramatic story into the realistic context of the boxing world Kubrick had come to know quite well (from the outside). The story is told in flashback, while the hero, a young boxer, waits in Pennsylvania Station. His situation vis-à-vis the heroine is established at the outset: both Davy and Gloria live in the same tawdry apartment block, across the court from each other, so that they know each other by sight and, we gather, fantasize about each other. Davy is said to be an up-and-coming fighter; Gloria is a hostess in a shabby dance hall, dependent for her job on keeping her boss, Vince, happy. One night Davy is awakened by a scream from Gloria, who has been fighting off the advances of Vince; he comforts her and stays the night. Gloria agrees to go home to Seattle with him, and he waits around for her outside the dance hall, where he has also arranged to meet his manager. While he is chasing after a boy who stole his scarf, Gloria and the manager both arrive, Gloria is summoned upstairs to Vince, and the manager is beaten to death by Vince's henchmen. For some reason Davy is suspected of this crime, but he hits back by following Vince through the night until they end up face to face and Vince takes Davy to his hideout, where the two henchmen are holding Gloria prisoner. There is a fight, and Davy manages to escape and runs until he finds refuge in a loft full of shopwindow dummies. The final fight takes place here, and Davy of course emerges triumphant. Now he is waiting for Gloria at Penn Station, and at the final fadeout she arrives to go off with him happily to Seattle.

In outline the story is obviously naïve, and there are too many gaps in its credibility. But one senses that Kubrick was more interested in it as an excuse for a number of things he knew he could do well, a thread on which to hang some bravura sequences without bothering too much about what happened in between (a perfectly respectable Hitchcock trick, after all). The film, in consequence, shows two distinct areas of strength, both of which were to be further exploited in later films. One is Kubrick's gift for capturing the minutiae of everyday life, when he wants to, as in the early sequences of the boxing ring and the dance hall here; he is well able to create vividly in a few shots the shabbiness of the underside of the boxing game and the grimy purlieus of Times Square's cheaper entertainments. But more significant than the grainy reality of the documentary background are those sequences in which they bypass reality altogether—the abstracted dream from which Davy is awakened by Gloria's scream, which is done in a long tracking shot in negative, with the camera whipping past an endless succession of otherworldly white buildings against a black sky (shades of the famous journey past and through flashing lights near the end of *2001*); the sequence in which Gloria tells Davy the story of her life while the screen is occupied with a ballerina dancing alone on a dark stage (this is loosely explained as being Gloria's ill-fated elder sister, but the explanation seems to be dragged in, like the sequence itself); and the finale in the mannequin store, which, though of course established as a bizarre but not entirely unbelievable location, does take on a strongly surrealist air and again, by its sheer oddity, carries the violent drama of the film's conclusion to the edge of black farce.

Killer's Kiss is by no means totally satisfactory, but it does, together with *Fear and Desire,* give us a premonitory image of Kubrick's mental and emotional world. In the context of the young filmmakers who were entering the industry at that time, it has its predictable elements, but much about it is strikingly different. This, after all, was the period of the vogue in American filmmaking for the shot-on-the-street-where-it-really-happened type of semi-documentary (or hopefully semi-documentary) drama. And, with the more obviously creative talents at least, Hollywood was preparing to welcome a new generation of rosy realists from television. The realistic, semi-documentary element is there, of course—there are sections of *Killer's Kiss,* for instance, which remind one of Dassin's *Naked City* or Robert Wise's *The Set-Up*. But they are not quite what stays in one's memory. Rather it is the elements of the bizarre, the extraordinary, the larger-than-life: it is as though Kubrick was already, albeit unconsciously, in training for the succession of great films he was to make in Britain in the 1960's and 1970's.

In comparison, *The Killing* (1956) is a disappointment. Not absolutely, for it is at the very least a superlatively well-crafted thriller, tight, sharp, and almost painfully vivid. But for all its virtues it comes across, particularly if seen again today, as the least personal of all Kubrick's films (except perhaps *Spartacus*) —more important to Kubrick, one could guess, as an indication to the industry that he was a serious professional capable of making a straightforward commercial movie to length and budget requirements and to the various other specifications insisted on by a major company (United Artists). By this time Kubrick had entered into a partnership with James B. Harris, a young man with some money of his own and a burning desire to get into movies. Between them they wrote the script, based on a novel (*Clean Break*) by Lionel White, sold Sterling Hayden on playing the leading role in it, took the property to United Artists and got from them the major part of the investment required, the rest being raised by Harris independently. Since the overall budget was $320,000—not so much for an A film, but far more than Kubrick had ever had to work with before—it was important that the film should be a commercial success, which, in its modest way, it was. As such, it led the way to *Paths of Glory* and Kubrick's later films.

The subject of the film, as several critics pointed out at the time, is akin to that of *The Asphalt Jungle,* in which Sterling Hayden also starred. It is the story of a carefully planned, apparently foolproof robbery which is carried out efficiently enough but then falls apart because of the human factor among the robbers. The structure is slickly devised (screenplay by Kubrick), with a lot of pseudo-documentary precision about time and place to keep us *au fait* with parallel events, to show us the various elements of the story pulling together and falling apart. There are five principals, each of whom has his own contribution to make to the total action (presumably —we never find out exactly the position of two of the five, but the neat dovetailing of the converging lines of action prevents us from being too irritatingly conscious of this). The brains of the outfit is Johnny Clay, just out of prison with, he thinks, a foolproof plan to put himself in clover for the rest of his life by knocking off a racetrack at the moment when everyone is distracted by the big race of the day. To help him he needs Kennan, a corruptible policeman, since managing the police plays an important part; O'Reilly, the racetrack bartender (to help with the diversion); George Peatty, the racetrack cashier; and Unger, an alcoholic whose necessity to the outfit is never made quite clear (we can at least guess that Peatty provides inside information).

We see the five in their separate private lives, the most significant for the plot being Peatty with his brassy, sluttish wife, Sherry, who is the most evident source of weakness in the combination, since Peatty is obviously abjectly subservient to her and she, as we discover, has a shifty lover on the side who is bent on intervening to their common advantage if he possibly can. The robbery itself is rather well handled; the device of the constantly emphasized time scheme as the action moves backward and forward to show the various elements of the crime converging helps to create a sense of urgency and excitement. According to the plan, a psychotic gunman Clay has hired will shoot the favorite in the big race from the parking lot (a particularly foolish place to do it, as it turns out) while Maurice, an enormous ex-wrestler Clay has also hired, creates a diversion by starting a fight in the bar. Clay holds up the racetrack office and collects the money, and Kennan, the unsuspected policeman, intercepts the money and takes it to a motel where Clay is to pick it up and bring it to be divided among the five in the gang. Before he can do so, Sherry and her boy friend jump the other four and shoot them down. Clay is warned that something has gone wrong by seeing Peatty stagger bleeding from the rendezvous, and decides to save himself, his dowdy girl friend, and the money. It looks as though he may get away with it, except that he is required to check the bag on the plane in which he is escaping and owing to a mishap during the baggage loading it falls onto the tarmac and bursts open, scattering money to the four winds. At the final fadeout the police move in on the couple.

This is all, obviously, fairly routine, cut in a standard mold of the perfect crime that went wrong; Hollywood has turned out dozens like it through the years. *The Killing* is a superior example in its slickness, tautness, and ruthless machine-like precision. But it is not greatly superior to others in its genre, and it lacks (deliberately, no doubt) the ambiguity, the expansiveness, the unexpected touches of poetry which distinguished its nearest competitor, *The Asphalt Jungle*. Nevertheless, there are moments vividly exemplifying Kubrick's taste for or interest in the bizarre and peculiar, the unreality or surreality lurking at the heart of the seemingly normal and everyday. The two diversions from the main action of the robbery, the shooting of the horse and the fight in the bar, are weird beyond anything that could be regarded as strictly necessary in realistic terms, and the fight staged by the massive wrestler, with its improbable onrush of policemen required, apparently, to cope with the man-mountain, has an inevitable overtone of the Keystone Kops—another point at which Kubrick seems to be knowingly edging drama over into farce. Some details of the robbery too, like Clay's choice of a grinning clown mask as a disguise, suggest a touch of surrealist humor, while the harsh, black depiction of Peatty's relationship with his sadistic wife is handled with a cold, relentless interest that seems to point the way toward Kubrick's handling of another perverse sexual relationship in *Lolita* and even toward some incidental details in *A Clockwork Orange*. In general, though, *The Killing,* while perfectly acceptable and even distinguished within its own rather closely circumscribed genre, seems, because of its very perfection in its chosen form, curiously impersonal, an exercise and a demonstration rather than a personal statement.

Paths of Glory (1957), the film *The Killing* enabled Kubrick to make, is a very different matter. It is as though Kubrick, having made two films with the accent on feeling, self-expression rather than precision, and then one film in which tightness, precision, and a rather cold, impersonal finish were of paramount importance, was able triumphantly to combine the two sides of his cinematic nature. *Paths of Glory* creates its extraordinary effect not only by the intensity of its feeling but, even more, by the way the intensity is kept under scrupulous control. The emotional Kubrick, the man who has an attitude toward life and its issues that he wishes to convey to his audience, is perfectly matched here by the technological Kubrick, the man who is fascinated by the sheer logistics of filmmaking, the way the pieces fit together, the adaptation of means to ends. The story comes from a novel by Humphrey Cobb which had had quite a success twenty-two years before and had meanwhile been forgotten. It would probably never have been filmed if it had not been for the enthusiasm of Kirk Douglas when he was shown the script (already the power of the star as independent producer functioning outside the old studio system was beginning to be felt). Douglas's say-so, plus the decent, unsensational success of *The Killing,* persuaded United Artists to put up the million dollars the film needed—especially since the film could be made entirely in Germany, thus using up some of the company's blocked assets in Europe.

If we compare the screenplay of the film (by Kubrick, the novelist Calder Willingham, and Jim Thompson, who had collaborated with Kubrick on the script of *The Killing*) with the novel we can see how Kubrick redistributed the emphasis in order to make a personal statement. A comparison with *Spartacus* (1960), Kubrick's next and (because of all the limitations it imposed on his control) least favorite film, is in order here. Both Cobb's novel and Howard Fast's stem from the same sort of 1930's left-wing liberalism, which basically is optimistic, perhaps naïvely so, in its belief in the possibility that things can be made to get better. *Spartacus* as a novel chronicles the triumph of a kind of democratic hero, a rebel slave who achieves, for a while at least, an ideal humane community; *Paths of Glory* as a novel deals with the fate of three ordinary soldiers in the First World War who are arbitrarily used as scapegoats for the incompetence of higher authority, and are shot *pour encourager les autres,* but by presenting two of the three as elementary proletarian heroes the novel contrives to suggest that though they come to a pathetic end their spirit goes marching on to a better tomorrow. Now Kubrick's outlook, as we will become aware in his later films, where he has complete control, is in general pessimistic—like Lindsay Anderson, he would no doubt say that once upon a time, in his naïve idealistic youth, he believed in the possibility of answers, of social betterment, but now he believes only in the enduring power of the individual to make his own way, define his own personality, accept and in a measure modify his own destiny. *Spartacus* as a film remains locked in its own liberal naïveté (even though Howard Fast apparently liked what Kubrick was doing, Kubrick was not allowed to modify the screenplay by Dalton Trumbo, another 1930's liberal, to any significant extent). *Paths of Glory* as a film takes on a completely different coloring, and one very characteristic of the mature Kubrick.

In the screenplay the focus of the story is modified by a total revamping of the structure and a radical change of emphasis, from the three doomed soldiers to the officer (Dax) who is involved as the unwilling go-between, resentfully carrying out his superiors' inhuman and sometimes totally irresponsible orders. Whereas the original novel can be taken as anti-war to the extent that it depicts, from the vantage point of some seventeen years after the event, the foolishness and evil of much that happened in the 1914–18 war, the film takes on an altogether wider significance, in that the Army and war are presented more as a microcosm of life in general—nothing happens in this disastrous military engagement which could not happen, in a less obvious form, in everyday civilian life. There is the same cynical division between Us and Them, management and labor, the officers and the men. In the novel the drama is concentrated largely on the men, the suffering, exploited classes, with Dax as little more than a cipher whose behavior is little explained and hardly at all developed; in the film Dax becomes the central character, with the three victims as ciphers, and the whole emphasis is shifted to the machinations of the officer class, the ruthless power game in which the soldiers are the merest pawns and in which Dax figures only because his most idealistically motivated moves in the game are (flatteringly) misread by his ultimate superior as the maneuvers of a careerist like all the rest of them, except a rather more ruthless and efficient careerist than most—a man, in other words, after his own heart, provided he is not after his own job.

The story is basically of a classic simplicity. At the outset

General Broulard, the highest-ranking officer we see, has orders, which he recognizes at once to be absurd and impossible to carry out, to capture a complex enemy citadel known as the Ant Hill. He hands these orders on to his subordinate Mireau, who after suitable demur recognizes that his promotion will depend on his handling of this operation and gives way. Mireau passes on the order to his subordinate, Colonel Dax, who just as clearly recognizes the impossibility of carrying out the order but nevertheless, because he is a soldier, and this is war, does his best to carry it out. The attack fails, and the high command is looking for scapegoats. When Dax suggests that he is a logical choice, his superiors cynically make it clear that of course this is not something that can or need affect officers—it is the men one must make an example of, and just one symbolic victim from each company will be enough to make the point, so let each company commander choose one man, however he wishes. Dax's gesture against this is to undertake to defend the three men so chosen, even though he knows perfectly well that the conclusion of the court-martial is foregone. The men are executed—none of them a hero or a villain, but just ordinary fallible human beings who would prefer possible life to certain, pointless death. When Dax retaliates by denouncing Mireau for firing on his own troops to drive them forward, Broulard first approves—a fool like Mireau deserves to be replaced by a tough cynic like Dax—but then realizes that Dax is a muddled idealist, and contemptuously dismisses him, back to his men, back to more pointless, bloody operations, and at best the sentimental relief of five minutes' respite for the men, weeping into their beer as a pathetic German girl sings them a sentimental song. The paths of glory, as Gray remarked, lead but to the grave, and only the cynics survive—and only the most ruthless cynics at that. And as for the men, the working classes, all they get is exploitation. But then, do they deserve any better? If they can be sufficiently reconciled to their lot by bread and circuses, or at least a *Fräulein*, a song, and five minutes extra to enjoy their beer, what good is there worrying about them?

The conclusions of *Paths of Glory* are impeccably logical, and absolutely consistent in their refusal to take sides emotionally—we are shown the pattern of human behavior bit by bit and left to make up our own minds about it. Just as in *Fear and Desire* it would be perfectly reasonable for us to regard the crazy, obsessed Mac as the hero—after all, he is the only effectual character, the one person whose *idée fixe* gives him the strength of purpose to carry through an action—so here it would be perfectly reasonable to see General Broulard as the hero. If he is a cynic he is a successful, effectual cynic. He has a purpose, a view of life, a comprehensive attitude toward his own role in the station in which life (and presumably his own deliberate effort) has placed him, and he carries out his plans unswervingly. Above all, he is not emotional about it. Everyone else is betrayed by his emotions: Mireau because he allows himself to become unguarded and hysterical in pursuit of his ambitions, Dax because he is fatally divided between his (possibly misplaced) sense of duty and his (also possibly misplaced) sense of humanity, the three victims because they lack the ability to understand their own plight or the strength to do anything about it if they did. Dax could be Spartacus if he would (both are played by the same actor, Kirk Douglas), could be the leader of a slave revolt. But the thought does not even cross his mind—he is hamstrung by his own training, his own absurd, self-contradictory (and therefore self-destructive) code.

All of this speaks well for Kubrick as a creative intelligence and as a writer, or guide of writers. By comparison with the film he has drawn from it, the book seems like a simplistic moral tract. But it would be unfair to Kubrick the filmmaker to leave it at that. For the first time in his work the subject is completely understood and exposed in cinematic terms. The film is based on a series of bold visual contrasts between the heavy, mud-gray world of the trenches, the world of the men, and the glittery, lacy, immaterial world of the rococo château from which the officers maneuver them like so many pawns on a chessboard. There is no connection between the two worlds, visually or emotionally: when Mireau reviews his troops in the trenches he no more makes real contact with them than a man from Mars might be expected to do. On and on, in a relentless, endless tracking shot, he strides past them throwing off formularized words of exhortation and encouragement, sublimely unconcerned with their replies, if any, and when reality, in the shape of a badly shell-shocked man, does actually intrude on his consciousness, he has it swept away ("There is no such thing as shell shock! Get him out of here. I won't have brave men contaminated.") By contrast, Dax, even in the château, always belongs emotionally and visibly to the world of the trenches. He is natural, sincere, remote from the hierarchic gestures of the high command and he always brings with him, figuratively if not literally, some of the mud of the trenches into the inhuman grace and fantasy of the officers' world.

The film is incalculably aided by the brilliantly subtle black-and-white photography of George Krause, capturing as it does the exact feeling of First World War front-line photography in the trench and battle scenes and contrasting this with the very careful, formal elegance of the château scenes. Also, for the first time Kubrick's masterly control of the soundtrack is in evidence—one scene which once seen (and heard) is never forgotten must be that of the three soldiers' execution, with its long walk to the posts at which they will be shot, in the flat gray morning light, accompanied only by the crunch of the gravel and the roll of drums on the soundtrack, and then, in the deafening silence before the shots ring out, a twitter of awakening birds. The whole sequence, in fact, staged like a ceremonial parade, with all the inhuman precision of a Busby Berkeley dance routine, sums up in microcosm the message of the film—war, like life as it is usually organized these days, is possibly wicked, but, much worse, it is *silly*.

From this dramatic presentation of the absurdity of war, the absurdity of life, it was only a couple of steps to *Dr. Strangelove,* in which this pervasive absurdity has been allowed to permeate the whole structure of the film, creating not so much a farcical drama as a dramatic farce. But before Kubrick could reach that point he had to make two more films, one an accident and a solecism in his career, the other absolutely essential to our understanding of him. The first, as I have hinted, was *Spartacus.* Now *Spartacus,* it should be insisted, is not that bad; indeed, it is not bad at all, merely rather disappointing and superficial as a Kubrick film. The spectacle as such is very well staged—the battles, as we might expect from *Paths of Glory,* are filmed with a clear eye and a steady hand, so that at least for once you know who is doing what to whom instead of merely watching the usual screen flurry of superficially exciting but incomprehensible activity. The first part of the film, when Spartacus is in the gladiators' school, is fascinating; again, one senses Kubrick's interest in process—how gladiators were taught, what they were taught, the indication of an active way of life by means of its external actions, with few words and no apparent attempt to influence the audience's attitude. Once the gladiators rebel, however, the film begins to lose momentum and direction; Spartacus himself becomes too much the conventional cardboard hero, mouthing the right liberal sentiments, and only toward the end, with the black and gruesome images of the multiple crucifixions, does some of the film's power return. Nor is it easy to take much interest in the characters, on any level—even the (at that time rather daring) implications of homosexuality between the dictator Crassus (Laurence Olivier) and his slave Antoninus (Tony Curtis) do not strike deep enough to allay the impression (borne out by Kubrick) that *Spartacus* as scripted was a chore in which its director could find only limited interest.

With *Lolita* (1962), on the other hand, we come to another masterpiece, or very nearly. In fact, to my feeling the only way in which it falls short of total success in finding an exact and telling film equivalent to Nabokov's novel is in its failure (imposed by the budgeting necessity to shoot in England) to capture much of the extraordinary vividness of the parts of the book in which Lolita and Humbert are on the road in America, driving around from motel to motel, eating at wayside hamburger stands, and so on. This is a part of the book which must surely have appealed very much to Kubrick, with his strong feeling for place and atmosphere, and in any case provides a necessary framework for the extravagant and very special emotions of the main story. However, with this reservation, the film stands up as the first full, mature expression of Kubrick's personality and point of view—more decisively, certainly, than *Paths of Glory,* fine though that is, because it enables us to appreciate fully for the first time the comic aspects of Kubrick's vision. Like Nabokov's, it is an anguished, violent, sometimes ugly comedy—the comedy of a man who has to laugh in order not to cry, who has to use a distancing frame of reference in order to make sense of an experience that could otherwise lead to black despair.

At the time, of course, many complaints about the film centered on its supposed watering down of the novel. This attack came on two distinct scores: (1) that Lolita is a little girl in the novel, and in the film a sexy, already well-developed fourteen-year-old, and (2) that what Nabokov tells us fairly directly about Humbert's sexual obsession with her (the book is, after all, in the form of a first-person confession) is in the film conveyed almost entirely by suggestion and innuendo. In both cases one could not help wondering whether the critics concerned had ever actually read the book and whether they had given any thought at all to the way the film (any film) works. True, at the beginning of the book Lolita is twelve, but throughout the vital central sections she is fourteen, and at the end she is a pregnant matron going on eighteen. As a matter of record, Sue Lyon was fourteen at the time she made the film, and if there is an evident drawback in casting her for the role it is not so much that she looks too old at the beginning as that she looks too young at the end. Of course, it all depends on what you have in mind when you visualize a fourteen-year-old (or a twelve-year-old, for that matter); it seems likely that most of those who complained about the casting of Sue Lyon had not bothered to take a close look at girls of that age group all around them, and were imagining a nine-year-old Curlytop Shirley Temple sort of figure rather than the teenage seductress (after all, it is finally Lolita who seduces Humbert, not he her) whose mixture of "tender, dreamy childishness and a kind of eerie vulgarity" is so well captured in Nabokov's writing and—surely—in Sue Lyon's performance.

The second criticism is in many ways linked with the first, and somehow suggests that critics were looking (no doubt with the highest principles) for something much more sensational and exotically perverse than either the film or the book offers. The book, after all, is by no means pornographic—the idea of a middle-aged man erotically obsessed with a twelve/fourteen-year-old may be alarming to many readers, but the crackle and jab of Nabokov's prose does not exactly lay things on the line. We could, I suppose, imagine a *Lolita* film made with the directness of *Last Tango in Paris* (which is not, when you come down to it, saying very much) or even of *Deep Throat,* but to what purpose? The subject is obsession rather than sex, and a sexual obsession which finally shows itself, too late, to have been love as well. Kubrick himself, in an interview included in *The Film Director as Superstar,* regrets that he was not able to stress the erotic element in the obsession more, but here it seems to me that he is rather short-changing himself: though the nature of Humbert's obsession is not quite directly stated (and how could it be?) it is, more importantly, dramatized, conveyed in a series of metaphors, starting with the shot behind the credits of an abject Humbert painting imperious Lolita's toenails (reminiscent of Joan Bennett's expression of her sexual power over Edward G. Robinson in *Scarlet Street* by presenting him with her foot and the taunt "Here, you're an artist—paint these!"), and in sometimes outrageous double-entendres, like Mrs. Haze's assertion as Lolita comes into frame that she is going to enslave her new lodger Humbert with her "cherry pie." And, above all, there is James Mason's extraordinary performance, which without exactly duplicating Nabokov's cowardly sensual hero does provide a perfect equivalent within his own definition of reality by showing unmistakably the hysteria about to break out at all moments from beneath the cool, suave, rather stiff-upper-lip exterior of the prim college professor.

A more legitimate complaint against the film might be the role (or roles) played in it by Peter Sellers, as Humbert's shifty adversary Quilty. The interpretation of Quilty as the embodiment of Humbert's paranoia makes sense conceptually—how otherwise is he so nearly omniscient and ubiquitous, even if he is in conspiracy with Lolita from the beginning?—but does not come across quite so clearly in the film, perhaps because we are always conscious of Peter Sellers doing his funny faces and funny voices rather than of a real character—I mean real even within the special reality of an obsessive's paranoid view of the world. There are, I think, moments when Kubrick indulges himself, or lets Sellers indulge himself, to the point where the outrageous humor of the Quilty-Humbert confrontations is transformed into a *Goon Show* turn —yes, of course, everyone remembers Sellers as Quilty as Dr. Zemon, Lolita's school psychologist, prefacing a generalization with "Vee Amerikans" in a heavy German accent, but as one stops to laugh at the idea the texture of the scene and its relevance to the overall dramatic pattern crumbles a little. However, even Peter Sellers does manage to achieve some extraordinary effects in the film, most of all his first head-on encounter with Humbert after the death of Lolita's mother, when they meet in a hotel otherwise (accidentally? actually?) occupied by a police convention and he drops all sorts of vaguely menacing, indecipherable hints about his connections with the police and Humbert's relations with Lolita before he has even had any physical relations with her. Here the tone, funny-sinister and hard to pin down exactly, the perfect fantasy language of paranoia, is beautifully sustained, by the filmmaker perfectly the master of his subject, perfectly in control of his performers.

Visually the film is not so distinguished in any way as *Paths of Glory,* or even, in its much simpler, Technicolor-spectacle fashion, *Spartacus.* Though there are flourishes, notably in Humbert's murder of Quilty, which starts the film (the major change restructuring the novel into the film), most of them take place in front of the camera rather than in the way the camera itself is used. Apart from the enforced anonymity of the exteriors, this seems to be deliberate, as though Kubrick chose a flattish, matter-of-fact style to keep his subject within bounds, and clearly in view. As he observed while shooting *Lolita,* a propos of Nabokov's famous prose style: "Style is what an artist uses to fascinate the beholder in order to convey to him his feelings and emotions and thoughts. These are what have to be dramatized, not the style." The script which Nabokov and Kubrick fashioned from Nabokov's book is in most respects a classic example of analyzing the essential elements of an imaginative concept as expressed in one medium and recrystallizing them in another—not quite so spectacular a job of total transformation allied with total fidelity as that which Harold Pinter achieved with Nicholas Mosley's novel *Accident* for Joseph Losey's film, but often within striking distance. In *Lolita* we see for the first time something like the whole of Kubrick, and see him clear.

Dr. Strangelove, or How I Learned to Stop Worrying and Love the Bomb (1964) is obviously in many ways, not least the use of Peter Sellers's powers of comic mimicry in a multiple role, a logical sequel to *Lolita,* and I am sorry I do not like it more. In the interview with Joseph Gelmis in *The Film Director as Superstar,* Kubrick has described how he reached the basic concept of the film by trial and error. His first notion on reading the novel *Red Alert,* a dramatic story of a brinkmanship situation that could conceivably drive both the major power blocs unwillingly into nuclear war, was that it was the ideal material for a film he had been wanting to make for several years about nuclear politics and the arms race. So he acquired the screen rights and began to rough out a script. But he kept finding that he had to throw out half his ideas because the situations, though logically arrived at and not necessarily in themselves unbelievable, turned out to be so absurd as to provoke laughter in quite the wrong places. Then eventually he began to ask himself if these *were* the wrong places, or should he perhaps not follow the logic of his own responses and accept the idea that the only way to handle the subject was in terms of farce. Well, for him at least it was in terms of farce; two other films around the same time elected to handle the subject in terms of high drama, one of them based on a competitor of *Red Alert*'s, Sidney Lumet's *Fail-Safe,* and the other, *The Bedford Incident,* curiously enough the first film by Kubrick's erstwhile partner James B. Harris as an independent producer-director, which is what, by this time, Kubrick himself had also become.

The initial premise of the film is that all the safety devices introduced into nuclear-war plans to prevent enemy interference and infiltration could also prevent the attack, once started, from being countermanded by those nationally in command. All it needs is the lunatic, and we meet that lunatic at once, in the shape of General Jack D. Ripper (only one of the funny names that to my taste help to belabor the obvious). He has developed a paranoid fantasy about the Commies sapping and polluting our precious bodily fluids. Since the powers that be in America are too cowardly, too enlightened, or perhaps just too infiltrated already to take the necessary steps, he does so himself by activating the attack plan for one of the nuclear bomber forces hovering twenty-four hours a day just two hours from vital strategic targets in Russia. He then cuts himself and his base off from outside communication, and the four planes, upon receiving their orders, do the same. He trusts to the natural impetus of events to give his policies definitive effect: after all, if America does not back up his attack with massive support, she will herself be blasted to nonentity by the Russians in retaliation. General Turgidson, his immediate superior in the Pentagon, is inclined mindlessly to agree—he is a great overgrown schoolboy who sees everything very clearly and simply in terms of black and white: when the President snaps at him that Ripper is obviously a psychotic he replies, aggrieved, "I don't think it's quite fair to condemn a whole program because of a single slip-up."

All the same, the President is not happy. Even if the chances of calling off the attack are small, Turgidson's logic fails to impress him—after all, he does not want to go down in history as the biggest mass murderer since Hitler (a comment which elicits the tart retort from Turgidson that he would do better to worry about the American people than the figure he will cut in the history books). Meanwhile the Army dispatches a force to enter Burpleson Air Base and make personal contact with General Ripper. While the B-52 commanded by Major "King" Kong, the only one of the four we see inside of, continues inexorably on its way toward its Russian target, the President decides on desperate measures: the Russian ambassador, De Sadesky (another humorous name, in case you hadn't noticed), is summoned to the War Room, and the President gets the Russian Premier on the hot line. As tactfully as he can (for how do you phrase such things tactfully?), he explains his dilemma, but the result is hardly satisfactory, since it seems that anything either side can do will be invalidated by the

"Doomsday Machine," a device which will destroy all human and animal life on earth for a century. Meanwhile the Army attack on Burpleson meets stiff resistance, and in the War Room we hear more about the Doomsday Machine, the information being elicited from the Russian ambassador by Dr. Strangelove, a sinister Germanic presence in a wheelchair who seems to be the scientific head of the American nuclear program. As he points out, the whole effect of such a device is invalidated if it is kept secret; the ambassador blandly replies it was to be announced at the next Party Congress—"The Premier loves surprises."

At Burpleson things go from bad to worse, with Ripper finally killing himself rather than run the risk of divulging the code and the invading forces compelled (against all the colonel's training in the sacredness of private property) to shoot open a Coca-Cola machine to get enough change to phone the President. Kong's B-52 is smashed up by an intercepting missile, but continues to limp on toward target, though the rest, with American connivance, have been destroyed by the Russians. Eluding all countermeasures, the B-52 reaches an alternative target and Kong manages to release the bomb, riding it himself, bronco fashion, to death and glory. But all is not quite over. In the War Room, Strangelove is cogitating the ultimate answer to the ultimate weapon—a select breed of people carefully nurtured in the deepest mine shafts to sit out the results of the Doomsday Machine. He gets so carried away that he starts to address the President as "Mein Führer" and his metal arm gets out of control, giving Nazi salutes and turning on its owner, while Turgidson pursues his own obsession about the possibilities of Russian retaliation to our retaliation to their retaliation. Finally in a paroxysm Strangelove discovers he can walk and staggers grotesquely toward the President as we go into a finale of newsreel footage of nuclear explosions accompanied by Vera Lynn's recording of "We'll Meet Again" on the soundtrack.

In our schooldays we used to be told that the first requirement of just criticism was to determine what the creator intended, and then we should consider how well he had carried out his intentions. Inevitably there is rather more to criticism than that, but it is a good start. Kubrick's intention in *Dr. Strangelove* is clear enough—to express the absurdity of the arms race in a form equally absurd, taking up the theme of *Paths of Glory* in a fantastic register, or for that matter accepting the moments of *Fear and Desire* where the action declines from being existentially Absurd to being merely absurd in a more basic sense as a viable means of expression. There are echoes of other earlier films—the reappearance of Sterling Hayden from *The Killing* as Ripper, the use of Peter Sellers from *Lolita* in three roles (this time playing three different people rather than one person adept at disguise), as Group Captain Lionel Mandrake, the very correct British aide to Ripper, as President Muffley, the mild-mannered liberal, and as Strangelove himself, the crazed German fanatic. If the tone can be seen as deriving from *Lolita,* where Kubrick seems to have learned the secret of playing comedy in deadly earnest and not being afraid to plunge right into outrageous farce when it suited his purpose, the character outlines can be traced back to *Paths of Glory* and even more unmistakably to *Fear and Desire* (no doubt because the four characters there are intended as permanent stereotypes anyway). The intricate dovetailing of parallel actions into a clear piece of exposition refers back to the construction of *The Killing,* and indeed in all sorts of ways *Dr. Strangelove* has the air of being consciously a kind of summary of Kubrick's work to date, a rehearsal of the lessons he had learned from film to film throughout his career.

I would admit, then, that if we are to judge *Dr. Strangelove* in terms of its creator's intentions, it is a triumphant success. I do not doubt that everything in it is deliberate, and meant to be exactly as it is. And yet it is the Kubrick film to which I personally respond least, and the only one which seems to me to diminish consistently with the passage of time. I would trace my dissatisfaction with it to two sources, which are somewhat related: the tendency to play for easy laughs with sophomoric irrelevancies, and the way Peter Sellers is used in it. Sellers is, I think, excellent as the President. His is a subtle, played-down piece of comic characterization perfectly in tune with the film as a whole, and to help matters still further, the President is given some of the best lines—his hot-line conversation with an irritable and quite possibly drunk Russian Premier is a model of perfect comedy timing and the extraction of comedy from the desperate attempts of a character to behave normally in a most abnormal situation. But his Mandrake is not very interesting, too close to a revue-sketch reading of the old-fashioned stiff-upper-lip R.A.F. hero, and his Strangelove I think goes right over the edge into the sort of self-indulgent burlesque which is quite beside the point of whatever the film is trying to say. Here too the writing is weak—Strangelove is too close to a wartime caricature of the mad Nazi scientist, and the desired audience response to him relies too heavily on easy recognition gags (the involuntary Nazi salute, etc.) . In other words, in the Strangelove sequences, it seems to me, the film is not doing its basic brainwork, it is having things altogether too easy.

This is another reason why the film seems noticeably dated today. To an extent this is inevitable and not necessarily to the bad—it can be of its period in its preoccupation with the arms race, nuclear disaster, and so on, and still achieve some kind of timeless, universal statement. But much more damaging in this respect is the film's relationship to a whole school of humor which had a temporary vogue around that time—the so-called satire boom in Britain. Looking back on *That Was the Week That Was* and *Not so Much a Programme, More a Way of Life* on television, committed cabaret at the Establishment Club, and kindred manifestations on stage and screen, the abiding impression is one of self-satisfaction and sophomoric pseudo-wit. Most of the funny names in *Dr. Strangelove* would come under the latter heading—one can imagine the three writers, Kubrick, Peter George (author of the original straight book and the very different book-of-the-film produced after the event) , and Terry Southern, really breaking themselves and one another up when they came up with ideas like Mervin Muffley, Jack D. Ripper, Colonel "Bat" Guano, Ambassador De Sadesky, and so on, but to let them linger on into the finished screenplay seems like a curious indulgence. Even more disturbing is the tone, characteristic of so much satire of the time, of complacency in speaking to one's friends, the right sort of people who of course have the right opinions on everything, so that you don't need to make your point—a passing reference will do to hook audiences into a whole world of semi-private humor. In consequence, *Dr. Strangelove* is frequently not funny enough to be accepted as really funny, and because of that, because it seems not to take its own comedy seriously enough, does not come across either as serious enough to be serious. Kubrick was no doubt wise to delete, before the première, a big final sequence of custard-pie throwing in the War Room, but I have the feeling it would not have been quite so out of key with the rest of the film as he thinks.

Now that Kubrick had at length reached the desirable status of producer-director, with no one to answer to very immediately but himself, he was able to go ahead with another project he had had in mind for some time, arising, like *Dr. Strangelove,* out of a long-cherished interest, the possibilities of space travel and the existence of intelligent life on other planets. The desire to treat such a subject coincided with his desire to get further and further away from literary, verbal expression on film. Already in *Dr. Strangelove* he makes consistent attempts to communicate in other ways than through our conscious intelligence—for example, the three locations of the film (the War Room, Burpleson Air Base, and the B-52) are shot in strongly differentiated styles, so that the shuffling of the locations has a dizzying subliminal effect on us, and the finale, with its succession of horrific/beautiful explosions to the soothing and in other contexts reassuring tones of Vera Lynn defies a single, precise interpretation. But in *2001: A Space Odyssey* (1968) Kubrick was to move much further in this direction, trying "to create a *visual* experience, one that bypasses verbalized pigeonholing and directly penetrates the subconscious with an emotional and philosophical content." Though the film runs 141 minutes in its final version, relatively little of it is verbal—only about 40 minutes.

To achieve this effect, Kubrick obviously had to go through a radical rethinking of his approach to narrative form. Up to *2001* he had always been particularly remarkable for his skill in telling complicated stories on screen, juggling the elements of several intrigues at the same time, as in *The Killing* and

Dr. Strangelove, or showing the pieces of a plot fall into place like a steel trap, as in *Paths of Glory* and *Lolita.* Certainly, either way his films had been very story-oriented. Now he was to go to the other extreme, to build a major film not on a complex intrigue, but on simple gestures with a minimum of words, and leave the psychological, emotional, and philosophical ramifications up to his audiences to provide. The master of the cut-and-dried, the precise, the forcefully explicit, had chosen to seek the vague, the general, the ambiguous; the filmmaker who had always approached his audiences very importantly through their minds was now looking to approach them "at an inner level of consciousness just as music does." The process of change and adaptation could hardly have been an easy one, as Kubrick, being the very antithesis of an emotional, instinctive filmmaker like Fellini, who can hardly approach his audiences any other way, had to work out an intellectual plan and then render it in nonverbal, inexplicit terms, suppressing the connections, disguising the thought processes by which he had reached his conclusions, and as it were rendering the intellectual progression embodied in his film by means of a series of metaphors and mimes, offering a sort of cinematic code produced from an analysis of the basic components of his subject, with enough hints of a key for spectators to break the code themselves if they insisted on doing so, but with the hope that they would not, would, to change the metaphor, soak up the film's significance by osmosis.

All of this is a roundabout way of describing the self-transformation of a prose artist into a poet, a psychologist into a myth maker. I think that any lingering doubts I may have about the effect of the finished film come from one basic doubt—that of whether one can become a poet simply by taking an infinitude of pains. It seems to me that the one big distraction the film presents, as far as the operation of its intended mode of communication is concerned, is the underlying awareness one has that it is a construct, intellectually arrived at, with a certain design on us which the creator perfectly understands but we are supposed not to. Jancsó once said, when questioned about his meanings, "I'm not a critic. I make films, and years later, perhaps, I begin to see what I was doing, what I put in them. But it's too early yet with *The Round-Up*. Anyway, if I ever do decide what it's about, I'll probably be wrong." I have no feeling that Kubrick could honestly say the same about *2001*, and that is precisely what is wrong with it. It works, or is meant to work, rather like one of the black basalt columns which crop up in it. Originally they were explicitly conceived of as teaching machines from outer space; later this idea was dropped (though it lingers on in the novel-of-the-film), but it still lies there somewhere beneath, as a possible explanation. The film too may be conceived of as a teaching machine from outer space, but its efficacy as such seems to depend on an expected failure to grasp precisely what it is or how it works on us, even though the clues are present for those so minded.

Interestingly enough, the novel-of-the-film by Arthur C. Clarke, Kubrick's script collaborator, gives us other clues too, by preserving notions which presumably were at one time in play between him and Kubrick but were finally suppressed. In fact, everything is pretty cut-and-dried in it, to the extent that it seems to represent an earlier, more explicit draft of the subject, blue-period Picasso, as it were, hiding behind an analytical-cubist Picasso. If we wonder about the sort of Claridge's hotel room in which the solitary astronaut finds himself near the end, we can discover a perfectly explicit explanation in the book, that it is a mental construct of his own, a tool to help him accommodate himself to mental experiences totally beyond his comprehension. In the film we are not told that, but just left to guess. Similarly with the monolith and the apes at the beginning: there seems to be some connection in the film between the presence of the monolith and the apes' learning how to use weapons and kill, but it remains an audience's hypothesis; not so in the book, where that is explicitly stated. And nearly all the other differences between the book and the film, which are rarely of more than detail, seem to show the same move toward vagueness, avoidance of the concrete in order to be more suggestive, more hauntingly ambiguous. Is not that the prose writer's notion of the way poetry works, rather than the poet's?

Let us look a little more closely at how the film does work. The plot can be quite briefly summarized. It is divided into two main sections, with a prologue and epilogue in which the significance of the body of the film may—or may not—be found. The prologue is called "The Dawn of Man" and shows, at some length, a group of ape-men discovering a new arrival on the scene—a mysterious black basalt column dropped seemingly from the sky—and shortly afterward working out for themselves how to make weapons out of bone. Then comes the first part of the main film. A similar column is found, around the end of this century, by men on the moon. It is clearly fashioned by some sort of intelligence, and it beams radio signals toward Jupiter when the sun is in the right position. In the second part we follow the journey of a group of astronauts toward Jupiter to find out exactly what all this means, and particularly the battle of two of them with a megalomaniac computer which has developed a yen to take over the expedition. Then comes the epilogue, which takes the craft to Jupiter and "beyond the infinite." Here the single survivor of the battle with the computer HAL goes through a succession of psychedelic/psychological experiences rendered in terms of abstract visuals before materializing again in the aforementioned room, where he seems to exist at various stages of his life right up to his death in extreme old age and rebirth as a "star child," a sort of human fetus close to birth floating near a transfigured earth in timeless space.

Kubrick has commented in some detail on his own ideas behind the film in the interview with Joseph Gelmis in *The Film Director as Superstar,* making the provision that "explaining" such a work "contributes nothing but a superficial 'cultural' value which has no value except for critics and teachers who have to earn a living." So, then, on "the *lowest* level, that is, explanation of plot," what happens for Kubrick in the film is:

> You begin with an artifact left on earth four million years ago by extraterrestrial explorers who observed the behavior of the man-apes of the time and decided to influence their evolutionary progression. Then you have a second artifact buried on the lunar surface and programmed to signal word of man's first baby steps into the uni-

verse—a kind of cosmic burglar alarm. And finally there's a third artifact placed in orbit around Jupiter and waiting for the time when man has reached the outer rim of his own solar system.

When the surviving astronaut, Bowman, ultimately reaches Jupiter, this artifact sweeps him into a force field or star gate that hurls him on a journey through inner and outer space and finally transports him to another part of the galaxy, where he's placed in a human zoo approximating a hospital terrestrial environment drawn out of his own dreams and imagination. In a timeless state, his life passes from middle age to senescence to death. He is reborn, an enhanced being, a star child, an angel, a superman, if you like, and returns to earth prepared for the next leap forward of man's evolutionary destiny.

That is what happens on the film's simplest level. Since an encounter with an advanced interstellar intelligence would be incomprehensible within our present earthbound frames of reference, reactions to it will have elements of philosophy and metaphysics that have nothing to do with the bare plot outline itself.

It is significant that Kubrick can and will provide such an explanation, even though he denies that he tried for ambiguity: "Once you're dealing on a nonverbal level, ambiguity is unavoidable." Opinions will obviously vary on the effectiveness of the various sections of the film as nonverbal communication, not to mention the effectiveness of the film as a whole. For myself I find it frequently presents the same problem as the passages of mime in nineteenth-century ballet—it seems to take a long time to communicate very little, and to choose a perversely roundabout way of doing it. The prologue with the apes, though stunningly beautiful to look at, especially in its use of slow motion at the end, when the first ape discovers the use of a bone as an offensive weapon (not much different in feeling from the slow-motion explosion at the end of *Zabriskie Point*), does go on and on, and I find the ending disappointingly glib and derivative after what has gone before, though this may only be the insuperable difficulty of ending a story which by its nature must take us further and further beyond the range of human thought. Perhaps also there is too much footage devoted to the slow maneuvering of the film-maker's giant toys, as the various spaceships turn and revolve and come little by little into port to the strains of a Strauss waltz (things happen so slowly in space). Of course, detail by detail the film is often staggering to look at—Kubrick designed and photographed all his own special photographic effects—and when it does decline into the merely verbal it is ingeniously scripted: in particular, the relations between the humans and the power-crazed computer are observed with a nice wit, and the most "plotty" moment is saved with much practical cunning for the intermission break—we know that HAL knows that the humans are conspiring against him, and are kept agog with elementary but effective thriller-type suspense to know how he will fight back. Indeed, it is not coincidence, and is not either merely frivolous to suggest, that the computer is the character with most "human interest" in the entire film.

Of course, Kubrick might well reply that it is a confession of failure (ours, not his) that one should be thinking in terms of plot continuity and "human interest" at all. (To which one could fairly reply that it is unwise for a film to comport itself like a plot piece, with a puzzle, a quest, and a battle for power, and then provide so little that can be interpreted as plot solution.) But I must confess also that there are times in the cinema these days when I begin to feel that perhaps I have a faint inkling of how the mammoth felt when the ice began to melt. This struck me with peculiar force when I went to see *2001* again with an ordinary paying audience in London. On second viewing, my pleasures, and my reservations, came in precisely the same places. I enjoyed and was held by the "plotty" bits, particularly the whole middle section, in which the human inhabitants of the spaceship find themselves locked in deathly combat with the rogue robot. I found the beginning as long-drawn-out, and the end as willfully obscure, as before. I admired the elaboration of the technical scenes showing the arrival of the spaceship at the space station and so on, but still tended to feel that they were overlong in relation to the film as a whole, as though Kubrick had had so much fun devising them that he failed, when editing the film, to appreciate that they would be considerably less interesting to an audience than they were to him.

But that apparently was where I was wrong. In the audience this time there were lots of children, especially boys, under fifteen, generally with fathers and sometimes with mothers in tow. A characteristic group sat just behind me: father and mother in their mid-thirties, boy of about eleven. And their reactions were fascinating. The mother was clearly a trifle restive. Like me, she was mostly held by the plot; otherwise, she kept asking her husband, *sotto voce,* what this meant, what was happening there, did he think a spacecraft would really be like that, and so on. To which he gave answers more hopeful than confident, I thought. But, evidently, what interested him above all was the purely mechanical side, the sort of thing that should appeal at once to Meccano addicts; the plot for him seemed to be incidental, like the plot in a musical, something that was there as the bread in the sandwich of really attractive items. The boy, on the other hand, obviously loved it all. He shushed his parents whenever their dialogue became too insistent, and at intermission kept bubbling, "Isn't it good? Do you like it? Don't you understand it? What's there difficult to understand?" Maybe, of course, he was just an infant genius, but I doubt it. He seemed an ordinary enough child. But clearly his attention was not functioning in the same way that his parents' was, and that mine was. He was, that is to say, not in the slightest worried by a nagging need to make connections, or to understand how one moment, one spectacular effect, fitted in with, led up to, or led on from another. He was accepting it like (dare one say?) an LSD trip, in which a succession of thrilling impressions are flashed onto a brain free of the trammels of rational thought. Nor can one put this down to his age and education: it is not, after all, a particularly childish way of seeing things. As any teacher will tell you, children tend on the whole, especially at that age, to be the most stuffily rationalistic of all, constantly demanding believable hows and whys.

No. It seems to me that what we have in *2001* is the first important attempt in the commercial cinema at a whole new way of assimilating narrative. It is not only children who exemplify it: many young and some not so young adults seem to accept things in the same way. What they want, or at least what they accept without demur, is a succession of vivid moments, not an articulated plot. They are, one might say, the audience envisaged by Artaud in his proposed Theater of Cruelty, ready-conditioned, perfectly prepared to abandon ratiocination and take drama straight in the solar plexus. Naturally, I have a theory to account for this, and it is hardly a new one. But it seems to me that, despite Marshall McLuhan and the sense he occasionally makes along with a lot of provocative nonsense, very little practical attention has yet been paid to the way that a life with television is affecting our mode of perception. With television, for all sorts of reasons—not least the manifold distractions of watching at home as against the narrowly directed attention to stage or screen required of us in a darkened theater—attention is always liable to drift away, and in a matter of seconds rather than minutes. What is needed, therefore, is not so much something which will keep one glued to the small screen every instant of a program—that would be too exhausting—but something which will keep bringing back the wandering attention with a new tidbit at regular intervals. How the transition from one tidbit to another is achieved remains fairly immaterial.

Hence, plot in particular does not matter greatly, and neither does an overall sense of form. Provided the attention grabbers are spectacular enough in themselves, no one is going to question the rationale behind them too closely. And once this habit of mind is established, it is bound to affect other fields of activity, notably the screen and the stage. I find myself worried quite frequently by evident weak points in plot but they seem to bother ordinary paying members of the audience not at all. To me, it would have seemed, for instance, a mark against the possible popularity of the Beatles' feature cartoon *Yellow Submarine* that it has no coherent plot at all, but simply makes up its feature length out of varied bits and pieces. Not at all, though: where it has been shown it seems to have gone down very well with audiences, and not necessarily highbrow audiences either, on its power to excite and enliven, moment by moment. I think it is this shift of sensibilities and gradual unnoticed change in audience expectations that Kubrick brilliantly seizes on in *2001,* rather than anything deeper and more significant. I doubt that *2001* is having a very deep effect on anybody—the lesson to be learned from it is rather that audiences these days are able and willing to accept a succession of purely visual and largely nonverbal experiences in the cinema without question or putting up intellectual barriers—in many respects this, and not explicable plot, is "the *lowest* level" of approach to a film today. If so, *2001* hits this level of audience acceptance with perfect aim—hence its vast popularity—and is significant as the first long, big-budget commercial film to do so. For that one can hardly fault it, even if one might still choose to find one's own most powerful visceral experiences of the cinema rather in Fellini's *Satyricon* or Lindsay Anderson's *If . . .* or Pasolini's *Teorema* or Jancsó's *Red Psalm*. Intellectual snobbery? Possibly, but to me it seems not to diminish Kubrick's stature too much to see him as a great popularizer rather than as a great innovator.

This brings us to Kubrick's latest, and I believe his best, film, *A Clockwork Orange* (1971). It is a pity that in English the word "confidence" so often brings in its train the word "trick." Confidence is the most extraordinary quality of *A Clockwork Orange,* but the confidence is no trick. From the first moment, the narrative moves with complete assurance: we meet the principal characters, we are shown the world in which they live, and are caught up in their progress at once, with no pause for explanations, no mess and untidiness. The whole thing works with, yes, the absolute precision of clockwork. Kubrick brooks no argument with his method; indeed, he seems almost not to conceive that argument is possible and because of that it isn't. The temptations to divagate from such single-mindedness must have been immense. Anthony Burgess's novel, on which the film is based, postulates a brave new world not so far hence, not so much different from our own, except that in some respects it has developed technologically, in others has frayed a little around the edges. Politically we do not know quite what's what, except that we may guess something from the Russianized English argot the younger characters speak. Socially various impulses are channeled through the ready availability of doctored milks which intensify one instinct or another—notably the urge to physical violence, which is what gets our hero into all his trouble. Environmentally the image is of an advanced urban society running out of control: in the brighter modern high rises the garbage is not collected, the vandalism unchecked. Kubrick's physical evocation of this future world is stunningly vivid, mainly because it is all strictly functional and never strays into the irrelevant picturesque. Again it is mainly a matter of confidence; nothing is insisted on. There are, I think, no purely atmospheric landscape shots in the film; everything is context for the people, and the color photography of John Alcott, which would in any other circumstances be dazzling, does not here dazzle because it never calls attention to itself at the cost of the film's overall effect.

And that overall effect is, first and foremost, as a piece of powerfully direct storytelling (which is surprising, perhaps, considering the novel, from which what everyone remembers is the trappings). Kubrick, back refreshed after his experiments with minimal plotting in *2001* to apply the skills of nonverbal filmic expression to a perfectly explicit story line, uses a technique which it is tempting to call comic-strip. Episode follows episode brusquely, with no lingering over transitions: the stages of our hero's accumulating misfortune following his indulgence with his three mates, or droogs, to use Burgess's argot, in a bout of ultra-violence—a therapeutic beating up of a shambling drunk, an all-out tangle with a rival group, a rape-cum-beating-up of a couple of country-dwelling intellectuals—are economically sketched in, with overwhelming logic. Each episode in the first half, when he is up, finds its mirror image in the second half, when he is down, drained of his violent and sexual impulses by a new conditioning course of cinematic forced feeding.

To get through so much so quickly Kubrick has to adopt a bold, caricatural style of playing for his cast. For the first time since *Dr. Strangelove* the acting plays an important part in the total effect (in *2001* the actors are ciphers, playing second fiddle to the machines), and as in *Dr. Strangelove,* many of the characters are played up to and over the edge of outrageous burlesque, yet always with a certain disturbing resonance. Or almost always: the only exception in *A Clockwork Orange* is the prison officer, played by Michael Bates. In other circumstances, as in his stage performance in Peter Nichols's play

Forget-Me-Not Lane, Bates has been able to bring complex overtones to a character who could be caricature but here he seems to be no more than a sort of *Carry On* figure of farce, and the discrepancy, though not a radical flaw, is disturbing. Patrick Magee, on the other hand, who can be the most execrably mannered actor, is beautifully used here by Kubrick: as the intellectual crippled in the first half by the wild bunch, he has a moment of extraordinary grandeur in the second half, menacingly inquiring of our hero whether his food and entertainment suit him while continually and clearly in a hysteria of hatred. As Alex DeLarge, the subject and object of all the action, Malcolm McDowell gives a performance of remarkable variety and controlled power, confirming the promise of *If . . .* that he would be one of the most striking actors of his generation. And the role is taxing, physically and emotionally, calling for considerable athleticism as well as unexpected moments of interior quality, as in the scenes devoted to his seemingly inconsistent passion for Ludwig Van and his Ninth. Incidentally, one cannot help wondering if it was this tissue of musical reference which first drew Kubrick to the book: certainly the music, Beethoven, Rossini, Purcell, and all, is used with a virtuosity reminiscent of the soundtrack in *2001* (from which everyone remembers the Strauss waltz and the recurrence of the "World Riddle" theme from Richard Strauss's *Zarathustra*), except again more functionally. There are no passages where we can sit back, listen, and admire. The film just hits, and hits hard. It works, as only a master could make it.

In *A Clockwork Orange* Kubrick seems to have found his ideal subject and his ideal form of expression. In all the lofty discussion occasioned by *2001* we have tended to forget (even with the box-office returns on that film to remind us) that Kubrick is essentially a *popular* artist, one skilled in adapting the latest techniques to the task of communicating complicated ideas to the largest possible audience. The look of *A Clockwork Orange,* contrasting the Pop/Op/Kinetic art trappings of the brave new world with the grubby makeshift of everyday life in a world run to seed, is smart and modern, but also perfectly functional, all there to convey something rather than indulged in for its own sake. Kubrick the master of dramatic-cinematic narrative is again functioning at full power, and it is arguable that *2001,* whatever one's reservations about its total success, was a step necessary for Kubrick to take in order to get to this point. Whether or not he has in the process proved himself an *auteur,* an inspired filmmaker, or merely, as I tend to believe, the brilliantly gifted cinematic intelligence who can occasionally turn out an inspired film, does not seem to matter too much at this point. No doubt with his next film, announced at the time of writing to be an adaptation of Thackeray's novel *Barry Lyndon* (which sounds on the face of it like a weird choice for a successor to *Dr. Strangelove, 2001,* and *A Clockwork Orange*), the question will present itself again, and again no doubt no definitive answer will be possible. But in the meantime we can at least take comfort in calling *A Clockwork Orange* a possible masterpiece, very likely to be one of the most influential films of the 1970's, and leave the rest to those "critics and teachers" who, as Kubrick justly remarks, do "have to earn a living."

Andy Warhol / Paul Morrissey

"BY THE WAY," PAUL MORRISSEY ONCE ASKED ME MATTER-OF-factly, "did you know that Jackie Curtis is a man again?" I did not, but in the Warhol world one should be surprised at nothing. Among the Warhol constellation Jackie Curtis is, or was, the large lady with the rather frizzy hair and spangled eye make-up who was to be observed in *Flesh* devouring forties fan magazines while Joe Dallesandro is otherwise engaged with the girl who is worried about whether she should have her breasts inflated with silicone. She was essentially the try-a-little-tenderness housewife who would like to be as glamorous as those movie stars up there but does not have the time, the money, or the self-confidence—as opposed to Candy Darling, most outrageously glamorous of the Warhol clan, every woman's dream of what womanliness ought to be.

Every man's too, I suppose, since both Candy Darling and Jackie Curtis are, or have been in their time, men. It seems that a few years ago, when Candy Darling had already decided to be a woman, Jackie Curtis wrote a play for her, to be staged by New York's Off-Off-Broadway Theater of the Ridiculous, his own brainchild. The play duly went on, but there were differences of interpretation, and as a result Candy Darling was fired and Jackie Curtis went into drag to play the role himself. Having settled on this new persona she stayed that way, accepting even the personal complications she cheerfully describes in Makavejev's *WR: Mysteries of the Organism*. Until, that is, the latest production of the Theater of the Ridiculous, written as a vehicle for herself. Here, it seems, the difficulties of interpretation arose with her leading man, and were resolved in a coup worthy of *Lonesome Cowboys:* the leading man was fired, Jackie Curtis shaved her head and took on his role instead, and to fill the heroine's role she had vacated, rehired none other than Candy Darling.

It all sounds rather like life imitating art, but in the Warhol world nothing is that simple—or perhaps I should say, nothing is that complicated. The essence of Warhol's art—and by extension that of the Factory he heads—is the straight look at things as they are, and acceptance of appearances as an important part, perhaps the most important part, of the truth. It is the same whether the object is a Campbell's Soup can or the Empire State Building or some people just living, just talking, just being in front of the camera. And if what people are is what they appear to be, what they appear to be is very importantly what they think they are, what they want to be thought.

This is where Jackie Curtis, Candy Darling, and, most shatteringly in *Trash,* Holly Woodlawn come in. Not because being men in drag makes them a spectacular special case, but precisely because it does not. We all define ourselves to some extent according to our own fantasies: the only difference with Warhol's drag ladies is that the discrepancy between the fantasy and the visible reality is likely to be more evident. But not to Warhol or his right-hand man, Paul Morrissey, with whose collaboration he has made most of his latest and best films. The point about *Flesh* and *Trash,* or for that matter *My Hustler* or *Bike Boy* or *The Chelsea Girls,* is that everything is taken on trust, everything is right there in front of the camera. Inevitably some of the people are more interesting than others, but we decide this fairly and squarely on the evidence; there is no snide angling from behind the camera. The Warhol films play scrupulously fair with their characters; the films do not build myths, they merely record them. They are documentaries, but documentaries of the human spirit, of subjective rather than objective reality.

No doubt that all sounds very grand and highfalutin as a way of describing films which, like *My Hustler,* were improvised during one day in the spirit of "if it works, fine; if it doesn't, forget it," or, like *The Chelsea Girls,* were destined to be projected simultaneously on two screens because (in the words of one of the film's creators) "most of it's much too boring if you have only one thing at a time to look at and listen to." All the same it is true: the sign of Warhol's coming of age as a filmmaker has been his acceptance, around the time that his collaboration with Paul Morrissey began, of that basic axiom of the cinema, that what the camera really photographs is not the outside but the inside of people. Therefore inevitably it can pick out a phony, and in Warhol's films it unerringly does so (in *The Chelsea Girls* the frequent tedium comes from an undue allowance of time to people who see their appearances mainly as an opportunity to strike what they take to be sophisticated attitudes).

But equally it gives full weight to the genuine article, however bizarre. Consider, for example, the part played by Holly Woodlawn in *Trash*. Holly is, in the more general sense of the term, living with Joe Dallesandro at the beginning of the film. She is dressed as a woman, speaks as a woman, but clearly there is something not quite right; we do not know for sure whether in the context of the film she is meant to be a woman or merely a man in drag. But as the film progresses, and further elements of plot are introduced—her sister, her decision to pretend to be pregnant in order to milk the Welfare Department—we realize that as far as the film is concerned she is a woman, and so as far as we are concerned she becomes a woman too. In this performance the power of inner conviction overcomes any prosaic misgivings we may have; just as certain actresses can convince us they are beautiful, despite all evidence to the contrary, simply by the force of their own belief in their beauty.

For this to work properly, though, the attitude of the filmmaker has to be right. One tiny hint that those behind the camera are laughing up their sleeves at those in front, and the effect is ruined. And whatever else may be said about the Warhol *équipe,* they are sublimely unpatronizing. They accept their "stars" absolutely on their own terms; the stars are whatever they want to be, whatever they think they are, and that is that. They are not representative of anything but themselves. And after all, why should they be? One could no doubt make out a case for seeing most of the Warhol films as parts of a large-scale survey of a certain homosexual/transvestite/drug scene in the margins of the New York art world, but it seems unlikely that there is anything systematic about it, or any intention to generalize, even about such a relatively small segment of the population. Empathy rather than abstraction and comment seems to be the aim.

And this is where the dottiest fringe of the underground joins hands with the most reactionary section of Hollywood commercial filmmaking. There is no reason why Holly Woodlawn, or Viva, or Joe Dallesandro should represent anything more than themselves, just as there was no reason why Garbo or Gary Cooper or the Marx Brothers should represent anything but themselves. In this respect the Warhol camp of taking nonentities and announcing that they are "superstars" makes a lot more sense than first appears. The people in Warhol films are treated just like Hollywood stars in their heyday. They are required primarily to be themselves, to irradiate any character they may happen to be playing with the rich, inescapable qualities of their own personalities. And, even more important, the emphasis of the films is entirely on them.

This is a Warhol principle; Warhol and his group believe that the increasing emphasis on the film director as superstar (the title of a recent American book of interviews, in which nevertheless Warhol figures) is putting film theory and, worse, the film itself off on quite the wrong road. Directors, says Paul Morrissey, are all very well in their place, along with hairdressers, camera operators, dialogue coaches, and such, but finally what counts, what has always counted, is the person up there on the screen, the star in front of the camera rather than the exhibitionist itching to get out from behind it. At the Cannes Festival the year *Trash* was shown he needed no persuading to see *The Trojan Women,* but was fretful about the way it was described: "Why do people keep talking about seeing 'the Cacoyannis movie'? What does that mean, 'the Cacoyannis movie'? It's the Katharine Hepburn movie, that's what it is." Equally, he loved *Death in Venice* not because of Visconti's directorial art, but for the very proper reason that, subject matter notwithstanding, it is basically a good old-fashioned star vehicle made in a good, glossy, old-fashioned style.

Logically, therefore, Warhol's own cinema should not be a

director's cinema at all. And in some very important senses it is not. Throughout his career as a filmmaker Warhol has worked very closely with collaborators, both individuals and the whole Factory. Just as with his graphics he has frequently said that the cult of personality has nothing to do with it—anyone in the Factory could turn out "Warhol" graphics just as well as he, without his ever seeing what they are doing, much less laying hand to it himself—so "Warhol" movies can be made, and have been made, perfectly well when the master himself is nowhere near; "Warhol" is much more of a brand name than an artist's signature. Perhaps it is true, as Gerard Malanga, a long-time collaborator of Warhol's, says in Bert Koetter's documentary *Andy Warhol and His Clan* (1970), that even if Warhol believes this in principle, he is furious if anyone puts the principle into practice by "forging" his work. All the same, it does seem that the main element which can be identified as Andy Warhol's personal contribution is, paradoxically, the idea of impersonality.

To see how this comes about, it is necessary to delve some way back into Warhol's personal and professional history before he became involved with filmmaking, which was as late as 1963, when he bought a movie camera and made a film called *Tarzan and Jane Regained, Sort of . . .* while on a visit to Hollywood. At that time he was thirty-five and had already gone successfully through two careers. Born of Czech parents in Pittsburgh, he had graduated with a degree in fine arts from Carnegie Tech in 1949 and very rapidly became a leading commercial artist in New York. He did drawings for fashion advertisements, designed book jackets (often for books by rather camp authors like Ronald Firbank and Baron Corvo) and some privately printed books of generally humorous drawings, and became best known for his playfully accurate drawings of cats and of shoes, real and fantastic. He was at this time a brilliant if rather precious draftsman. This phase lasted for about ten years; by the early 1960's, though, he had changed direction, becoming a painter (his first important one-man show was in 1962) and then giving up painting proper for silk-screen printing, sometimes touched up by hand. It was at this point he first gained widespread fame as the painter of Campbell's Soup cans, and consequently became a rallying point for those interested, either as creators or as connoisseurs, in Pop Art. There was a certain internal logic in this transition—having made a living from drawing for advertisements, Warhol would seem to be carrying over the same sort of subject matter into the fine arts. But this was hardly apparent from the works themselves, for whereas his drawings had been highly personal and, in the series of shoes for instance, whimsical and fantastic, his early paintings often seemed to originate in photographs and aim at a harsh, precise, mechanical finish, as though photographically reproduced. And after painting meticulously detailed pictures of Campbell's Soup cans and Coca-Cola bottles, Warhol rapidly went to the obvious next stage, by ceasing actually to paint and silk-screening photographs on canvas or paper instead, so that the works could be multiplied ad infinitum (it is, after all, a considerable job to paint by hand hundreds of virtually identical canvases, as was allegedly the case with the soup cans) and the personal element in the work was even further reduced—to the choice of the photographic material at the start, and to the way it was colored or touched up with additional color after reproduction.

Another factor that was possibly significant for Warhol's development in the direction of filmmaking was the way that the images were placed in relation to one another, the sizing and grouping of them within an overall multiple image. For by this time Warhol had become interested in repetition as an artistic effect: generally the multiplication of a single image —"stars" like Marilyn Monroe, Elvis Presley, or Jackie Kennedy; photographs of deaths and disasters—but occasionally a variety of different images, as in his "Robert Rauschenburg" (1963). Of course, owing to the technical limitations of the silk-screen process, no two reproductions would be exactly alike in texture, color, or whatever, and Warhol was fascinated by the accidental variations which resulted; also images within the same frame might well be deliberately varied by the application of extra color, as in the Elizabeth Taylor and Marilyn Monroe pictures or the "Flowers" of 1965. This kind of "serial" art might seem at first sight a logical step toward the cinema, as were Muybridge's serial photographs analyzing animal movement in the 1870's. But it should be remembered that nearly all Warhol's multiple images are deliberately non-narrative, repetitions of the same image with only the slightest variations, and that an essential part of their effect comes from simultaneity of vision—the effect of seeing fifteen images of an electric chair arranged in a rectangle of canvas is very different from seeing them, slight variations and all, projected one after another onto a screen as slides. If the artist who was fascinated with this effect on canvas was going to develop into a filmmaker, it might be supposed that his films would be far from conventional.

In any event, that was how things turned out. The films of Warhol's first period as a filmmaker threw most of the normal assumptions of filmmakers, even consciously experimental ones, out the window. They are based, like his serial paintings, on repetition with minimal accidental variation or on unblinking scrutiny of an object which remains uniform through a small cycle of change. The first famous film was *Sleep* (1963), a six-hour silent picture of a man sleeping. Warhol says that of course he could have shot continuously six hours of a man sleeping, but actually he shot six hours of ten-minute segments over several weeks, then arranged them, threw out half the material, and repeated the other half, "faking" it, as he says, "to get a better design." In other words, given that we are dealing with ten-minute strips of moving picture instead of individual, fixed images, the technique of assembling the film is very similar to the technique of assembling a serial painting. The subject is deliberately limited, open to only slight variations, and even so there is a lot of literal repetition as well as overall uniformity. To the complaint that it is boring Warhol might well reply (though he seldom bothers to defend or explain his work) that it is meant to be—repetition, after all, is one of the familiar techniques of both Eastern and Western religion to induce a tranced concentration which may itself be a mystical experience or within which mystical experience can flower. A controlled boredom, drugging the first levels of consciousness, is part of the film's psychological design.

Thus, though the films are in a certain sense, owing to the nature of the medium itself, experiences in time, they are always working against that, manipulating time and dulling our awareness of it. The film itself is indeed often manipulated in these early Warhol films, so that we get the impression of a tranced slowness even beyond that created by their total lack of conventional progression: some of them, for instance, like *Kiss* (1963), were shot at a normal twenty-four frames a second but shown at sixteen frames a second to give a slow-motion effect; in others, like *Eat* (1963), in which a man takes some forty minutes to eat a mushroom, the "performance" itself was directed to take place as slowly as possible. A dozen other films were made in the years 1963–64, of which the best known are *Couch, Blow Job,* and *Empire.* In *Couch* a number of people become variously entangled on one couch, against a background of Warhol's "Flowers" painting; in *Blow Job* we concentrate for thirty minutes on the face of a man who is supposedly experiencing a slow orgasm orally induced (out of camera); in *Empire* we fixedly observe the Empire State Building for eight hours through a cycle of day and night.

In 1964 Warhol the filmmaker moved into his second phase. It was distinguished from the first phase by the introduction of sound (directly recorded) and the intrusion of some sort of story content (most of the Warhol films of 1965 were scripted by the poet Ronald Tavel). This phase was also marked by the arrival of the "superstar" in Warhol's work, the first famous example being the transvestite Mario Montez. Already in films like *Harlot, Kitchen,* and *The Shopper,* we can begin to see the way Warhol deals with his human material. In a sense it would seem that he uses his performers as actors—they are directed, after all, they follow a prearranged program, and even, if possible, say actual lines written for them. But a lot of this is unessential and irrelevant, just a means of getting at and freeing the essential element for Warhol, the characteristics of the people as people. Warhol maintains that no one was really interested in the characters Marilyn Monroe was playing. Her audiences were attracted rather by the continuing insight into Marilyn Monroe as Marilyn Monroe that the various films offered—and that is the true nature of star quality. This does sometimes involve a problem, in that for me at any rate Mario Montez, playing Jean Harlow in *Harlot* and Hedy Lamarr in *The Shopper,* is really not interesting enough as a person or a screen presence to carry the films as far as intended on a human level. Or maybe he does carry them just as far as Warhol intends, since maybe at this stage he is interested above all in the complete nonentity of his superstar, weaving about him/her a cunning pattern of abstract camp.

Technically the films are rough, though with a roughness that is often intentional. One aspect which at the time was often regarded as primitive—Warhol's usual technique of keeping the camera stationary and staging action within a fixed frame—we know from Ronald Tavel and others to have been a deliberate decision, maintained against much argument from his associates. And indeed working with the camera he then had, in a sort of tradition of hand-held underground cinema, it would have been just as easy and far more conventional if he had moved the camera. In not moving the camera he was making a deliberate decision, and taking film style in a direction which would later be adopted by filmmakers as different as Godard and Straub. It is probable that many of the other creative decisions taken in these films were less thought out, if not entirely unconscious—all Warhol's associates testify to his unerring instinct in artistic matters, so that even real mistakes are somehow used, become part of the texture of his artwork. One incidental effect of the unmoving camera is that our attention is distributed with extraordinary evenness over the whole frame of vision—the settings and props assume as much importance as the people, the whole scene becoming, as it were, a weird, complex, not wholly explicable *objet trouvé* selected through the special sensibilities of the artist and then displayed with a minimum of further intervention.

Even the inferior quality of the sound recording plays a positive part in the effectiveness of the films. In *Harlot,* for example, the action consists of a long-held composition with minimal movement within the frame—mainly Harlow (Mario Montez) eating bananas while reclining on a sofa, leaning against a very tough-looking lady with a white cat on her lap, and behind, two men, one looking generally toward the ladies, the other out at the camera and us. Meanwhile, on the soundtrack, we hear, or half-hear, very indistinctly, the voices of three "readers" (poets Ronald Tavel, Harry Fainlight, and Billy Linich), who were apparently asked to come along and read something, anything they liked, but in fact ended up just talking, somewhere off screen, where they could observe the action in front of the camera and comment on it, diverge from it, improvise in varying counterpoint to the visuals. Of this rambling chatter we hear in fact very little; the effect is the aural equivalent of the roughly silk-screened, blown-up, blotted, tinted, and otherwise obscured photographs Warhol used in his contemporary serial paintings, creating the same kind of vague unease in audiences.

Unease and disturbance are obviously part of the intended response to these films. As Ronald Tavel (as quoted in John Wilcock's *The Autobiography and Sex Life of Andy Warhol*) describes his intentions in the script of *Kitchen* (which was subsequently staged with little or no change as a play), the performers within the cramped, impersonal kitchen

> might just be crapping around, on the other hand it's terribly organized. . . . It's all very real and there's a way of driving them to become very real because the script was geared in a way to make them just go insane, and then you pick people that are just on the verge of going nuts so that there is never any security. Just as the audience would feel secure and think they're actually making a movie, or it's a play about people making an underground film; just as they get into that we stop. . . . It has this obviously fake ending of killing the girl, and you sit there and think well it's obviously a fake ending, and they just have to get this over with so they're killing the lead, and on the other hand you're forced to confess that that kind of behavior will lead to murder and this is like a final parody; it's fake and it's real and it's a perfect equation.

Something of the same kind of ambiguous discomfort is appreciable, in varying degrees, in most of the films made in this phase and the next, up to the major work which in many respects summarized Warhol's films thus far, *The Chelsea Girls* (1966). There seem to have been disagreements within the group in this period, and sometime in 1965 Ronald Tavel left and was replaced as writer by Chuck Wein, the friend of one of Warhol's current superstars, Edie Sedgwick (though Tavel did have a hand in preparing *The Chelsea Girls*). But since what was written tended to be used merely as a starting point, and otherwise disregarded, the distinction between the two periods is more apparent than actual. More important for the future was the arrival in the Warhol group at this time of Paul Morrissey, who was to exert a dominant influence on the later films of the group and who was a distinguished creator in his own right. He was born in New York, studied English at Fordham University, and worked for an insurance company and in the New York Welfare Department (a significant job in relation to *Trash*). Further, he had already made some short underground films, including *Taylor Mead Dances* (1963), featuring one of the Warhol group in an imaginary striptease with tin cans. In 1965 Morrissey visited the apartment where Warhol was filming *Space,* with Edie Sedgwick (never printed or released): Warhol asked his opinion about whether the camera should move at one point, he said that it should, as there were too many people in front of the camera, and this was the first recorded pan or zoom in a Warhol film.

From this time on, Paul Morrissey was generally around while Warhol was filming, as assistant, associate producer (a grand term for a part in such informal proceedings), and cameraman on several, including parts of *The Chelsea Girls, Nude Restaurant* (1967), **** (1967), and *Lonesome Cowboys* (1968) before beginning to make his own personal films with *Flesh* (1969). The first film planned after Morrissey's arrival on the Warhol scene was one to be made on Fire Island on the subject of hustling, *My Hustler* (1965), which was to prove in many ways a presage of things to come. It is not very good but it is undeniably likable. Paul Morrissey recalls that it was made in one day with direct sound on a system new to them, and abandoned when they found the soundtrack unplayable, only to be taken up again later when by chance they discovered that the fault was in their playing equipment. It is also interesting in that it sketches, in the course of two long-lasting shots (about thirty-five minutes each, making up the film's total running time), the theme of *Trash* and of one important scene in *Flesh*.

The basic idea it shares with *Trash* is that of a beautiful, relatively nonreacting young man as the object of other people's fantasies and desires. The most effective part of the film comes in the second reel, when the young man (prefiguring the plain lad in *Flesh*) questions an older, more established hustler about career prospects in that line while they shower and shave together in the bathroom of a Fire Island beach house. Before we come to that point, though, there is rather a lot of affected camp talk, only occasionally funny, from a character who seems to see himself as the Firbank of Fire Island and a would-be sophisticated but disastrously inarticulate "fag hag" neighbor who aims to take this latest young man away from him. As they talk, the young man suns himself on the beach, the camera drifting away from the talkers on the sun deck, over toward the young man and back again, then back to him as they grow concerned (particularly his protector) at his getting into a conversation with someone else—the older hustler, who is an old friend of the observer, as it turns out. After the conversation indoors in the second reel between the experienced hustler and the neophyte, full of practical hints on what cologne to wear and how to go about things, we see a succession of people making the boy offers in exchange for his sexual response (as in *Trash*), and (again as in *Trash*) none of them seems really to connect—the boy is so caught up in his own world that the fantasies of others scarcely impinge on him. Compared with the later Morrissey films, *My Hustler* is weak and tentative, in that too many of its characters spend too much of their time striking attitudes rather incompetently in front of the camera. No doubt there is some attitudinizing in the later films also, but if so their characters prove to be far more interesting people when they wear masks forced on them by circumstance rather than masks of their own choosing.

The flavor of *My Hustler* is more realistic than in the earlier films, with the accent much more on characterization and on dialogue which is meant to be heard, though improvised, during shooting. Much the same sort of character is visible (or nearly visible) in *Poor Little Rich Girl* (1965), in which Edie Sedgwick, extremely out of focus, wanders around her apartment talking about her money and how it has all gone, and showing us some of the results of her spending, such as a coat of which she is very proud. It is also appreciable in most of the segments which go to make up *The Chelsea Girls,* which Warhol was shooting at this time, probably with no clear intention at the outset that they should all come together as part of one three-and-one-quarter-hour film. For during this period Warhol was filming every day that he could, with no fixed aim necessarily in view, just as later on he would start obsessively tape-recording everything that went on around him, an activity that eventually produced, more by accident than design, his "novel" *a* and his "play" *Pork.*

In any case, whether or not the segments of *The Chelsea Girls* were originally intended to go together, at a certain point the overall design of the film occurred to him, and the finished film is quite intricately structured, leaving room for the arbitrary and the accidental but quite carefully circumscribing the areas in which they can function. Briefly, *The Chelsea Girls* breaks down into seven half-hour segments, the materials of which are apparently unrelated, though since the order of the sequences within the half-hour segments and the order of the segments within the whole are predetermined, we find ourselves inevitably reading the film in a linear, continuative fashion, finding connections where none were put except fortuitously. But what I have been describing is only half the film—either half. For the film is actually seven hours long, its two parts shown simultaneously on twin screens. The two halves of the film are again apparently unrelated, except fortuitously, and though the order of sections in each half is fixed, the two projections are not exactly synchronized, so that each showing will differ slightly from any other. The left-hand half is in color, and quite a bit more finished in photography, sound recording, etc.; the right-hand half is in black-and-white, and seems much more casual (possibly the material used on this side was shot earlier). Both halves have soundtracks, which could presumably be played together, though in all showings I know of only one track has been played at any particular moment. You can therefore watch either image, or both, but can listen to only one half at a time. Visually the experience is akin to the appreciation of one of Warhol's serial paintings, with movement and sound added. It is difficult to watch both screens with equal concentration, and impossible to concentrate fully on both (Paul Morrissey says, perhaps not altogether frivolously, that this form of presentation was a good way to distract attention from some material which was by itself too weak to withstand scrutiny), but at the same time it is impossible, however closely one is concentrating on one screen, to ignore completely the other—resonances and apparent cross-references, or at least a continuous nagging counterpoint, must always be present in the spectator's consciousness.

I have seen the film both in the form intended and with the two halves played separately, so that each can receive total concentration. And at least I can attest (as one would hope and trust) that the form intended is better. For one thing there is the question of the inherent interest of the people in the various episodes. This is always a potential problem in films made the Warhol way—insofar as all his and our attention is concentrated on the people and what they can be persuaded to reveal of themselves in front of the camera, it can be mildly disastrous if the people so scrupulously examined do not justify the scrutiny. In *The Chelsea Girls,* watched episode by episode, there are sections of considerable intensity and fascination, but there is also a lot of tiresome attitudinizing by people who seem to regard themselves, mistakenly, as turners of fine phrases and tossers-off of sophisticated epigrams they can never quite manage to carry through to a satisfactory conclusion. When the less interesting episodes are set off by another episode on the other screen (even if that episode is not in itself any more interesting), the effect is balanced out, and of course our attention can be further directed by which soundtrack we are permitted to hear at any given point.

So, the total effect of *The Chelsea Girls* is complex, evidently more than the sum of its very uneven parts. The context must always be borne in mind when discussing any individual sections—but the fact remains that there are sections which stand out in the memory and could well stand alone as short Warhol films. The opening sequence (one of the opening sequences, that is) is a quintessential expression of one aspect of Warhol's film work, the very free, very casual-seeming camera pursuit of the object, showing in minute detail the fabric and texture of one person's life—in this case that of Nico, a glamorous blonde who is trimming her hair in what eventually turns out to be a kitchen as she moves around and the camera drifts away to show a child on the floor, then back to Nico, while some kind of outside reference is provided by a few more or less incomprehensible remarks from off (and presumably behind) camera. Other sequences, like that between Marie Menken and Gerard Malanga as an Oedipally involved mother and son, are entirely "acted," having a fictionalized dramatic structure, possibly written in advance (Ronald Tavel apparently scripted eight of the episodes completely, even if the end result diverged considerably from his original conception). Some of them are acted in a different sense—that with Mario Montez doing a pathetic, would-be provocative drag act seems like the compulsive acting out of a private fantasy (I find it hard to see any kind of satirical comment here, either on the superstar's part or on Warhol's—editorializing would be out of character for him). And some of the most memorable sequences exist on that mysterious borderline between reality and fantasy—that in which Eric Emerson delivers a long and beautifully written (if it was written) monologue while supposedly tripping on LSD, telling us of his doped fantasies and ambitions toward oneness with others and with the world; or the famous final sequence in which another superstar, a man known as Ondine, starts playing a role as a Pope hearing confession and then apparently gets freaked out (really) when a girl penitent starts to talk about God, slaps her around, chases after her shouting and raving, comes back into frame, wheels on the camera ("Turn the fucking thing off!"), and those behind it grind inexorably on, recording it all, one would say voyeuristically except that the regard is cool, uninvolved, and the purpose of the protagonist/victim is undoubtedly communication of a sort. Many commentators have felt that this sequence is the finest thing Warhol has ever done on film, and though I would not necessarily agree with that, it is a remarkable tour de force, even if, like *The Chelsea Girls* as a whole, somehow more interesting as a conception than as an executed film.

If *The Chelsea Girls* looks like a sort of summary of Warhol's work up to 1966, a collage made up of bits and pieces of different kinds, in different styles, rather like one of Warhol's few "narrative" silk-screen paintings, such as "Jackie" (1965) or "7 Decades of Sidney Janis" (1967), the next couple of years showed a development in a new direction, one faintly hinted at in *My Hustler:* toward feature-length films shot in color, with fair amounts of dialogue that is meant to be heard, and something approaching plot, or at least narrative structure. Admittedly **** (1967) hardly falls within this category, since it was originally (and for one showing only) twenty-five hours long, made up of half-hour episodes, and the two-hour version which survives is considerably disjointed. But *Bike Boy* (1967), *Lonesome Cowboys* (1968), *Fuck* (also known as *Blue Movie*) (1968), and *The Loves of Ondine* (1967) all fit in more or less. *The Loves of Ondine* is by general consent of the Warhol clan terrible, and I have not seen it. *Fuck* is an hour-and-a-half contemplation of Viva and Louis Waldon going at it on the floor, in bed, in a bathtub, accompanied by a free-ranging, freely associative soundtrack in which they chatter on about this and that, life and sex and sundry irrelevancies. The best of this group, I think, is *Bike Boy;* the most famous and I suppose one would have to say the most successful with critics and public alike is *Lonesome Cowboys.*

Bike Boy constitutes a significant step on the way from the Warhol of *The Chelsea Girls* and its predecessors to the later, narrative, "Hollywood" Warhol. It is also directly in the line from *My Hustler* to *Flesh* and *Trash:* it is perhaps significant (and perhaps not) that *My Hustler* was the first Warhol film planned after Paul Morrissey joined the group and that he was the cameraman for *Bike Boy*. In any case, *Bike Boy* has a structure and an informing idea very much like that of the second reel of *My Hustler* and *Flesh* and *Trash.* In every case the attractive young man is the object of a succession of approaches and attacks, throughout which he retains his cool (either admirably or culpably, depending) and in most of which he seems to be an excuse, the nearest object to which the others can attach their fantasies, rather than a true catalyst. Joe Spencer, a stranger from Los Angeles and genuine bike boy, turned up at the Factory to ask how he should spend his time in New York. Warhol had the idea of putting him in contact with a number of seasoned Warhol performers in front of the camera and seeing what developed. Thus in *Bike Boy* he is shown taking a shower, buying clothes in a boutique attended by a funny group of screaming faggots, then meeting a series of women—a girl in a flower shop with whom he talks rather boringly about flagellation; an older woman in a blonde wig whom he resists; Ingrid Superstar, who tries to seduce him in her kitchen while she talks about cooking; Brigid Polk, who taxes him with impotence in front of her impotent husband; and Viva, who finally bludgeons him into sexual action. Apparently the Viva sequence was shot last, with the intention of injecting a bit of sex, and the shower scene added at the beginning with a similar purpose; otherwise the scenes are shown much as shot, edited in the camera with the flash frames and soundtrack blips left in, though there was also some trimming in the editing room afterward. The film is slight and boring in parts, but the boutique scene and those with Ingrid and Viva are very funny, and the collision of the unknown quantity with the known produces some typical and provocative results.

Lonesome Cowboys is altogether more "plotty"—the most detailed of all Warhol films to date from the point of view of plot. The action takes place in and around what seems to be a Western ghost town. Romona (Viva) lives nearby with her nurse (Taylor Mead). In town one day looking for company they meet Mickey (Louis Waldon) and his brothers, who chase them out of town, but not before Romona has had a few cutting words to say about Mickey's dubious relationship with his brothers. The next morning, Eric, one of Mickey's brothers, rouses him roughly to ask who Tom, the man he's sleeping with, is—apparently they picked him up on the trail a few days earlier. They fight, and Eric is beaten. Then the brothers ride over to Romona's ranch and rape her (she is not entirely unwilling). The sheriff (Francis Francine) refuses to take action, saying he is too busy, and the brothers settle down on the ranch. Romona seduces Tom, the nurse makes a play for Joe (Joe Dallesandro), the sheriff performs a long drag act, and finally Tom and Eric decide to go off together westward to the surf, leaving Mickey complaining and uncomprehending. This is fine in principle. The idea of a Western community in which all the men are homosexual, and the evidently attractive Viva has great difficulty in getting herself even slightly raped, is rather charming. Some of the incidental jokes are funny, and virtually everyone in sight is easy on the eye. But, even though some very lofty and highfalutin readings of the film have been put forward, notably Peter Gidal's in his book *Andy Warhol: Films and Paintings*, which goes on at some length about "the consistent oneness of reality and fantasy" in the film, it somehow just does not come across like that—its prime, indeed sole intention appears to be that of giving us a good giggle. And there for me it does not succeed. So many of the cast seem to be high so much of the time, the audience is left feeling rather like the only sober man at a party where everyone else is rolling, rollicking drunk. One can well believe that everyone had a ball making the film, but as so often happens the fun at the time does not turn itself into fun for mere spectators after the event. It was obviously a riot if you happened to be there, but there is no comic discipline, timing is all haywire, and in the cold light of the morning after it is neither funny enough nor significantly unfunny enough to work.

If these films pointed the way toward a clearer narrative structure, something more psychological and involving, rather than rigorously exterior and distancing, it took a completely irrelevant happening to confirm the change and inaugurate the latest period in the Warhol canon. It had often been said that Warhol paintings could be executed by anybody—they frequently were, since the personal touches of traditional art were irrelevant; indeed, the more mechanical and impersonal they seemed, the more abstracted from mere human intervention, the better. Similarly, Warhol's first novel, *a,* was probably the first novel never to have been read by its author, consisting as it did of unedited transcriptions by a secretary of a series of jumbled and undecipherable tapes recording everything during a day in the life of Ondine. It seemed reasonable to assume that Warhol films could be made in the same way, though in practice they rarely were—often, indeed, Warhol was his own cameraman as well as everything else. But the test came in June 1968, when Warhol was shot and seriously injured by Valerie Solanis, who had appeared in his film *I, a Man* (1967) and who apparently resented having a script she had written turned down. At this point, Warhol had been planning to make a film with Joe Dallesandro about a day in the life of a hustler. In Warhol's absence, Paul Morrissey, who had devised the original idea, went ahead with writing, photographing, directing, and editing the film, *Flesh.* Though many Warhol films carry skimpy credits or no credits at all, we know therefore that one of the best and most famous was made entirely by Morrissey while Warhol was in the hospital; and *Trash* bears all the marks of (dare one say it, after being so strictly enjoined to accept impersonality as the norm?) the same creative personality.

The most immediate effect of Morrissey's influence might be regarded as "going commercial." Not that that seems to have been the prime intention; rather, Morrissey seems to be a much warmer, more outgoing person than Warhol, and his films therefore have a far more human touch. While the news that *Flesh,* having progressed in Britain from uncertificated club showings to a limited (uncut) showing with an X certificate, was to be booked on an experimental basis into a number of Odeons for a few weeks up and down the country did seem, in relation to our usual expectations of Odeons and the underground, almost unthinkable, it is certain that such a reversal would be impossible with any of the "purer" Warhol works. *Flesh* has a charm and good humor, and even (no less important but quite against earlier Warhol principles) a plot to make it accessible to any reasonably open-minded audience.

Above all, *Flesh* is sharp, funny, serious, completely clear about what effect it wants to make and how best to make it. It is the story of a day in the life of a young married New Yorker who is driven out to work by his wife after arguments about the laundry and who shall mind the baby. That sounds normal enough, though it is perhaps slightly odd that the wife should want money so that her girl friend could have an abortion, and even odder, except in the Warhol world, that the work Joe Dallesandro does is hustling. During the day we see him picking up a number of men who want him for various sexual purposes, or passing his spare moments giving friendly advice to a sublimely unlikely tyro hustler and chatting to a former girl friend about whether she should have her breasts enlarged with silicone (after she has delivered the deathless soap-opera line "Do you know what it's like to dance topless in front of someone who's raped you?"). Several of his encounters are very funny in various not so obvious ways—notably that in which he is picked up by an elderly gentleman (played by Maurice Bradell, a revenant from *The Shape of Things to Come* and other British films of the 1930's) who claims to be an artist, wants him to pose naked, and chatters on endlessly about the Greek ideals of physical beauty without ever getting to the point or apparently understanding what his guest is.

And the opening sequence captures perfectly the Warhol-Morrissey vision of normalcy within the heart of the extraordinary. The opening shot, obsessively held, of Joe's head asleep on a green pillow while a gramophone somewhere blares a Fred Astaire record is classic Warhol minimal cinema, but the scene soon opens out into the play between husband and wife, a sort of grouchy/sexy ritual of awakening, and the famous, rather touching sequence of Joe naked on the floor playing with his child and feeding her a small tart. Contrary to what one might expect, the final effect is of a nice little film full of bizarre touches of characterization which add up to a curiously believable picture of a way of life. The film has what few if any films in the Warhol *oeuvre* up to now have had, charm. And technically it is far from the usual willful slapdash of Warhol—it is photographed with considerable skill and control (almost glossily, at least by comparison), and gives the impression of being planned with some care, and capably, deliberately constructed within a simple, circular form (it ends where it began, with Joe going to sleep after his hard day's work, having learned that the abortion is not necessary after all). It is clearly the work of a highly talented, individual filmmaker—and it would be difficult to believe that it comes from Warhol alone, since its positive qualities are so at variance with all his theory and most of his practice.

It was as a result of the success of *Flesh* that Paul Morrissey's name first came to be known outside the Warhol circle; though the film originally carried no credits, he was fully credited on publicity material connected with it. Up to that point he had been photographer, assistant, and general odd-job man around the Factory, so that it would be difficult to say just how much or how little he had to do with any given film, so much was he part of the communal effort. He was also, it appears, business manager of the enterprise, unwillingly, in the absence of anyone else to do the job. After *Flesh,* of course, he had a reputation of his own, and has since made a series of films which are explicitly his own creation (*Trash, Heat*) as well as continuing to take a hand in most of the Factory's other productions. The first of his films after *Flesh* was *Trash,* also starring Joe Dallesandro and featuring one or two other people from the earlier film in a story that might almost be a sequel to *Flesh*. At first sight, *Trash* (1970) is unmistakably a very good film; reseen, it has sections at least when it looks like a great film. What it takes on along the way is subtlety and density; far from being improvisatory and hit-or-miss, like most of the earlier films by the Warhol group, it proves on examination to be, like *Flesh,* very tightly plotted, scrupulously constructed to make even the smallest passing comment pull its weight in the overall dramatic argument. In this the two films are defiantly the work of Paul Morrissey, not only highly personal, but in several vital respects the antithesis of Warhol's theorizing about the *gratuit,* impersonality in filmmaking, and the beyond-boredom principle.

The true subject of *Trash* is presented neatly, as a sort of formal statement of theme, in the opening sequence, during which Geri Miller (the girl who was considering having her breasts inflated with silicone in *Flesh,* and has now apparently done so) tries everything she can think of to excite Joe Dallesandro, who remains resolutely, and not too concernedly, as unaroused by her manipulation as by her elaborate go-go dance. Geri is worried in an almost maternal fashion about Joe; the trouble, she says, is the drugs he takes. Why can't he trip on sex instead? It's cheaper, nicer, and a lot healthier. Can you trip on sex? asks Joe. Of course, says Geri; isn't it great when you come? No, says Joe; it's over.

The comment resounds through the rest of the film, one way or another. Behind practically everything that happens and is said there is a quiet, almost suppressed anguish over the evanescence of experience, the search for something that lasts, and the retreat, most evidently in Joe's case, into drugs as a deadener, as something which, in removing the desire for anything more lasting than the next fix, removes also any capacity, physical or mental, to do or experience anything else.

In each of the major sequences of the film the themes stated at the opening are restated with variations. In all of them the basic situation is that characteristic preoccupation of the Warhol group, first clearly presented in *My Hustler,* the way that apparent communication often shows itself when examined to be merely the bouncing of one's own feelings off someone else who happens to be around at the time. In this case, because of his complete impotence, in every sense of the word, Joe is the sounding board for other people's fantasies. There is the crazy lady who carries a bag full of toys and is searching desperately for LSD, which she is convinced against all reason that Joe must have concealed somewhere on his person. There is the rich young wife who finds Joe trying halfheartedly to burglarize her nearly empty apartment and nurtures hopeless fantasies of rape. There is even the man from the Welfare Department who does not really connect with anyone else at all, pursuing relentlessly his fantasy of the silver Joan Crawford shoes and their self-evident suitability for conversion into a chic and unusual lamp.

But above all there is Holly Woodlawn. Holly, needless to say, is one of the Warhol drag queens. And it really is needless to explain: the first time around one may be intrigued at the outset by the problem of what she is exactly, but before long one accepts completely that she is what she says she is, a woman. It does not matter what she was born as and may still, if we may judge from her appearance in Larry Rivers's film *Tits,* anatomically be. She is a woman giving a performance, and a performance which is by any standards mesmeric. Apart from Joe, she is the only recurrent character in the film; he shares a room with her, and is the object of her concern and often exasperated, resentful affection. We see her gathering junk, with and without Joe's assistance, and in a very funny, very sad scene in the first half setting about seducing a high-school lad who is desperately eager to establish his own sophistication and has been dumb enough to think he can buy some grass from Holly (which is not what he gets at all).

The character gradually builds, though, and comes into her own in the final scenes, when her sister's pregnancy gives her the idea that she and Joe will impose on the Welfare Department as parents-to-be. Unfortunately she comes home one day to find Joe attempting (ineffectually, of course) to ball her sister, and launches into a great scene of entirely illogical recrimination. Then comes the funny scene with the man from the Welfare Department, broken up finally when the cushion she has stuffed under her sweater drops out in a moment of mobile fury. She and Joe are left exactly where they were at the start, with no money, no prospects, and no chance of communication even on the most elementary, physical level; yet, for however much or little it may count, with each other.

It is in these final scenes that the point of Morrissey's method really shows itself: they summarize the film and pull its pieces together and build dizzyingly to a succession of climaxes, and to the final anticlimax, with complete certainty and economy. In them Joe is, as he has been established, the still, dead center around which other people's passions revolve, while Holly is the dynamic element. And while what she says and does is often fiercely funny, she does bit by bit acquire her own dignity. Morrissey's treatment of her is masterly. How far what he elicits from her is properly speaking a performance could be argued at length, quite fruitlessly; what we get is what nearly all cinema ultimately is, the physical embodiment of private dreams. And it works here so immaculately because the people are so scrupulously respected in their quite possibly crazy integrity.

Paul Morrissey's is a cinema of complete human acceptance: however odd the characters are, they are never patronized, never made fun of, never presented as material for a quick camp giggle. The angle of regard is the most important thing in *Flesh* and *Trash;* the fact that the technique is in its own way stunning seems incidental—Morrissey belongs to that select band who make films in such a way that the film becomes a transparent envelope, through which we can enter, telepathically, their minds.

In the years following *Trash,* Warhol and Morrissey, variously combined, made three features, *Women in Revolt, L'Amour,* and *Heat. Heat,* like *Flesh* and *Trash,* is a solo effort by Paul Morrissey; *L'Amour* is mainly Warhol, shot in Paris, with some of the exteriors and particularly the ironic finale shot by Morrissey; *Women in Revolt* seems to be all Warhol, though with Morrissey generally in attendance. Compared with *Flesh* and *Trash* they are fairly minor works. But they all have pleasing things about them. *L'Amour* is probably the least effective. It features two young American girls eager to live a way-out, bohemian life in Paris. There they meet Michael, an effete millionaire, the heir to a deodorant empire, with designs on a young French hustler, whom he announces he wants to adopt. In order to do this he devises the plan of marrying one of the girls. Their marriage is not very successful, though it does lead to a funny bed scene in which the bride and groom eat their way with unadulterated greed through all the goodies they can lay their hands on. In the end, no one gets anyone he or she wants, and the conclusion is a camp-funny affectionate parody of the *Stella Dallas* ending, with one character watching the happiness of others through a rain-spotted window and then walking away, alone. The film is mostly rather jolly, but with one or two bitter undertones to give it a distinctive flavor.

Women in Revolt was originally called, with classic simplicity, *Sex.* There was a slight worry that Mae West might sue, on the grounds that she owned the word, if not the concept, but that seems to have blown over, and the retitling was apparently more on grounds of topicality than trepidation. The film (and this is quite a change) had its official world première as part of the Los Angeles Film Exposition, where it actually played in Grauman's Chinese Theatre. This circumstance is curiously appropriate, since an important theme in the film, and finally the dominant one, is the determination of Candy Darling to become a Hollywood star while there is still a Hollywood to star in. Two of the film's best scenes are concerned exclusively with this, one in which she has a long interview with an agent (played by the man who plays the social worker in *Trash*) and goes through her gamut of Kim Novak imitations while he tries, without success, to strip her on his couch, and the final interview (after she has achieved stardom and is making *Blonde on a Bum Trip*—or is it *Bum on a Blonde Trip?*), in which she eventually comes to blows with a determinedly insulting columnist who wants to record the details of her incestuous and lesbian experiences for *The New York Times*.

Up to then the film has followed a highly characteristic, if totally unpredictable, course. It stars the three most famous of Warhol's drag ladies, Jackie Curtis, Holly Woodlawn, and Candy Darling as—but of course—pillars of Women's Lib. Jackie is the moving spirit, a simple schoolteacher in forties print dresses, Candy is a dizzy socialite who has turned to lesbianism after tiring of incest with her brother, while Holly, for all her theoretical enthusiasm, likes men too much to pay attention to anything else. Jackie manages to get money out of Candy to further the cause, but then spends it on getting herself deflowered by Mr. America, and is last seen battling with the baby she has as a result. Holly takes to drink, and Candy gets her wish, only to find that success has turned to dust and ashes. All highly moral, in the Russ Meyer manner, and hysterically funny. Sadly, Holly Woodlawn, so sublime in *Trash*, is given little opportunity to show what she can do. But Jackie Curtis has wonderful moments and Candy Darling really steals the film, looking absurdly glamorous and acting out what used to be every teenager's dream (well, admittedly, not boy teenagers, but who's quibbling?). *Women in Revolt* is perhaps not a major addition to the Warhol-Morrissey *oeuvre,* but it is a funnier comedy than *Lonesome Cowboys,* with never a dull moment, and, sensibly considered, scarcely a dirty one.

Heat, which Morrissey made along the traditional Warhol lines on location in Hollywood itself, is a sort of updated version of *Sunset Boulevard.* Joe (Joe Dallesandro) is an ex-child star from television who has come to Hollywood in the hope of starting off an adult acting career. He settles in a motel run by a vast and lecherous lady and otherwise occupied by such strange people as two brothers who make their living in a live sex show—one of whom, a Harpo Marx-like mute, masturbates constantly, to the consternation of passers-by—and Jessica, a young unmarried mother living with her baby and her lesbian lover. Jessica and her ménage are supported by her has-been screen-star mother, Sally (Sylvia Miles). When Joe and Sally meet, she immediately takes him over. He is attentive to her, in the hope that she will turn out to be useful somehow, or at least will support him for a while. This she does, moving him into her mansion. But she does not prove very helpful, and the return of her daughter and grandchild does not help matters either. Sally has to ask her ex-husband for financial aid, while Joe runs back to the motel and is discovered by Sally in the act of flirting with the motel owner. Naturally, she shoots him and he falls, William Holden-like, into the pool.

The idea is funny and the film has some splendid sequences, but the principals are not so fresh and vivid as they are in other Warhol/Morrissey films. I suspect that this is because Sylvia Miles is a seasoned professional, and so, even delivering lines that are largely improvised, makes her effects too cleanly and precisely, excluding us by her technique and leaving no gaps through which the irrelevant, life-giving insights can emerge to tell us more about Sylvia Miles the woman than about the character she portrays. Joe Dallesandro too is having some difficulty in maintaining his amateur status—he has made so many film appearances that he runs the risk of falling into tricks of characterization instead of just existing with the requisite intensity and conviction in front of the camera. In consequence, the film is just slightly off, though by no means an unworthy successor to *Flesh* and *Trash.*

Since making *Heat* Paul Morrissey has spent some time in Rome making, back to back, a 3-D version of *Frankenstein* and a non-3-D version of *Dracula.* The *Frankenstein,* sometimes known as *Flesh for Frankenstein,* is actually a film of great charm and uninhibited gusto. Obviously nobody connected with it took it very seriously, so it does have strong elements of parody, but at the same time they took it seriously enough, in the right way. It evidently springs from an almost childish delight in the tattiest kind of monster movie, an unaffected enjoyment of all the silliest shock tactics of 3-D in the *House of Wax* era, and a cheery determination to do likewise. Thus, though a lot of the film is quite funny —notably the scenes between the ravening Baroness Frankenstein (whether Frankenstein's wife or sister remains unclear—perhaps both) and the new hired hand, played by Joe Dallesandro, and the dinner-table scene in which Joe recognizes the head of his best friend, recently removed in a night attack, on the shoulders of Frankenstein's mute new "guest"—at the same time, when it wants to pull the horror stops out, as in the aforementioned decapitation scene, it proves perfectly capable of doing so. Visually the film is surprisingly elegant, the improvised dialogue, delivered in a variety of impenetrable accents, is more funny than revealing, and the gleeful dangling of bloody entrails in the face of the audience or the setting at us of very palpably three-dimensional bats does make for a pleasurable gasp or two with absolutely no offense. The *Dracula,* originally known as *Blood for Dracula* and finally sold as "Andy Warhol's Dracula," is if anything even better. It is based on a consistent new idea which gives the film an amusing line of narrative continuity: Dracula, it appears from this version, can be satisfied only by the blood of a virgin, and finding virgins (accessible virgins at any rate) rather thin on the ground in Rumania, he decides to go to Italy, where the girls are, he understands, more devout and less guarded from vampires. Unfortunately the family he picks on, an aristocratic one ruled eccentrically by Vittorio de Sica, of all people, and decidedly down on its luck, is not too strong on chastity, and he has two sickening experiences before finally (but too late) the old maid of the family gives herself to him. The mixture of cheery absurdity (the plentiful bloodletting is so extravagant and explicit as to move far beyond gasp-and-gulp reactions into the area of loud guffaws) and real delight in the operatic excesses of the genre as traditionally practiced is very much like that in the *Frankenstein*. But it is more controlled, more precisely balanced, more idiosyncratic in its details (the characterization of Joe Dallesandro, all-purpose servant and deflowerer of daughters, as a young communist prophesying the imminent collapse of capitalist society, is particularly fetching), and the look of the film, untrammeled by the special requirements of 3-D, is sensational, worthy at times of Visconti. Perhaps *Frankenstein* and *Dracula,* both of which have had a wider showing to a more genuinely popular audience than any earlier "Warhol" film, will prove to inaugurate the popular-entertainment phase of the Warhol-Morrissey career, like the sexy-episode films in Pasolini's. Perhaps not; only time will tell.

It is not too early, though, after ten years and unnumbered films (literally—no one seems to know how many the Factory has made), to suggest some of the impact Warhol and his films have had on the American underground cinema and latterly, as a result of the considerable commercial success of some of the recent films, on the American cinema in general. Only someone who remembers the tortured preciosity and anguished solemnity of the Markopolos-Brakhage generation will appreciate the breath of fresh air that the simplicity, directness, and thoroughly un-arty approach of even the first Warhol films brought in. And right from the start, even when they were making eccentric, hermetic films, the Warhol group never followed the conventional intellectual-underground disapproval of Hollywood and all it stood for—the star system and the whole idea of broad popular appeal. In most of the public statements of Warhol and Morrissey, the same ideas—of popularity, audience involvement, the restoration of all the qualities of the unpretentious entertainment which the American film stood for in the good old days of studios and stars, before the domination of the director became absolute—turn up too frequently to be dismissed as merely camp.

The same can be said of the internal qualities of the films, their coherence and (at least after the event) inevitability as a development. The themes and ideas retain a general consistency from period to period, but with a constantly increasing sophistication of technical means—to such an extent that it would now be by no means impossible for Warhol to accept the blandishments of Hollywood and make Hollywood movies —except, why should he bother when obviously Hollywood needs him much more than he needs Hollywood?

Inevitably, there are limitations to what the Warhol approach to filmmaking can achieve. The Warhol clan may admire *Death in Venice,* but they could never achieve a *Death in Venice,* nor would they think it desirable that they should try. More immediately, even within the range of their own current activities there are things they do noticeably less well. *Lonesome Cowboys* is an example. The notion of parodying the Western in such terms has a certain camp appeal, but, as the *Carry On* team found out to their cost in *Carry On Cleo* and *Carry On Screaming,* sustained parody has certain built-in disciplines of its own which can be ignored only at grave peril. Especially dangerous in the light of what the Warhol films do best, it requires consistency of tone and style within a consistently artificial context; with no style (making films stylelessly has, after all, been Warhol's great aim) and no detailed directorial control of timing, even good jokes are likely to fall flat.

In other words, one is driven to the surprising conclusion that Warhol's cinema, which seems at first glance to be built entirely on camp, finally works best when it is not camp at all, and fails to the degree that the self-indulgence of camp is allowed to creep in. The material may be camp in *Trash* or *Flesh* or *Bike Boy,* but the treatment is something else again. It accepts things as they are, entirely seriously, but mercifully without sociological solemnity. The methods of the Warhol Factory may be deliberately hit-or-miss, but when things fall out right, when the superstars in front of the camera are glowing at maximum power and Paul Morrissey behind the camera is letting them, the results can stand comparison with anything else the cinema of today has to offer.

Satyajit Ray

WHEN THE FILM INDUSTRY OF A COUNTRY HITHERTO UNSUNG IN film history comes to international attention, it is only natural that we should start off with mistaken, or at least grossly unbalanced, ideas about it. It took quite a while after the first startling impact of Akira Kurosawa's films in the West for us to realize that he was not the be-all and end-all of Japanese cinema, but in fact just about the least Japanese of Japanese directors. Similarly, Buñuel had some severe shocks in store for those who had too readily assumed that the lush exoticism of the Fernández-Figueroa type of film was "typically Mexican." Are we, then, likely to prove equally wrong about the Indian cinema if our ideas of it are based exclusively on the Apu trilogy and other works of Satyajit Ray, even though he is generally conceded to be the dominating figure in the Indian cinema? On principle, one could say almost certainly. And yet the urge to generalize persists. In recent years the discovery of Shadi Abdelsalam's *The Night of Counting the Years* from Egypt or Daryush Mehrjui's *The Cow* from Iran at once set in motion speculation about a renaissance (or naissance, as the case may be) of a national school of cinema in those countries, even though it should be evident almost at a glance that both films were highly individual and eccentric, and could not possibly reflect anything other than the talents of the individuals responsible for them.

Similarly, the immediate and obvious answer about Ray, even without additional knowledge of what is going on elsewhere in the Indian cinema, is that one can never generalize from the work of great individuals. Ray is a great director, and *ipso facto* cannot be typical of anything, perhaps not even reliably himself (it is the prerogative of all great artists constantly to take us by surprise). But it seems reasonable to assume that he must have come from something and fit into some sort of context. And so of course he does. Not particularly a cinematic context: eighteen years after the appearance of *Pather Panchali,* the first of the Apu trilogy, he is still a solitary figure, a unique talent in Indian cinema, and the Indian cinema apart from him has hardly moved on from the kind of nonsense he gently satirizes in the filmgoing sequence of *Apur Sansar,* all trashy, theatrical, sentimental, and fantasticated. But a literary and artistic context is very much there, to begin with in his own family, the literary and artistic activities of which Marie Seton in her biography of Ray traces back exhaustively through fifteen generations. Without going into any such detail, it may be accepted readily that Satyajit Ray's background was highly literate, artistically sophisticated.

More important, no doubt, is the general cultural background. Ray is a Bengali, and all his films have been made in this minority language (spoken by some twenty million, however), a literary language far antedating the now official language of India, Hindi, which is distilled from the dialects of the central plains. Ray's first films, the Apu trilogy, at once place him in a certain tradition by being based on a modern classic of Bengali literature, the semi-autobiographical novels by Bibhuti Bhushan Bannerjee; a more personal kind of placing is implied by his much later filming of a famous children's book by his grandfather, *Goopy Gyne Bagha Byne.* The kind of cultural society from which the young Ray sprang can be observed more directly in his film *Charulata,* which shows something closely comparable to the cultural level and high-minded seriousness suggested in the works of Ibsen and Chekhov. If Ray seems in many ways the most Western of Oriental filmmakers, it is because the traditions in which he was brought up are most closely analogous to those of Western life.

Not only the literary side of Bengali culture has been influential in Ray's career, however. A trained musician, he has composed music for all his own films since *Teen Kanya,* as well as for James Ivory's film *Shakespeare Wallah.* His training in the graphic arts has been no less far-reaching; indeed, for some ten years before he made his first film he worked as a commercial artist in advertising, book illustration, and design. As a writer he has written not only all his own scripts but also a number of critical articles and has worked on and off as a journalist, as well as more recently blossoming into an author of children's stories. And during his filmmaking career he has acquired other skills—ever since *Charulata,* for instance, he has been his own camera operator. This is not to say that he was necessarily first-rate in any of these other, specialized fields of activity: his music is a charming but not very complex combination of Western and Eastern elements, his graphic work not especially distinguished, though well above the normal level in India. But an independent and proven ability in all these fields, as well as giving us some insight into the versatility of the man, has enabled him to exercise remarkably complete and detailed control over all aspects of his films—technicians such as the art director, cameraman, and editor come much closer in his films than in others', except perhaps in the films of Chaplin, to being pure executants of the director's ideas rather than contributors of their own creative personalities.

With all his many interests and gifts, the cinema would seem to have been from the start the natural outlet which would best enable Ray to combine them all. But easier said than done. Ray began, by his own account, reading books on the cinema when he was still a teenager studying at Tagore's famous school at Santiniketan. Shortly afterward, in 1943, as a young commercial artist of twenty-two, he set seriously about trying to break into films. He came very close to doing so when an adaptation he had written of Tagore's novel *The Home and the World* was accepted for production. But Ray's ideas, which included such notions, deeply alien to the Indian cinema of that time, as shooting exteriors on natural locations and using nonprofessional actors, were found unacceptable by the producer and director, and despite some possibility that he might find work instead as an art director he drifted away. In 1945 he was commissioned to illustrate a children's edition of *Pather Panchali,* and the idea of filming it began to germinate in his mind. In 1949 he had some brief but inspiring contact with Jean Renoir, who was shooting *The River* in India, and in 1950 he was sent to London for six months by the advertising agency for which he was working. There he "saw all the film classics he could cram in" and began serious work on writing a script for *Pather Panchali.*

When I got back to India I set about raising the money and getting a crew together and finally we began. I had never worked in films before, my cameraman had never shot a film, my art director had worked on only one before and my editor had edited only two. Many of the actors were non-professional and the rest not experienced in the cinema. We had to feel our way tentatively, working only at weekends when we were free from our everyday jobs, and stopping for months at a time when the money gave out, until finally the government stepped in with the money to finish it.

The result was not, even with government help, particularly well regarded in India, where of course there were various pressures and factions associated with its partial government sponsorship. The shooting took a long time, with many interruptions, and the film, completed in 1955, did not appear at all in India until the beginning of 1956. It seems to have achieved a measure of popular success if little initial critical acclaim. Nonetheless, it was entered in the Cannes Festival of that year and actually won a prize. This was something very new for the Indian cinema and established Ray as a name to be reckoned with at home. On the strength of this success, he was able to go ahead with the sequel to *Pather Panchali*, *Aparajito,* which did even better by winning the grand prize at Venice in 1957. At the time he had no intention of turning the Apu films into a trilogy, but in 1959 he decided to complete the sequence with *Apur Sansar,* having meanwhile made two other, totally unconnected films.

The Apu trilogy is the work which first established Ray's fame, his style, and his approach to his subject matter. It therefore occupies a crucial place in his career, and if not necessarily his finest work (though some would still maintain that it is), it calls for fairly detailed consideration for the light it throws on Ray's work as a whole as well as for its own inherent interest. It is difficult to believe that the three films were not conceived at the same time, as one unified work—even though Ray tells us the notion of the trilogy came to him gradually. They are based on two books, the materials of which are symmetrically divided among the three films: the book *Pather Panchali* (*Song of the Little Road*) takes us up to the halfway mark of the film *Aparajito* (*The Unvanquished*), when Apu and his mother return from the city to the country; the book *Aparajito* takes up the story a few years later, and tells of the later stages of Apu's education and something of his life as an adult. In reshaping the material in cinematic terms Ray has imposed a different order, giving each section of his trilogy a dramatic center and point of its own—unobtrusively he has found or invented shape, or rather three shapes, out of the much more loosely organized material of a *roman-fleuve.*

It is useful to know this if we are to counter the supposition, current at the time the trilogy first came out, that Ray is a kind of primitive, instinctive creator who somehow manages to hit it right from time to time. Merely as adaptation of material from one medium to another, the Apu trilogy is an outstanding example of creative rethinking. And the result is three films each of which can perfectly well stand on its own and yet which gain immensely from being seen together, when the subtle lines of continuity, the recurrent yet constantly developing images and ideas, can be properly appreciated. The first section, *Pather Panchali,* takes only as much from the books as concerns Apu's life in the village with his whole family. For the second, *Aparajito,* Ray looked at the remainder of the material and found in it, running through parts of the two novels, a unifying theme, that of the growing Apu's relationship, close but gradually becoming less so by force of education and circumstances, with his mother, Sarbojaya—a theme which is naturally concluded with Sarbojaya's death some way into the second book. *Apur Sansar* (*The World of Apu*), the third film, uses what is left of the literary material, and is to my mind the least satisfactory of the three, but even here the structure is perfectly calculated (perhaps even too obtrusively so), the film being built around Apu's (unconscious) preparation for marriage, the marriage itself, which occupies the central section of the film, and then the aftermath of his wife's death. Equally, *Apur Sansar* is unified by another theme, that of Apu's determination to be a writer, which is bound up with his young manhood, and is finally put aside along with his immaturity.

The plot content of the films is, in fact, by Western standards very slight (and even more so in comparison with the average Indian film). The films are built up from a succession of little incidents, at first glance linked together by no more than the "and then . . . and then . . . and then . . ." of a children's story. But to counteract the danger of shapelessness Ray has devised a whole network of subtle pictorial and aural references to articulate his clear understanding of what, essentially, each film is about. However wayward the detail may seem to be, it is controlled by a strict criterion of relevance, which we can always feel to be guiding things even if we are not from moment to moment consciously aware of precisely what it is.

The first, and in many ways the subtlest, ensurer of consistency is the angle of regard Ray turns upon his characters and events. The first we see of Apu in the first film, apart from a glimpse of him as a baby, is as a shape sleeping beneath a blanket; then his sister shakes him and finds a way through his protective covering, and then we have a close-up of his closed eye, which promptly opens. One inference, which has been too readily drawn, is that Apu's is the eye we see through in the films, that we are seeing things from his point of view, as though this is a first-person narrative. But a moment's consideration shows that this is by no means true of the films as a whole, and that this particular shot indicates rather the reverse: seeing Apu's eye open to consciousness, we recognize immediately that we are seeing more than he does, spying on him as it were, observing him from the outside: we are at once conscious of our eye seeing his eye, and that the two are quite different things. This attitude is observed with absolute consistency throughout the trilogy: it remains firmly, if unobtrusively objective, using Apu, it is true, as a central figure but keeping him within a context which is observed by another, more analytical eye. In *Pather Panchali,* for instance, we may observe the child's wonder at new things—a theatrical troupe, a train—but we are not invited to share it, and the same is true of his reactions to the city at the beginning of *Aparajito:* we watch the child in his context, not the context through the child.

In other words, Apu is always a character in the films, not an enveloping consciousness. And therefore there is no danger of the filmmaker becoming lost in his creation. This is as it should be, for Ray's theme is nearly always community, living together and finding ways of doing it without compromising the individual's individuality too much. We see Apu throughout as part of an evolving group, seeking solutions and finding answers. In *Pather Panchali* the group is largest, consisting as it does of his father, Hari, an unsuccessful holy man; his mother, Sarbojaya; his sister, Durga; and Indra, the aged aunt they look after as best they can. In *Aparajito* the group is reduced by death to just the two, Apu and Sarbojaya. In *Apur Sansar* Apu begins alone, and feeling the lack of a group to relate to, acquires a wife, Aparna, who gives some stability to his life again (though perhaps at the expense of his own individuality, his writing), then suffers a breakdown when that relationship is ended by Aparna's death in childbirth, and finally finds himself again in the potentiality of a relationship with his young son. For Ray, Apu truly exists only in relationships with others.

Given this unity of regard, each film is meticulously constructed to exemplify Ray's basic concept: if the comparison often made between *Pather Panchali* in particular and Italian neo-realism has any validity, it is not because of any rough documentary quality the Ray film may seem to have or its supposed concern with the underprivileged (these, insofar as they exist at all as formulated, are respectively accidental and incidental), but rather because Ray has something of the same cool, distancing quality that Rossellini at his best (the side reminiscent at once of Brecht and Godard) has. Everything in Ray is demonstrated, externalized in some way. This is not to say that his films lack richness or subtlety, but that their "poetry" is of a classical rather than a Romantic variety, depending on the exact management and constant redefinition of images, so that they take on a complex of associations without ever losing their immediacy and propriety as literal statements of fact.

This can perhaps best be demonstrated by an examination of the two principal recurrent images in *Pather Panchali,* the train and the pond (the train indeed is the pervasive linking image throughout the trilogy). I call them images rather than symbols because images is what they are, in the most literal sense of the term: things we see (or sometimes, with the train, merely hear), factual props in the life of the family. They do not "symbolize" anything, in the sense the term is normally, if imprecisely, used, to suggest an exact equivalence between a concrete fact and an abstract idea. But gradually, by a process of accretion, each takes on a coloring of metaphor. The train moves, and suggests travel, progress; it is also a man-made machine, and therefore suggests the modern world at the limits (physically as well as mentally) of the village with its traditional forms of life. The pond is static, stagnant, a place to sit aimlessly by, a place to bury unmanageable, unwanted facts: it suggests the world of tradition from which Apu is destined to escape (by train, of course).

Much of the action in *Pather Panchali* is built on the alternation and elaboration of these two images. The train is first heard, as a distant sound in the night, while Apu is bending over his books, being taught to write by his father, the association thereby being directly established between the train and education, which is what will eventually separate Apu from his family background and make him part of the modern world. The pond is first importantly present shortly afterward, when the aged Indra stands miserably by it as the children, Apu and Durga, run carelessly past on the way to new experience—the traveling players at the village fair and, immediately following, direct confrontation with the physical reality of the train: the pond is clearly associated with the past, old age, passivity, resignation, in contrast to the children's carefree rush toward the future. But neither the train nor the pond is there just as a metaphysical trapping: Ray appreciates to the full the point once made by Pasolini:

> Metaphor is an essentially linguistic and literary figure of speech which is difficult to render in the cinema except in extremely rare cases—for example, if I wanted to represent happiness I could do it with birds flying in the sky. . . . The cinema represents reality with reality; it is metonymic and not metaphoric. If I want to express you I express you through yourself, I couldn't use metaphors to express you.

So it is the reality of the train, the reality of the pond, which the cinema expresses: what associations they gather are something else again, and yet inexorably they gather them as the film progresses.

We may see how this comes about by a more detailed examination of the sequence in which Apu first actually sees the train. It is in fact quite elaborately intercut with another, parallel sequence, the death of Indra after she has been turned out of the family home. It is not the first time—the same thing had happened to her in the moments immediately before the play scene when she stands by the pond—for she is old and useless, and it is impossible for the family to support her, so close are they to the borderline of starvation. The play scene, the effect it has on Apu, is the main cause of the events which lead up to the first sight of the train; Durga quarrels with Apu because he has appropriated some silver foil from her small box of childish treasures to make himself a crown in emulation of that worn by the principal actor in the drama he has just seen. As a result of the quarrel (in which Sarbojaya automatically sides with her son), the children run off into the open country and rapidly begin to forget their disagreement. At this point, we come back to Indra, clearly ill and begging rather humbly (at least compared with her earlier defiance) to be taken back into the family home. Sarbojaya refuses. Then, out in the country, we see Durga and Apu coming close to a reconciliation. Back at the hovel, Indra begs for water, and is told to get it herself, but Sarbojaya does finally make a gesture of assistance. That is all, though; she is adamant, and Indra is compelled to gather together her few belongings and hobble away forever.

From here we cut back to the children, who have now wandered farther from the village than usual. The sequence begins with a shot of electric wires and the distinctive hum of wires in the wind on the soundtrack. Then we see the wondering (and in Durga's case slightly fearful) reaction of the children to a pylon, and Durga's gesture of forgiveness toward Apu. Then Apu lost joyfully in grass higher than his head, appreciating to the full a strange new world of experience.

And then, finally, the train—first as a moving puff of black smoke in the distance, then crossing the horizon, then, as the children run toward the embankment, it approaches nearer and nearer until it fills the whole of the foreground, cutting off our view of Apu on the other side of the tracks, so that we catch sight of him only in flashes between the passing wheels. The shape of the episode is rounded off by a shot of Apu and Durga, all differences completely forgotten, going home together (perhaps days later, though the effect is of close continuity with the previous scene), their finding of Indra sitting alone in the woods, the joking attempt to startle her, which proves that she is dying, and their running away to fetch help.

In description the sequence possibly sounds naïve: the opposition of youth and old age, death and the incursion of the modern world, poverty and progress, sounds simple and too schematic. But it does not affect the spectator that way. To begin with, though the juxtapositions might sound like opposition, in fact the effect is rather the reverse; it makes us conscious of unity rather than diversity, the integration of the new experiences—the actors, the train, the grasses, death—into Apu's developing consciousness. This is achieved as much as anything by the consistency of regard already mentioned, and by its most obvious physical manifestation in Ray's mastery of the long shot. Ray can also be, when necessary, a master of the meaningful close-up, but his characteristic method is to establish the physical and mental situation of his characters and places in long shots, often sustained while people and things move in and out of frame, or are followed around by the camera.

Most of the family scenes are handled this way. We always know where everyone is in relation to everyone else about the house and yard through expressive long shots, as in the scene of our real introduction to Apu, which first shows us the three female members of the family each going about her separate business within one moving-camera shot. The important scene of the quarrel when an angry neighbor accuses Durga of theft is handled the same way, refusing all emphasis and allowing the action to develop naturally in all its emotional complexity and us to make of it what we will. In the episode of the train and Indra's death, there are two classic long shots—that in which Apu actually sees the train up close for the first time, when he is physically integrated into the same field of vision as the train, but reduced to a flashing speck intermittently glimpsed beyond it (we are left again to divine his reactions, we are not shown them directly) ; and that in which the happy homecoming children are shown in the same panning shot as the dying Indra, physically related to her yet emotionally contrasted, as their singing continues on the soundtrack beyond our moment of realization that Indra is close to death, if not dead already. There is no comment by artificial and obtrusive emphasis—the comment is implied, absorbed into the form of the film.

One final example from *Pather Panchali.* In an early scene Durga, as we have noted, is accused of stealing a necklace from the rich landowning neighbor. At that point her guilt or innocence is immaterial: the tensions under which the accusation puts her family, and particularly her mother, Sarbojaya, are instead used to trigger action which helps to illuminate the character of those involved and their relationship to one another within the family—particularly in the conclusion to the scene, where Sarbojaya, pushed beyond endurance by the shame of the accusation and what it implies about her as a mother, turns almost reasonlessly on the girl she has just been stoutly defending and drives her out of the yard. The incident is not totally finished, however. After Durga's death, and while Apu is preparing to leave with his family for Benares, he pulls down a dusty bowl from a high, forgotten shelf, and there is the necklace. So Durga was guilty after all, but what can that signify now? Apu takes it, tells no one, and throws it into the pond. The weeds, disturbed by the impact, settle again into place: the stagnant pond swallows the past as Apu turns toward departure, the future in Benares, and, of course, the train that will take them all there.

Aparajito, the second of the trilogy, seems to be generally considered the least satisfactory. Even many sympathetic critics feel that it is broken-backed and lacking in unity (especially since the period of time covered requires two different boy actors to play Apu), and that at best it makes formal sense only as a hinge between the two flanking films. I cannot agree with this—partly, I suppose, because by chance *Aparajito* was the first of the trilogy I saw, and I found then that it made perfect sense formally and intellectually taken by itself, without knowledge of *Pather Panchali* or of the yet unmade *Apur Sansar*. What gives unity to it, despite its apparent break in the middle (the interval between the two novels), in which Apu and his mother return from Benares to the country (her parental village home this time) and Apu grows several years into another actor, is its continuing theme of Apu's relations with Sarbojaya, and the tug between education and new experience on one hand and traditional ways of life on the other which coincides almost with that between his own individuality and the claims of his mother.

The form of the film is freer, more expansive than that of *Pather Panchali*. Again, the train provides the main linking image, before becoming pervasive in *Apur Sansar;* the very opening shots of the film are from the train carrying Apu's family toward Benares. The first sequences evoke lightly and freely the life of the family in the city, particularly that of Apu, who relishes to the full the new experiences it brings him, his ability to wander almost at will through the strange and wonderful sights on the banks of the holy Ganges where his father works and becomes reduced in importance to little more than one of the things Apu observes during his wanderings. Everything is necessarily disconnected, impressionistic, though again it must be insisted that we are not seeing things through Apu's eyes: we are seeing him experience them.

The connecting link here is the decline, illness, and eventual death of Hari, who has, in any case, not counted for much as a character and merely continues the gradual reduction of the family by death to two, Apu and Sarbojaya—and then finally, by her death, to Apu alone in the world. Hari's death is marked in the film by a shot of many pigeons suddenly taking wing, which has been interpreted as one of Ray's more obvious metaphors (the soul leaving the body). Curious that this very idea—birds flying free—should be that cited by Pasolini in the passage quoted as an obvious metaphor for happiness. What did Ray mean by it? Probably everything his commentators find and more. If the shot was meant as an exact equivalence, it fails, because one cannot be sure what it means. But if, like Ray's recurrent images, it is there for its suggestive power and its rich ambiguity, then it is remarkably successful, producing exactly the sense of release into a new dimension that the film at this point requires.

The rest of *Aparajito* concentrates directly on Apu's growing away from his mother. Her decision to move back to the country may be read as an economic necessity (though the point is clearly made that she has an alternative in continuing with the work she has taken during Hari's illness, cooking for a prosperous family), but it can also be seen as, unconsciously at least, her first move in the battle to keep Apu, to enclose him in her own little world of quiet, passivity, and withdrawal from the challenge of life. The first view of Apu in the new village is of him in the gateway of his grandfather's house, watching the train passing by in the distance, as though it has become as unattainable for him now as it ever was. The central section of the film, that in which Apu and Sarbojaya are shown virtually alone in the village, while Apu is still a child, defines the grounds for the eventual, inevitable separation. Above all, it is caused by education and Apu's desire, even need, for it. Sarbojaya is, both temperamentally and socially, fixed in the past: she cannot cope with the modern world, the city, learning, and mistrusts them. There may be some selfishness in her obstructiveness toward her son's development, but there is no malice, only fear and the inability to develop herself beyond a certain point—she fears because she knows that in his development Apu is sure to outstrip her.

The whole complex of emotions is nicely conveyed in a very small scene near the middle of the film in which Apu tries to give her some idea of astronomy, and her fascination in what he is saying because *he* is saying it, her natural motherly pride, are balanced by her obvious timidity, which drives her toward impatience with anything she does not understand, and her shame at not being able to understand, at already knowing less than her own child. A similar complex of emotions is evoked in the more important scene in which Apu tells her that he has been offered a scholarship with ten rupees a month to study in Calcutta. She is proud, no doubt, but her first reaction is one of hurt—the immediate selfish one of "who will look after me?" When Apu says he does not want to be just a holy man all his life (like his father), she at once picks up the implication and slaps him. But later her motherly feelings win out and she gives him her savings, telling him he can go. He accepts her sacrifice with an equanimity that is almost callous. And when he does leave he heads down the road toward the train without a backward glance—that same train which is quietly evoked on the soundtrack at the moment Apu first tells his mother of his wish to leave and his opportunity to do so.

The final section of the film is built on an alternation of scenes in Calcutta while Apu studies and scenes in the village during vacations. Apu seems at home in Calcutta, relishing his new friends, new learning; back in the village he views with boredom all the things that used to delight him as a child, and though he delayed his arrival he refuses to postpone his departure, by even a day, to please his mother. Clearly she sees the situation as a struggle to keep him, and one which she has already lost—and would have, we suppose, even if she had refused to let him go. When the time comes to leave, he goes, but relents at the last moment, deliberately misses his train, and returns. But it is merely a sentimental gesture and does not alter the true situation. Once Apu is back in Calcutta they correspond, but she has cause to chide him for not writing more frequently, and we see her visibly fading away, getting weaker and weaker, while he writes evasively back. The end of the film recapitulates various motifs which have become familiar: Sarbojaya sitting pathetically under a great tree, as Indra sat among the bamboos to die in *Pather Panchali;* the sound of a train in the distance, with Sarbojaya hoping against hope it will bring Apu back to her (the train, once a cause of fear and separation to her, now represents hope and the possibility of reunion); the props of village life—the barking dog, the house enclosure, the pond—as Apu returns at last, summoned by a letter telling him of his mother's illness. She is already dead when he arrives, and he makes an almost instantaneous decision in favor of a return to his new life, he will immediately go back to his examinations. The film ends with a decisive visual rejection of the old life, the old man standing at the door of the house enclosure as Apu walks off toward Calcutta, the train, and the freedom implied by the open sky of the very last shot, with Apu just a small silhouette at the bottom of the frame.

If the train and the railroad seemed constantly recurrent in *Pather Panchali* and *Aparajito,* they are a dominant factor in *Apur Sansar*. Immediately after the credits, train noises invade the soundtrack as we see where Apu lives in Calcutta after having to leave school on account of lack of funds. His home is a garret by the railroad tracks, and Apu is actually awakened by a particularly insistent whistle. He has entered the world of trains, with a vengeance. In certain ways he seems acclimatized to it (he has, after all, chosen it himself), in some ways not. The sequence showing his ineffectual search for work and his receipt of a letter accepting one of his stories for magazine publication conveys the mixture of confidence and timidity, ambition and impracticality, in his nature, especially when it is usually mirrored in his walk home along the tracks, where what he sees mixes squalor with abounding life. Again we get a clear indication of it in the next sequence, where Apu is taken out to dine by his friend Pulu. Apu, though he has chosen the modern world, still wears a dhoti, whereas Pulu wears a shirt and slacks; Pulu eats with a fork, Apu in the traditional manner with his fingers. He still remains, whether by accident or from choice, a mixture of the old and the new.

This prologue leads into the central section of the film, that in which, by a strange turn of events (at least to Western audiences) he marries, without any preparation, a total stranger. He goes with Pulu to the country to attend the wedding of Pulu's cousin Aparna (arranged, of course, like most Indian weddings even today). Her bridegroom turns out to be hopelessly insane, but according to custom and belief she will be forever cursed and unmarriageable if she does not marry on this very day, selected by astrology. Apu's first reaction to this news is: "But we are living in the twentieth century"; his second, as Pulu's best friend and accepting the notion that it seems to be somehow meant, is to marry the girl himself. This may well seem much too arbitrary to Western audiences, though Indians tell us that such happenings are by no means unusual in Indian society; but even here Ray prepares us in every way possible for Apu's change of situation, by bathing the country scenes immediately before the wedding in a magical, mysterious atmosphere (this is the only section of the whole trilogy which can be described as primarily atmospheric, yet even here the objectivity of regard is not wholly lost), so that we are ready to accept the marriage almost as a part of a dream the hero seems to be living at this time, in this place.

If dream it is, we, he, and his bride are soon restored to reality when the film comes back to Calcutta. The bride's first reaction to Apu's home, the dirt, the noise, and the strangeness is tears, but before long the marriage, beautifully evoked in tiny details of casual intimacy and tenderness, comes to seem inevitable, the necessary complement of Apu's solitary life, for Ray can never stand to see his characters alone for too long—they live by interrelation. Thus when Aparna goes back to her village to bear their child and dies separated from Apu, we understand his at first violent reaction (he hits Aparna's brother, who brings the news) and then complete desolation: the death comes with the full weight of Ray's belief in the need for togetherness, and with the accumulated force of all those deaths which have gone before: Indra's, Durga's, Hari's, Sarbojaya's. At this point the train plays its last important part in Apu's story: he nearly kills himself beneath it, succumbing to the forces in the world which he temporarily feels he cannot begin to understand or cope with. Immediately before the news of Aparna's death is broken, we see Apu walking happily along the tracks toward his home, reading her last letter to him; he picks up a small child wandering dangerously near the track and returns it to a safer spot. After he has heard of his wife's death the effect is reversed. He is lying in a state of numbed lethargy, scarcely conscious of the kindly interfering of his neighbor. Then he gets up and looks at himself. As he does so, the clock stops ticking, and then we hear a train whistle. An inner emotional logic takes him immediately to the rails, where he stands waiting to jump beneath a train. But he does not die; instead a stray pig is run over, and its shriek brings him back to his senses. Images and associations from all the earlier train scenes, right back to his first encounter with a train, are all capsulated here, and the effect has the sort of emotional intensity which does not just happen, but has to be hardly won.

The rest of the film forms a kind of epilogue. For a while Apu wanders, and rather histrionically burns the manuscript of his book at dawn on a mountaintop (his inability to get on with it had been the only blot on his otherwise perfect marriage). He takes an ordinary menial job in a mine. Finally, he determines to go to see his son before setting off abroad to make a new start. Here, in his son, is evidently the prospect of togetherness, a new family situation; but Apu has deliberately rejected it. When he arrives, however, he finds that his son, Kajole, though ready enough to call on his name as an abstract ally in his absence, rejects him, fearful, disappointed, shy—we are never told exactly why. But given Ray's attitudes, the whole course of the trilogy, the shape of Apu's life, reconciliation is inevitable, and when Apu leaves at the last with Kajole on his shoulders, heading toward who knows what future, the effect is devoid of all sentimentality: in it human necessity and structural necessity are one, nature and art perfectly combined.

The Apu trilogy is unmistakably Ray's longest and most ambitious work, and contains much that is unforgettable. But it is an early work by a beginner and for all its astonishing maturity and mastery it has weak points and fumblings, particularly in the third part—one has the feeling, very slightly, that Ray is more interested in Apu as a child and a youth than as a man. (Much the same is true of the most obviously comparable work of cinema—surprisingly not mentioned at all in Marie Seton's or Robin Wood's books on Ray—Mark Donskoi's Maxim Gorki trilogy, which, though at the time Ray had seen only the first section of it, could almost be the model for the Apu trilogy: in Donskoi's use of recurrent images, the river instead of the train; his splendid use of an old actress, Massinilitova, as compared with Chunibala as

Indra in Ray's film; and the rich ambiguity of his attitudes toward old and new, sensitivity and ruthlessness, in the formation of a writer.) Nor does the trilogy by any means exhaust the range of Ray's interests, sympathies, and abilities as a filmmaker. It is unfortunate, and quite unfair, that it has so often been used as a stick to beat Ray's later films.

Ray's next films after the first two parts were very different in subject matter and style, both from the trilogy and from each other. The trilogy so far might have helped to tag him as a rustic neo-realist concerned principally with the peasant classes, but *Paras Pathar* (1957) takes place entirely in the city, among the middle classes, and *Jalsaghar* (1958) is the first of a series of films dealing with the zamindar class, the rich landlords of British India. Moreover, *Paras Pathar* (*The Philosopher's Stone*) is of all things a satirical fantasy, closest, if it is close to any neo-realist film at all, to De Sica's *Miracle in Milan*. This miracle in Calcutta concerns a mild and harmless little clerk who suddenly, for no particular reason, finds himself in possession of the philosopher's stone and able to turn base metal into gold at will. The first part of the film manages to tread its tightrope of whimsical fantasy with considerable grace and precision—the first reactions of the poor Duttas to their new-found riches are very funny and believable enough to keep us in touch with reality despite the extravagance of the point of departure. Particularly appealing is Dutta's drive around the city daydreaming of his future life as a rich man, ending with him discovering in a scrap-iron dump the ideal materials to practice his new gifts on, a pair of cannon balls. Later on, though, the comic tone is not kept up—the Duttas' situation becomes too seriously uncomfortable, and the satirical lines directed at Calcutta bourgeois society are rather lacking in subtlety. All the same, it is a pity *Paras Pathar* is not better known, for it shows a gift for fantasy in Ray which he was not to exploit again until *Goopy Gyne Bagha Byne* in 1969.

If *Paras Pathar* is unarguably minor, *Jalsaghar* (*The Music Room*) is a major work, and remains one of Ray's finest. It is curious that it should come immediately before the third part of the Apu trilogy, for while *Apur Sansar* is expansive, *Jal-*

saghar is the most concentrated and restrained of his films, a long, lyrical meditation on a single theme, the decline of an aristocratic family. The film is deliberately underdramatized; the decline is a *fait accompli* from the first, and the whole story is told from the point of view of its principal victim (perhaps, too, its principal agent), an aged and solitary nobleman now near death. Above all, this is an atmospheric piece, set in the sad moldering remains of a once splendid country house on the edge of an empty, mournful estuary, almost the only sign of life apart from the few, slow remnants of the household being the one horse and the single elephant left to wander idly across the sandy flats.

Exactly why the family's fortunes have sunk so low we never learn. Is it the excessive mourning and withdrawal from the world which follows the death of the hero's only son, or the natural extravagance and impracticability of a nature in which all is subordinated to a love of music and the arts? It does not really matter; the entire film is a dying fall evoking a situation with the poet's sublime disregard for worldly whys and wherefores. Though there are one or two places, usually in action scenes (notably the hero's ride across the sands near the end), where this leads to perfunctory handling (Ray has always been least sure in his direction of pure action, particularly violent action), in general *Jalsaghar* is one of Ray's most masterly films, exquisitely photographed and directed with a complete, unquestioning mastery of mood and tempo which matches the work of Jean Renoir at its best. Most wonderful of all, perhaps, are the two big sequences in the music room itself, that leading up to the storm in which the hero's son is lost and that in which with a grand gesture he spends the last of his money on just one more, crowning performance before he dies. In particular the first—with its long concentration on the mounting intensity of the Moslem singer's song, the physical signs of the rising storm in the shaking mirror and the swaying chandeliers, at first unnoticed by the rapt guests, the insect drowning in the zamindar's glass of wine, and then the full fury of the storm—is unforgettable as a piece of musical, dramatic, and visual construction. *Jalsaghar* is not the easiest of films, especially for a Western audience, since it lacks the more accessible appeals to sentiment of the Apu trilogy, but for those willing to place themselves under its hypnotic spell it offers pleasures of unique delicacy and refinement.

The same cannot be said of *Devi* (*The Goddess*), the film Ray made in 1960, immediately after *Apur Sansar*. Though some like it very much, it never seems to me to come through with the force and conviction that it should. Easy to feel, but hard to say exactly why. The plot is both interesting in itself and, for a Western audience, exotic enough to offer a bonus of Oriental glamour. A young wife is identified by her fanatical father-in-law as an embodiment of the goddess Kali, becomes more than half convinced when an apparent miracle is performed through her agency, and is finally destroyed by the combined effects of her intellectual husband's skepticism, the religious pressures of the village, and the failure of a second miracle to materialize. It is, in fact, an unusually coherent, tightly knit plot, one of the best-organized plots in Ray's *oeuvre,* and perhaps this is what is wrong with the film. Ray's is an expansive, rhapsodic talent, and it seems to blossom best when it has time to work by indirection, by the cumulative effect of recurrent images and delicate hints of character and motivation, and is least confined by a strict external form. *Devi* is more a matter of uncluttered storytelling than of atmosphere and the loving accumulation of detail. The story is, admittedly, quite well told, if a little slowly, but somehow in the process much of the life of the film, the life which we normally expect of Ray's films, seems to have drained away. Of course, there are remarkable things in *Devi* all the same, especially in the hypnotic scenes of the religious ceremonies in which the unfortunate heroine is involved, and these introduce another element into our knowledge of Ray's range of effects: his ability to handle successfully a florid style with flashy camera work and obtrusive editing effects. But by and large the film does not seem quite to live up to its ambitions, and it is interesting in Ray's progress mainly as marking a shift from a narrative to a more dramatic approach.

The year 1961 was the centenary of Tagore's birth, and so it was perhaps only natural that Ray, once a pupil of Tagore's at Santiniketan and the son of one of Tagore's closest friends, should make films in tribute. In fact he made two, the documentary *Rabindranath Tagore,* commissioned by the Indian government, and *Teen Kanya* (*Three Daughters*), a three-episode film based on Tagore short stories, later shorn of one of its episodes and shown in the West as *Two Daughters.* Though a commissioned work, *Rabindranath Tagore* was obviously also in many ways a labor of love. As organized, it sets out to trace Tagore's life partly by the use of documents (paintings, photographs, books, and manuscripts) and partly by reconstruction with live actors. On the whole, it reflects Ray's technical skill and superior tastes rather than his most personal gifts as a filmmaker, but even so it is often fascinating, with its glimpses of moldering architectural splendors and its revealing snapshots of both the great and the insignificant in the early years of this century. There are, however, three sequences worthy of Ray at his best and most personal: that in which the young Tagore, played by a boy with a radiantly expressive face, first starts to explore the world about him, which yields images as beautiful and astonishing as anything in the Apu trilogy; the passage evoking the onset of the rains, a frequent subject in Tagore's poetry; and the wordless demonstration of the evolution of Tagore's painting from early doodles in the margins of his writing to the highly sophisticated work of his seventies. For those sequences alone the film deserves an honorable place among Ray's works.

Teen Kanya is longer and more substantial, though its material is essentially slighter. In its original form the two primarily comic episodes known in the West as *Two Daughters* were separated by another new venture for Ray, a ghost story called "Monihara," which Ray felt would make the film, at nearly three hours, rather too much of a good thing for non-Indian audiences. *Two Daughters* is as it stands one of Ray's most wholly delightful films, showing his till then largely hidden gift for comedy to the full. The first story, "The Postmaster," is hardly more than an atmospheric sketch of the affection which springs up between a lonely young village postmaster, exiled from Calcutta, and his diminutive orphan housekeeper, but it is beautifully done, and the performance of the girl (Chandana Bannerjee), especially at the end, when the postmaster leaves without warning, is remarkable. The episode is built up with tiny touches of local color and character, as in the opening scene, in which the rather stuffy but ostentatiously self-possessed postmaster is terrorized by a wild-looking lunatic in the outlandish remains of a soldier's uniform, only to be even more put out when a tiny orphan girl firmly drives his tormentor away. Later a friendship grows between them, with Ratan helping the postmaster to find his way around the unfamiliar village and its ways, while he teaches her to read and write. But if the theme of education seems to bring some scenes of "The Postmaster" close to *Pather Panchali,* the conclusion, when, after a bout of malaria through which he is nursed by Ratan, the postmaster decides to return suddenly to the city whence he came, has a strange bittersweet quality quite different from anything in the earlier film: we feel, for all the comedy of the earlier sequences, that something sad is happening, that probably Ratan, who came so near to developing into a mature woman capable of coping with the modern world, may never do so now. The balance of comedy and sympathy in this slight, erratic tale of a brief contact between very different people is perfectly brought off by Ray, in a fashion which one would not otherwise have suspected him capable of.

The second story, "Samapti" ("The Conclusion"), is a social comedy about an unlikely marriage that works out all right in the end. Though the episode tends to go on too long, and the interludes of swift action are too brief to leaven effectively the hypnotic slowness of the rest, some of the individual scenes are very funny, particularly the hero's unfortunate visit to inspect the pudgy but domesticated bride his mother has picked out for him. This owlish law student pigheadedly chooses to marry instead a tomboyish young woman, despite everyone's warnings, with nearly disastrous consequences for both of them. The plot is spun fine, but never quite allowed to snap altogether, the humorous observation of character is generally acute, and the part of the reluctant bride, a sort of Indian Baby Doll more interested in her pet squirrel than her husband, is made by director and actress at once funny, irritating, and completely believable. In adapting a rather rambling and uninteresting story by Tagore, Ray has developed the comedy so as to make the drama into a kind of Indian *Taming of the Shrew,* constructed along much the same lines: like "The Postmaster," it is a study in the maturing of a child-woman, though this time in absence rather than presence: Pagli plays the tomboy-child all through her wedding and wedding night, shinning down a convenient tree to escape her sleeping husband and play with her pet squirrel instead. It is only when he has gone, after assuring her that she is still too immature for marriage but he will be ready when she signifies she is ready, that she begins to develop and put aside childish things. The truce and happy ending between her and her husband are finally arrived at through a compromise: she will not send for him and he will not come of his own accord. But he comes in answer to a transparently contrived summons to his mother's fictional sickbed and then forgets his promise far enough to go and look for his errant bride down by the river where they first met.

It is interesting to see Ray, even in this very lightweight context, constructing his drama on recurrent developing images just as he did with the most serious sections of the Apu trilogy. In "Samapti" there are two of these: the mud flats on the riverbank where Aparna's romance with Pagli begins and ends (and playing a vital part elsewhere in the story, particularly during Aparna's abortive attempt at engaging himself to the other girl) and the tree Pagli climbs down to escape from her wedding night and finally climbs back up again to signify her readiness for it. Three if we count Pagli's pet squirrel as an image rather than a character—and indeed, he is both: his behavior and death are perfectly naturalistic, but during the story his various recurrences come to be associated in our minds with Pagli's childishness, and his death therefore implies her complete break with childhood and readiness to accept womanhood.

The third episode, "Monihara," might well create too strong a contrast of mood within *Teen Kanya* as a whole, being really a horror film quite different in style and material (apart from their common origin in Tagore) from the other two. The story concerns a prosperous businessman obsessed with his frigid wife, who craves nothing but jewels, which he constantly buys her in a desperate attempt to gain some show of affection. One day his business is ruined, and his wife, fearing he may want to sell her jewels, takes flight with a mysterious servant who seems to have a blackmailer's hold on her. Whether he kills her or not, she vanishes, but reappears in ghostly form to claim the last gift her husband had brought her from the city. All of this is framed in the narration of a schoolteacher, who may be mad or drugged, directed toward a cloaked figure who at the end announces that he is the ghost of the husband and vanishes. Though this twist at the end is more comic than horrific, for the most part the film is horror taken straight, leading from a slow build-up to a spectacular set piece of melodrama in which the inanimate objects in the house seem to come malevolently alive to the terrified husband as he awaits his wife's ghostly return. The story remains an isolated essay in a genre alien to Ray, but within its confines done with surprising effectiveness.

Ray's two ensuing films, *Kanchenjunga* (1962) his first color film, and *Abhijan* (1962), have had little showing in the West. This seems reasonable in the case of *Abhijan,* a picaresque adventure story centering on a taxi driver and his romantic and dramatic entanglements, which apparently Ray undertook to direct at the last minute and has little to commend it apart from the interest of seeing Ray handle a subject much closer to the Indian commercial norm than any of his other films. But *Kanchenjunga* is one of Ray's subtlest and most personal films, and perhaps the most concentrated example of his preoccupation with interrelations within the family and the difficulties as well as the joys of togetherness. It is, incidentally, the first film based on an original story by Ray himself. Essentially it is a conversation piece. Its action strictly observes the unities, the film taking exactly the one hundred minutes that the action it represents takes. On one level the script is simple—merely eight members of one family drifting in and out of camera, talking often at random, with a couple of outsiders to influence the course of their meandering afternoon. But within this framework the drama is carefully and precisely patterned.

One element is a walk the younger daughter, Monisha, takes with the unappealing but eligible Bannerjee, during which he is supposed to propose and she to accept him. Monisha and Bannerjee have their reflections, or projections perhaps, in the elder daughter, Anima, and her husband, Shankar, who proved to be an unfortunate match and with whom now she constantly quarrels (while their little daughter looks anxiously on from a distance as she rides her pony around the hill—Observatory Hill in Darjeeling—where the family is spending its afternoon). Do Anima and Shankar represent what Monisha and Bannerjee may become if she does not summon up the strength to resist her father's will? Possibly. At any rate, in the end she rejects Bannerjee and seems to be looking instead toward the other outsider, the poor tutor Ashoke, whom her father, Indranath, has found himself disconcertingly unable to buy. The other characters are Indranath's cowed but not stupid wife, Labanya, and her widower brother Jagadion, who is now interested in nothing but bird watching; and Indranath's son, Anil, who is interested in nothing but bird watching of a rather less literal sort.

In a sense little happens; in a sense a great deal does. The drama here is much more interior than usual in Ray's films, and the surface is much more apparently literary, in that there is a lot of dialogue. But only apparently, for in this story the characters seldom say directly what they are thinking, or indeed anything particularly germane to the central issues of the drama, which are all thought and fought out beyond, between, and beneath the words they speak. The visual aspect of the film is cool and elegant, not overstuffed with effects or even images apart from the main one, which is an image of absence, the mountain of Kanchenjunga they cannot see till the end because it is cloaked in mist. Its final unveiling has been taken as a piece of naïve affirmation; as a monumental rebuke to the pettiness of these human entanglements; as a touch of irrelevant picturesqueness inspired by the fact that the film was, after all, being made in color. Actually, the presence/absence of the mountain has a not quite definable contribution to make to the edgy atmosphere of the afternoon, and its final appearance resolves nothing—the story is left, as Ray likes them, open-ended. We have seen the family, separate yet together, we have spent a hundred minutes in the company of idiosyncratic, believable human beings and got to know something of them, and we come away with a Chekhovian sense of human fragility, human durability, and the mystery behind the simplest happenings. We cannot ever be sure of what, so how can we hope to know exactly why?

Kanchenjunga is a high point in Ray's career; *Charulata,* which he made two years later, again basing his script on a story by Tagore, is another. In between comes *Mahanagar* (*The Big City*) (1963), which I do not find by any means so compelling, though it deals with a theme that obviously has some special importance for Ray, since he deals with it also in *Apur Sansar* and again in *Pratidwandi*: the search for work in a big city. Clearly the film has considerable importance thematically in India, because it confronts the problem of the working wife, and whether wives should go out to work, as this is absolutely against tradition. It also, incidentally, raises the question of the Anglo-Indians and their status, poised between two cultures and completely accepted by neither. This said, though, much of the film strikes me as thin and rather summary in the staging, lacking the rich suggestivity and complexity of Ray's best work. What it says it states, and that is about all. Arati, the wife of an impoverished young bank clerk compelled to support his pernickety old ex-schoolteacher father and his younger sister, determines to go out to work to help support the family.

Despite her tradition-bound father-in-law's resistance she persists and gets a job selling knitting machines. She is very successful and enjoys the work, and also becomes friendly with a fellow salesgirl, an Anglo-Indian named Edith. Her husband insists that she resign, but relents just in time when his bank fails and he is out of work. Her father-in-law is incapacitated by a heart attack. Her idle husband develops unfounded suspicions about her fidelity and spies on her. Finally she discovers that Edith has been dismissed from the firm on a trumped-up accusation of immoral behavior which she knows to be false, and she herself resigns in angry sympathy, so that at the end of the film both husband and wife are out of work, if still determined to look on the bright side. Though there are some nice moments of sly social comedy in Arati's introduction to the selling of knitting machines, and the character of Edith is interesting on a purely informational level, the second half of the film has too large an accumulation of bare happenings, some of them decidedly melodramatic and all of them losing conviction by their number and rapid succession. Ray still does not stage action well (witness the father-in-law's heart attack on the stairs with the cliché of the dropped stick clattering down), and seems out of his element in a plot-bound situation which does not leave his characters enough room to grow and develop by interaction. He does not seem creatively involved with much of *Mahanagar,* however much importance he may as a man attribute to the ideas and attitudes expressed in it.

Charulata, on the other hand, is by any standard one of Ray's masterpieces. Dealing with a moneyed and highly literate section of the zamindar class in the 1870's, it is, to steal a phrase from the advertising campaign for a very different film, "almost a love story," concerning the elusive, implicitly emotional relationship between the young wife of a newspaper proprietor and her husband's artistic cousin. The husband, Bhupati, is constantly preoccupied with the paper and with politics, and gets so excited about whether Gladstone or Disraeli will win the next British election that he never has time for Charulata, and she naturally becomes more and more involved with her literary soul mate, Amal, now competing with him, now wheedling him, now brusquely rebuffing him. Things come to a head when Bhupati is defrauded by his brother-in-law and Amal begins to wonder guiltily if he too is committing a betrayal of faith, even though, as they say in Hollywood films, "nothing has happened."

The whole story is told in hints and sidelights; in fact, in a real sense nothing does happen: it is all atmosphere and suggestion and unstated, even unconscious, emotional responses. *Jalsaghar* had already demonstrated, if demonstration were needed, how well capable of dealing with a subject as sophisticated as this Ray was—the days, if they had ever existed, when he could reasonably be regarded as a gifted but chancy primitive were long past—and in *Charulata* he brings the whole battery of his talents to bear, with sometimes breathtaking results. The sheer visual beauty of the film is extraordinary and the more showy technical devices—fast tracking shots, zoom lenses, etc.—are used with exemplary discipline and discretion. The acting of the principals too, on occasion the weak point in Ray's films, is here impeccable, catching exactly the Morrisian fervor relieved with heavy playfulness which makes this stratum of Indian life seem, oddly, more English than England itself.

Charulata has its recurrent images, notably the ornate carved-wood Victorian bed in Charu's room, where we first see her embroidering a gift for her husband and near and around which a number of other key scenes take place. A curious choice, in a way, because though justified realistically in the sense that much of Charu's life is lived in her room—hence her bored sense of confinement and neglect by her fond but preoccupied husband—the bed obviously has strong sexual overtones, which are, as is Ray's way with his images, just allowed to gather around it, and largely to be supplied by us, rather than being in any way directly insisted on. And in this, after all, the bed is an apt image for the drama as a whole, which is one of largely unrecognized sexuality. Charu and Amal drift into a friendly companionship, encouraged by Bhupati, with no notion of falling in love, unaware that they may be doing so. Charu's softening and unconcerned (because unrecognized) abandonment to her new feelings is brilliantly conveyed in the famous garden scene where Charu swings higher and higher (another disguised sexual reference?) while Amal reclines writing in the background under a tree, carrying out his part of their friendly literary competition. And again little is actually said; the growth of love, mainly Charu's for Amal, is shown in a number of tiny details—the song she hums and he takes up, the slippers she was embroidering for her husband and gives to Amal instead. Only when Charu steps out of the Victorian convention of reticence and declares her love for Amal does the situation become impossible: Bhupati might (were he conscious of what is happening before it is too late) echo the thought of one of Stendhal's characters—"If once the word 'love' is born between them, then I am lost." In fact, all three are lost. Amal leaves in shock and fear of his own feelings; Charu stays on, but her husband recognizes what has happened, leaves, and then comes back to an emotional stalemate, where everything is known between him and Charu but nothing can really be said.

Charulata, it is tempting to say, is Ray's most Western film—in discussing it one thinks at once of Ibsen or Strindberg (more in this case than Chekhov, who so often seems to offer close parallels to Ray's dramatic practice). But that is begging the question whether most of Ray is not Western. Obviously there are qualities in his films, such as their frequently very measured tempo (slowness, unsympathetic critics would say), which are easiest to discuss as part of his Indianness. But apart from his subject matter it is hard to be sure that there is anything in his films that derives specifically from his Oriental background and heritage: he is very much a world filmmaker, influenced more by Renoir, Donskoi, Welles (the swinging scene in *Charulata,* and the film's whole loving re-creation of its period milieu, has more than a hint of *The Magnificent Ambersons* about it), and even by the theories of Pudovkin, which were among his early reading, than by Indian cinema and its circumstances. And Ray himself, in his cultural background, is, in any case, poised between East and West. There is nothing in his films which has to be related to anything but his own artistic development and taste as an individual; like any artist, he is finally independent of his background, and whatever use he may choose to make of it is ultimately self-determined.

The films of 1965–67 may be taken as an interlude between *Charulata* and Ray's next major work, *Aranyer Din Ratri* (*Days and Nights in the Forest*). One of them, *Chidiakhana* (*The Zoo*) (1967) I have not been able to see, but it would seem to be of no importance—a competent detective story started by Ray's assistants under his supervision and then completed (mainly for financial reasons) by Ray himself: he does not regard it as one of his films. *Kapurush-o-Mahaparush* (*The Coward and the Holy Man*) (1965) is deliberately slight but agreeable: the first of the film's two stories concerns a second meeting between young lovers, some years after the young man ran out on the girl, who is now married to a decent bore, and is mainly about how nothing happens because she chooses to stay with her husband; the second develops as a knockabout farce concerning the unmasking of a fake holy man by the relatives of one of his gullible followers—a genre for which on this showing Ray would seem to have little gift, whatever his talents in subtler comedy.

Nayak (*The Hero*) (1966) and *Goopy Gyne Bagha Byne* (*The Adventures of Goopy and Bagha*) (1968) are both more substantial, but each in various ways is disappointing. *Nayak,* the second film from an original screenplay by Ray, is an evocation of the life and personality of a successful but dissatisfied film star during a train journey to Delhi, where he is to receive a prize. In the course of the journey he strikes up an acquaintance with a woman journalist, who at first regards their conversation as a useful opportunity to get material for a salable story, but eventually realizes that their relationship has become personal to the extent that it would not be ethical to use the information he has given her and tears up her notes. For his part, he is impelled to a sort of confession by a nagging sense that despite his evident success he is fundamentally mediocre and has not had the courage and the perseverance to make the most of what talents he has. He is also disturbed by a dream which represents his fear of money—his fear of corruption by the money he has, his fear of not having it any more. There is another dream, this time about fears of death, and there are seven flashbacks that detail to us in bits and pieces the course of the star's former life. This film is efficiently enough made (though the dreams could be characterized, like little else in Ray's work, as naïve), but the imaginative pressure is low, and for all its incidental touches of intelligent observation, *Nayak* seems to escape the sensational exposé genre only to fall rather too far into the world of soap opera.

Goopy Gyne Bagha Byne (also known simply as *Goopy and Bagha*) is another attempt on Ray's part at something new—or at least something he had not ventured on since *Paras Pathar*—fantasy. It is evident that *Goopy Gyne* was a film Ray very much wanted to make, and certainly one that he had to fight to make, considering its large budget and spectacular resources compared with his other films and the fact that it came at a time of crisis in the Bengali cinema. But one cannot help wondering if the reasons for Ray's determination and persistence really had enough to do with strictly artistic necessity; whether he was not perhaps pushed too much by family feeling and by love for his grandfather's book, on which the film is based, without considering closely enough how suited the material was to his temperament and skills as a filmmaker. There might also be another consideration at work: as well as being a fantasy, *Goopy Gyne* is a musical, with no fewer than eight full musical numbers in it, and the opportunity it offered Ray as a composer may well have tipped the balance unduly in its favor.

At least we can say that *Goopy Gyne* was a labor of love and no mere commercial chore (though, oddly enough, it became Ray's biggest box-office success, even in India). One of the main pleasures to be derived from it is a sense of relief and relaxation—we feel that Ray is content to have fun with his subject, and though solemn analyses of the subject in relation to Ray's attitude toward war and violence have been produced, the feeling of the film is primarily that of a romp. It is a rambling (too rambling) and picaresque tale of two rather dopey musicians, Goopy, the singer, and Bagha, the drummer. Wandering one day in the woods, they encounter the King of the Ghosts, who first terrorizes them (in a very jolly dance sequence all shot in negative) and then makes them the gift of three wishes and a pair of magic slippers which will carry them anywhere. Naturally confused by this stroke of good fortune (if it is good fortune), Goopy and Bagha fly off into the middle of a war between the good king of Shundi and the bad king of Halla. Actually, the bad king is not so bad as all that—he is bloodthirsty only when under the influence of a drug given him by his evil prime minister, and in his natural state he is so shy and retiring that he does not even want to be king. The natives of Shundi have all been struck dumb by a plague, and the royal family pretend to be dumb in sympathy, though in fact they have escaped the plague. A series of adventures separate and reunite the two heroes, get them thrown into prison and nearly executed, and enable them finally, with the help of their magic, to intervene in the war, avert the imminent battle, and marry the daughters of the two kings, now peacefully reunited in friendship.

This is all very nice, if a bit long-drawn-out, with too many twists and turns of plot to try the audience's patience. It would be easy, reversing the judgment on *Charulata,* to say that *Goopy Gyne* is Ray's most Indian film, and in a sense this may be true—undoubtedly with its comedy and romance and fantasy, its songs and dances and spectacle, it is nearer than any of Ray's other films to the sort of Indian cinema best known in the West, as exemplified by Mehboob's *Aan, Savage Princess.* Of course, it is immeasurably superior to its parallels, but a slight feeling remains that it is disappointing from Ray—less personal, less felt, less intensely realized than even the lightest of his other works, like *Teen Kanya* or *Kapurush-o-Mahapurush.* It is true, also, that purely technical limitation may have something to do with this: a fantasy of this kind has to be physically absolutely convincing, and suspension of disbelief is not aided here by shaky back projection and traveling matte or obvious economies in sets, costumes, and spectacular highlights. Nor indeed by the fact that the film, for financial reasons, had to be made in black-and-white (bursting into color only right at the end), when it obviously begs to be made in color throughout.

After these four films *Aranyer Din Ratri* (*Days and Nights in the Forest*) (1970) was a decided return to form, and enforced some clear rethinking of attitudes toward Ray which were beginning to become set in critics' minds. It has always been easy, too easy, to pull out the conventional epithets for Ray's films. "Measured," we say, to suggest that they are slow, but are obviously meant to be that way. "Poetic"—for Ray's approach to character and event is clearly far from documentary, and his films seem often to be built to music unheard as well as to his own heard, and highly expressive, scores. "Humane"—because his sympathy, and ours, goes out to even the most unlikely objects, realizing in practice that usually somewhat unrealistic maxim that to understand all is to forgive all. But these ready formulations leave the magic of his films unexpressed. The very opening of *Days and Nights in the Forest* is a perfect case in point. A group of four somewhat ill-assorted friends from Calcutta are out for a few days runaway holiday in the country. They joke and mildly quarrel as they drive, the particular humorist of the party chattering on about the forest and the various failures of the others to respond to the adventure of their situation. Then without warning one of them says to him, "Look to your left," the camera moves, and there, suddenly, flashing past the car window, is the forest. The tempo slows, in comes the music, and we go into the credits. Magical is the only word to describe the effect, achieved with apparently the simplest, most naïve means.

There are many such moments in *Days and Nights in the Forest,* and it is not even, I would say, one of Ray's really top-notch films throughout: just a better-than-average middle-range work. There are sections, particularly in the first half, which are rather too measured for comfort, and the build-up to the appearance of the feminine interest is too long-drawn-out. But even this slight wearisomeness pays eventual dividends in that we really feel we have been living along with these people. There is, indeed, something Chekhovian about Ray's wayward, indirect means of character revelation. The picnic scene, near the end, in which nearly all the characters agree to play an idiotic memory game, is almost a perfect Chekhov scene, conceived in cinematic terms, with all revealing more and more of themselves by the way they play or refrain from playing. And the restrained climaxes to two of the three romantic elements in the story—abortive in one case, possibly pointing toward something further in the other—are among the best scenes Ray has ever done.

In the wake of *Days and Nights in the Forest,* Ray embarked on a film in which the political theme, implicit in *Days and Nights in the Forest,* came to the fore. And by the time he came to make his next film he became aware that what he had was a second trilogy, less closely-knit than the Apu trilogy, but united by recurrent themes indicative of social change in modern India. In *Pratidwandi* (*The Adversary*) (1970) we return to the theme and the world of the opening of *Apur Sansar* and *Mahanagar*. The hero, Siddhartha, is compelled by his father's death (much as Apu was by his mother's) to give up his studies and look for a job. Like Subrata in *Mahanagar,* he has a family to support, a mother, sister, and brother. But he cannot manage to get a job, because though, like Apu, he has intellectual qualifications, he has neither the drive nor the right contacts. So in practice the family is dependent on the earnings of his sister, Sutapa, a modern young woman of considerable ambition and determination. Siddhartha, on the other hand, is a curious mixture of the old and the new, like the adult Apu, considered a fuddy-duddy conservative by his younger brother Tumu, who is caught up in student revolutionary politics. He is conservative even in his attitude toward sex: his reaction to a visit to a prostitute organized by one of his college friends is horror and revulsion. A more settling and suitable romance with the daughter of an income-tax inspector also comes to nothing when she becomes emotionally confused by the prospect of her widowed father's remarriage to her aunt. And Siddhartha cannot cope with life—he still cannot even get a job, and when he is about to have a crucial interview he gets so worked up against his prospective employers for their callousness that he turns on them, in circumstances somewhat similar to those which brought about Arati's resignation in *Mahanagar,* and refuses the job.

In the final sequences we see Siddhartha settled (like Apu at the mine) in a humble job selling medical supplies in a small town. He has achieved a sort of balance, but still cherishes ideas of returning to the city, reclaiming the girl he loves, and improving himself at last. In the following film, *Seemabadha* (*Company Limited*) (1971), we see as it were the reverse side of the medal. Back in Calcutta, Ray shows us the new bourgeoisie functioning in a Westernized setting of big business. The central character, or at any rate the character who provides the moral center of the film, is a girl who comes to the city to visit her sister and brother-in-law. Like Siddhartha, she is in a state of indecision about the future shape of her life, and the main reason she comes visiting is to renew contact with her brother-in-law, for whom she had strong feelings when she was in her teens, six or seven years earlier. It is a sort of sentimental journey, a journey to her own emotional past, and a checking up: how has the young man she once had a crush on developed, what effects have life in the city, an executive job in a big business, had on him? And by implication, is this a way of life she herself would wish to accept, or should she return to her revolutionary boy friend in the country? She finds nothing very encouraging in the aura of social success and urban glamour provided by her elder sister and the brother-in-law. At first they seem to have acclimatized well to the new way of life, but when a crisis comes at the brother-in-law's office, as a result of faulty workmanship at the factory where the electric fans he markets are made, he proves to be as obsessed with his career, with self-preservation, as any of his Western peers. He is essentially the reasonably honest middle-class man, reasonably decent, provided he is not pushed too far or cornered, but once he is, he is willing to fight dirty and sacrifice anyone who gets in his way. He does so, and he succeeds: he ends up with his ambitions fulfilled (for the moment) with a directorship of his firm. So he is quite happy, but his sister-in-law is much less so. She feels she cannot but reject his standards, his way of life—but whether that means she feels enough for her revolutionary to go back and marry him, embrace his standards wholeheartedly, is another matter, and one about which we feel no final certainty at the end of the film.

Company Limited is technically quite straightforward, particularly when compared to *The Adversary* and its elaborate structure, with its flashes forward and back, its adventures into negative in certain sequences, and its instantaneous glimpses of potential action going on in its characters' heads. It is also a lot funnier, with much mordant humor in its observation of business methods and the contrasts of social life in Calcutta. It is rather as though the satire present within the fantasy of *Paras Pathar* has been transmuted by contact with the realistic observation of, say, *Mahanagar* to produce a satisfying new tone in Ray's work. The sociopolitical observation of the new trilogy is consistent in its humor and its underlying sadness—sadness rather than bitterness, for Ray does not seem to be the stuff of which revolutionaries are made. He observes human follies and failings, but remains sympathetic and understanding toward his characters—his sympathies can embrace the young executive in *Company Limited* as well as the naïve, idealistic sister-in-law, and one feels that the revolutionary boy friend, if we ever saw him, would be no more likely to figure as an unequivocal all-round hero. Ray's is a world of complex human beings, in which most people mean more or less well, and nobody gets to carry the banner of Ray's sympathy or the stigma of his total disapproval; it is a fallible, human world we can all recognize.

If something of a new tone was perceptible in *Company Limited,* Ray's latest film at the time of writing, *Ashani Sanket* (*Distant Thunder*) (1973), suggests a departure in quite a new direction for him, an extraordinary development in his talents. Though there are certain points of detail in common between it and some of his earlier works, these generally seem to be something in the nature of deliberate references, like the recurrent shots of the pond and the tree near the hero's house, which cannot but remind us of the similar shots recurring in *Pather Panchali.* What is different about *Distant Thunder,* based on a novel by the author of the Apu trilogy, is its whole tone, scope, and approach to character. It comes very near to being an epic drama in the Brechtian rather than the Hollywood sense of the term. Its subject is the onset of the great Indian famine of 1942, and the numerous characters, though no less vividly created than those in the earlier films, are kept quite deliberately as figures in a landscape, parts of a larger pattern. At first this is not apparent: the character of Gangacharan, the impecunious Brahman with plans of making a living from running a village school and officiating at the local (for some time disused) temple, has a vague, bookish charm a little reminiscent of Nandal in the "Postmaster" episode of *Teen Kanya,* and his wife, the squirrel in a cage separated by her caste and her upbringing from those around her and expected to lead a relatively leisurely life of refined domesticity, could be Pagli from the "Samapti" episode once she has been settled a little by marriage. We might reasonably suppose that we are about to witness another personal drama of life in a village, played almost entirely upon nuances of human character and behavior.

Instead, the great world outside and its problems gradually

sneak up on us, as on Gangacharan and his wife. Some talk of a war in faraway Singapore (who knows where that might be?) seems utterly remote from rural Bengal, something to talk about theoretically for a while and then dismiss from mind. But then the price of rice starts to increase. Only a local scarcity, perhaps, something to worry the next village. But slowly, inexorably, the trouble spreads, and we see the gradual erosion of normal standards of behavior under the external pressures of hunger and poverty. The delicately nurtured wife, who could not consider taking any kind of work because that way they would lose respect in the eyes of their lower-caste neighbors, starts husking rice for a small payment in kind; later, out of necessity, she goes out with other village women to dig for edible roots, and before the end she is seriously considering the offers of the hideously scarred man at the brick kiln promising rice in return for favors received. Other (in principle) decent enough, scrupulous enough women do not endure so long—they have never been tested seriously, and hunger is a powerful argument. But then all the niceties vanish under pressure. Before long law-abiding villagers are pillaging rice stores, rapists lurk in the woods, people are set upon and beaten to death almost casually, for what does one death more or less matter when hundreds are dying of hunger on the roads every day? Gradually the accepted patterns of caste and other social relations crumble, and Gangacharan and his wife, who seemed initially to be the center of the film, dwindle down almost to the vanishing point, absorbed in a sea of humanity, just as, in the film's stunning final shot, the family of the poor Brahman from the next village is instantly lost in an outward zoom which seems to show the whole population of India coming relentlessly over the hill. There are details of great visual beauty in the film, particularly in its use of color, which Ray is here using in a feature for only the second time. But whereas Ray has often seemed in the past to be essentially a miniaturist, or at least an intimist, here it is the grand design of the whole which works on the spectator: the film is built on a monumental scale which belies its relatively modest length and overwhelms one as surely as the rising tide.

Now in his fifties, Satyajit Ray is a filmmaker of world reputation, at the height of his mature powers. He has lived through, and lived down, a number of pigeonholing reputations. There was that of being an Indian filmmaker, *the* Indian filmmaker, as opposed to a filmmaker *tout court:* with its implication that he was a special case, requiring sympathy, tolerance, patronage, special standards of judgment. Then there was that of the neo-realist primitive, an instinctive artist whose first films just happened to come out right because of "sincerity" and humane values, rather than because of any conscious art. Then there was that of the poetic symbolist, dependent on the manipulation of obvious (and often too obvious) visual metaphors for his effects. Then there was that of the filmmaker of unfulfilled promise, who had shot his bolt with his earliest works and was now overproductive and disappointing—the Apu trilogy has often been used as a stick to beat his later films with, both because they are different and because they are not, even by critics who did not particularly like the trilogy when it first came out. And all this time Ray has continued to make films in his own time, according to the dictates of his own artistic development, and influenced as little as possible by critics or by commercial considerations.

Sometimes he may choose a deliberately simple, unadorned style, as in the "Postmaster" episode of *Teen Kanya,* when he feels that it matches the material, but in films like *Jalsaghar, Devi,* and the "Monihara" episode of *Teen Kanya,* his style can be as rich and highly wrought as any in the cinema today. Similarly, the pace of his films may often be slow (and not only to Western viewers), but the slowness nearly always justifies itself as the only way of adequately exploring the material, and when he wants to, Ray can pick up the pace with complete mastery and conviction, as in the swinging episode of *Charulata.* Admittedly, in his constant experimentation with new styles and materials, some weak points have emerged—he is not at home with the staging of violent physical action or of broad farce—but to balance this he has scored decisive successes in some unexpected genres, such as the horror film ("Monihara"), social comedy ("Samapti" and episodes of *Mahanagar* and *Days and Nights in the Forest*), and the highly sophisticated atmospheric conversation piece (*Kanchenjunga*).

Understandably, the assumption which still crops up among Western critics, that he is a natural, untutored genius, unconscious of his art and unthinkingly warbling his woodnotes wild, rankles a little, but in spite of the critics, and in spite of commercial pressures at home, he goes on making films in his own fashion, with conscious and consciously developing art, on the principle that if they do not please him they are unlikely to please anyone else. As he says: "In the cinema you can't be a primitive; you can pick up a pen or a brush with no training, but to make a film you have to know what you're doing."

Miklós Jancsó

It is, some might say, the mark of the true *auteur* that he is, in a sense, always making the same film in different guises. The problem with Miklós Jancsó is that he has sometimes seemed to be making the same film over and over again in the same guise. There is no filmmaker today who has more instantly recognizable subject matter, a more limited range of recurrent images and situations, a more highly mannered and idiosyncratic camera style. There are times when one feels that the sequences of any Jancsó film could be shifted to any other Jancsó film with no sense of dislocation or incongruity whatever, except for the minor consideration that some are in black-and-white and some are in color. The wide Hungarian plains, the horsemen constantly circling, the ritual stripping of men and women, the dialogue in short, barked-out orders and commands, the revolutionary songs and dances, the faces of the same players continually recurring, the patterns of humiliation, the intricately choreographed shifts of power, the camera ever on the move, twisting and turning, rising and falling, as though in response to an obsessive kind of abstract patterning rather than from any evident functional connection with the matter in hand—all these are the familiar components of Jancsó's small, intensely pictured world. Perhaps too familiar; and perhaps the world is too small. But at his best Jancsó can evoke his own private world with a hallucinatory power that thrusts aside all urge to question. He is a magician whose spells sometimes work more potently than at other times, and sometimes do not work at all. But when they do work, as for me they do most spectacularly in *My Way Home, Silence and Cry,* and *Red Psalm,* the effect is so extraordinary, so daring, so utterly unlike anything else in the cinema that it is not only possible (it should always be possible) but very easy to forgive the other occasions where he has tried grandly and failed.

Jancsó is older than one might think, or than his films would lead one to suppose, probably because of his rather late arrival on the international scene with *The Round-Up* in 1965, when he was already forty-four and, unbeknownst to us, a filmmaker of some fifteen years' experience (which included sixteen short films of various kinds, three features, and an episode in a fourth). For some time he must have seemed the perennial student: he studied law first, then folklore and art history, and took his first diploma in 1944; then he went on to the Budapest Academy of Dramatic and Film Art and graduated in 1950. From there he started filmmaking, working first in newsreels and directing his first short, a documentary called *Autumn in Badacsony,* in 1954. In 1958 he directed his first feature, *The Bells Have Gone to Rome* (*A Harangok Rómába Mentek*), which he now dismisses as entirely uncharacteristic and quite unsuccessful, and which has never been shown, so far as I can trace, outside Hungary. In 1963 came his second feature, *Cantata* (*Oldás és Kötés*), and in 1964 at last his first mature, fully personal work, the feature *My Way Home,* which was, incidentally (or perhaps not so incidentally), also the first work in which he collaborated with Gyula Hernádi, his regular script collaborator on all his subsequent films.

There is very little in either *The Bells Have Gone to Rome* or *Cantata* to indicate the way Jancsó would develop. Evidently he is still feeling his way in both films, trying on different styles and subjects. *The Bells Have Gone to Rome* does in fact contain the germs of the kind of situation out of which Jancsó was to make something highly personal in his mature works. But the film is a muddle of conflicting influences—a mild, very realistic approach to character, à la Donskoi, is disturbingly mixed in with attempts at ambitious symbolic overtones which suggest Bergman studied not wisely but too well. The story is set in the last days of the Second World War, with the Russians advancing toward the borders of Hungary. A group of schoolboys are press-ganged into service by the Germans. At first they are not really ill-disposed toward the venture, but gradually they come to question what they are doing there, whom they are fighting, and what for. The spirit of revolt crystallizes when they help a girl to escape on her way to a concentration camp; after this, they all go into hiding on an island until the war is over. The teacher in charge of them covers their flight and dies protecting them. The possible connections with later Jancsó subjects, like *My Way Home* and *The Red and the White,* are obvious—the scene of confusion at the end of a war, the conflicts of loyalty or more precisely the tendency to reject any rigid pattern of loyalties are typical elements of the later films' make-up. But whereas in the later films this sort of scene is made the stage for playing out a complicated drama of power, domination, and subservience, with everything reduced as close to abstraction as possible, here the narrative is anecdotal and the details generally dominate the overall picture. Also, the script is talkative, with everything worked out, not too effectively, in heavy dialogue exchanges, where later everything is done with a minimum of dialogue, and as much as possible the dialogue is precipitated by events.

With *Cantata* the most obvious influence is that of Antonioni, for whom Jancsó has always professed the greatest admiration. The drama is almost all internal, "psychological," and to that extent it may be said to resemble more closely Jancsó's later work. But whereas in the later films all the psychology is crystallized into action, in *Cantata* it is generally expressed in talk, and is clamorously explicit compared with the mysterious indirection of, say, *Silence and Cry*. The story is about a confrontation with the past. An apparently successful, happy young doctor, who comes from a peasant family and is therefore a walking testament to the efficacy of the new order in providing opportunities and breaking down class barriers, has nevertheless a hidden memory which torments him. A few years earlier, he had failed, while at the university, to defend a girl he was involved with from untruthful accusations, thereby safeguarding his own position at her expense. His subsequent life has been professionally successful, but he has achieved success only by suppressing his human feelings and hiding his early emotional experience like an unhealed sore. Finally a meeting with an old teacher whose relative lack of brilliant success has been compensated for by a growth in wisdom and humanity brings the doctor to a realization of his shortcomings and an acceptance of his need to face and come to terms with his past cowardice before he can develop into a rounded human being.

The style of the film is rather chilly and formal—one has the feeling that Jancsó is still trying on styles to see how they fit—an impression confirmed by those of the shorts Jancsó was making during these years that I have seen, which vary from a very simple, documentary, almost newsreel approach to the rather self-consciously extravagant style of *Immortality,* an art film about a working-class sculptor of the interwar years which evokes his life and work through a lot of thoroughly showy, virtuoso camera work and cutting. With *My Way Home* (*Igy Jöttem*), though, a distinct, distinctive personality emerges, and all at once. The film establishes the essentials of Jancsó's world—the landscape, the ideas, the power play. Admittedly *My Way Home* seems a lot more expansive and romantic than any of his later films—it has a certain freshness, innocence, almost, which makes one understand why Jancsó should have professed such admiration for Donskoi's Maxim Gorki trilogy and *Ballad of a Soldier,* which would otherwise seem absolutely alien to his mature work. *My Way Home* is Jancsó's warmest, most approachable, in every way most likable film; but all the same one would never for a moment mistake it for the work of anyone else.

The very beginning is typical—the situation which fascinates him above all others, that of confusion in the wake of a war (the Second World War in this case), presumably because of the detachment from conventional loyalties and established hierarchies that it produces in people, setting them loose to fend for themselves psychologically as well as physically. In such a situation, Jancsó presumably figures, people find their natural level—the leaders and the followers, the dominators and the dominated. Or in some cases, perhaps the strongest, perhaps the weakest—maybe both—drop out altogether. Again and again in Jancsó's films the field is crossed and recrossed by opposing groups (*The Red and the White, Agnus Dei, Red Psalm*), with individual figures and groups drifting backward and forward, being captured, escaping, changing sides. Frequently, indeed, no individual does clearly emerge, but *My*

Way Home is an exception—it has a clear "hero," a central character who runs through the whole story, traversing a series of vaguely picaresque incidents and actuated at most by a vague desire to make his way home—wherever home may be. He is a young Hungarian (played by András Kozák, for long Jancsó's favorite actor, and the one who most generally seemed to represent Jancsó's point of view in his films) wandering around during the last weeks of the war, while the Russian army is invading Hungary. At the beginning of the film, he and his companions are often caught literally between two fires, the advancing Russians and a scattering of retreating Germans, for neither of whom they seem to have any feeling other than mistrust and a desire to stay out of the way.

The first episode—as it turns out to be—shows the hero with a group of other young people. He becomes lightly involved with a girl, and so in a way the rival of another boy, but when he chooses to go off on his own way the girl remains with the group—that is the casual way things happen, with people thrown together or drifting apart without any particular reason or pattern. He has not been on his own for long when he is surrounded by Russian horsemen (the image of circling horsemen on the wide Hungarian plains is to become obsessive in Jancsó's films) and captured. He is put into an improvised camp, and detailed to help fetch water. An escape is attempted, but he stands by, keeping his own counsel (strength or weakness?) until, quite arbitrarily, he is set free because the female guard finds that she had made a mistake in counting, and cannot balance her books with him included. Thus set free, he has no particular purpose or direction, except the continuing vague urge to go home, so it is not surprising that he is almost immediately recaptured.

This time he is set to herding sheep with a young Russian soldier. At first they cannot communicate at all verbally, since the only word they have in common is the Russian for bread. But all the same an intimate comradeship springs up between them: even without language they are hardly more than a couple of schoolboys sharing a jolly open-air adventure. At first our hero thinks of escape, and even tries, perhaps rather halfheartedly, to get away on one occasion. His guard motions him to come back, seems almost threatening, but when he shoots it is only to detonate a mine in the young man's path, to show him that he is walking into danger as soon as he leaves the charmed circle of the sheep station, and when he is offered a further chance of escape by a passing group of refugees, he refuses so as not to get his guard into trouble. Later they become so at home with each other, so trusting and trusted, that at one point the Russian, after a little target practice by a river, hands over his gun to his nominal captive to have a go also, and the captive, just as naturally and unhesitatingly, hands it back afterward. The relationship between these two young men forms the core of the film, emotionally and structurally—their natural high spirits, which expresses itself sometimes in games and horseplay, their desire to understand each other across the language barrier, their shared concern for their animal charges—and is beautifully handled, with a light, gentle touch which will seldom subsequently recur in Jancsó's work.

The idyll—for that is really what it is—is rudely disrupted at last by the unexpected illness of the Russian. He has an old, partially healed wound which begins to give him trouble. (Is this why he has been set to something as relatively undemanding as sheep herding? We never know.) The Hungarian boy is desperate to help him, but does not know what to do, how to make himself understood and get medical assistance. Finally he decides the only solution is to put on his guard's uniform and, disguised as a Russian, commandeer help. He forces a doctor at gunpoint to come and examine the Russian, but it is too late; the Russian dies anyway and the boy is again left to his own devices. So he sets out homeward once more—only to meet the doctor again at a railway station. Here he gets into trouble because he cannot explain his former masquerade—or if he can no one will listen. But still he is on his way; life goes on and he with it. He may not be indestructible, because no one is that, but he will clearly survive and find his way home eventually to a new life: the film's final images are of him setting out philosophically on foot, like some hero of a Russian socialist-realist, optimistic social drama.

But though this may sound naïve, *My Way Home* is in every way far from naïveté. The joyous simplicity it shows in parts is only one side of the picture Jancsó presents. The episode on the sheep station with the Russian soldier is very much a "time out of war," an interlude of peace in a world where sudden death, casual violence, and complete emotional and intellectual disorientation are the order of the day. Elsewhere in the film characters come and go like figures from a half-remembered dream. In the first few minutes, for example, we meet the group which the young hero belongs to, or seems to belong to, and two of them, the girl and his rival for her interest, are sharply, individually etched, as though a whole plot is to be built around the hero's relations with them. Then all at once they vanish, never to reappear. The whole film, in fact, has a mysterious, almost hypnotic quality: actions which seem to be, and from the point of view of plot are, crucial, are deliberately underplayed, while seeming unessentials (which prove, of course, to be nothing of the sort, but vital clues to character and relationships) are accompanied by a positively Pre-Raphaelite profusion of detail.

In this, as in many of its purely visual elements, the film prefigures *The Round-Up* (*Szegénylegények,* literally *The Hopeless*) (1965), which first made Jancsó a figure of international importance and established once and for all the image of his work in the minds of filmgoers. Its reputation began with its showing at the Cannes Festival in 1966, though it had already the previous year received the major award of Hungarian critics. At Cannes, though surprisingly it received no award, the film was an instant revelation. The purity of its style, its obsessive concentration, the mysterious, elliptical nature of its plotting, the exoticism of its locales, all signified something completely new in international cinema—a film unlike any other, a director whose style and approach were unmistakable, and as the release of *My Way Home* outside Hungary on the heels of *The Round-Up*'s success immediately demonstrated, no flash in the pan either.

It is always tempting, in such situations, with a career that begins, as far as international audiences are concerned, with such a bang, to overreact afterward, to underestimate the element of sheer surprise and novelty in the initial impact, and so maintain that this first seen film is the director's best. We criticize him if he continues to work in the same vein (he is repeating himself), and we criticize him if he changes (he is deceiving the expectations he originally aroused). Jancsó has indeed come in for criticism on the first score (not entirely without foundation, it must be said), with the result that it has become difficult to look clearly and freshly at *The Round-Up* itself. But even returned to in the light of Jancsó's later work, *The Round-Up* holds up very well in its own unadornment, its inexorable concentration on the logic of betrayal, subordinating all merely picturesque elaborations to the basic telling of the story.

The story itself is at once simple and hauntingly strange, taking on a curious ritual quality as the pieces fall into place through a series of ruses and cat-and-mouse games. The action takes place in a fort in the middle of the Hungarian plains, where a lot of peasants are shut up under the surveillance of the soldiery after the Kossuth rebellion of 1848. Among them are a number of Kossuth supporters, and perhaps even Sándor, the chief of the pro-Kossuth rebels. The imprisoning forces need to identify the hidden rebels, and they set about their plan by guile and indirection. In the first stage, an old woman reports the men she has reason to suppose murdered her husband and son. One of the men thus arrested confesses to five murders, and from then on the pattern of progressive betrayal is set in motion. He is promised his life if he will name one person even more guilty than himself. On these terms he becomes an informer. When the other peasants find out about this, his life is in danger, and for his own safety he is shut up by the police in a prison cell. The next morning he is found there strangled. Suspicion falls on the occupants of two other cells, which were left unlocked, a father and son. Both deny everything, but are eventually persuaded, in order to save themselves, to denounce the actual murderer, for whom they had unlocked the door during the night. All three are then put in irons. Meanwhile, the search for Sándor, the rebel leader, goes on, though in fact he is not in the compound. At last another stratagem is hit upon. An amnesty is announced for all the ex-rebels if they join the imperial army. The peasants enroll, and then in front of the assembled troops the colonel reads a decree announcing that Sándor can now come out of hiding, as he too has been granted amnesty. The ex-rebels burst spontaneously into a triumphant song in praise of their leader before the colonel continues reading the decree, which goes on: ". . . while all his followers will be put to death." At which they are all shot down—the round-up is complete.

All this is realized in a rather simple-seeming style—the film is shot in uncompromising blacks and whites, set against the unvarying gray of the great grass plain stretching away as far as the eye can see. Every shot is meticulously composed to convey the maximum by the minimum, to keep us almost as unnerved and on edge by the constant shifting of power in the stages of psychological warfare as those directly involved. In *The Round-Up,* compared with Jancsó's subsequent films, there is surprisingly little spectacular camera movement—as a rule the camera moves very short distances, with a very precise purpose, concentrating closely on the people as individuals and elucidating their relationship with one another within the overall power structure. The film is tight and rigorous, that is to say, as much in its visual style as in its plotting—everything in it is concentrated absolutely on its analysis of the politics of terror and the Kafkaesque machinery with which it works. Indeed, on the strength of *The Round-Up* one would think Jancsó the ideal director to film Kafka—an impression rapidly belied by his later, more extravagantly expansive work.

It was difficult to come to any but the most provisional conclusions about the development of his talents from his next film, *Csillagosok, Katonák* (*The Red and the White*) (1967). For one thing, the rather special circumstances of its making must have had much to do with its shaping, though not, maybe, as much as might have been suspected at the time. It seemed, and seems, likely that when Jancsó was given the chance to make a film in Russia in celebration of the fiftieth anniversary of the October Revolution, the very idea was irresistible: a gamble to see whether, in these unlikely circumstances, he could manage to play his own game, keep his own counsel, and make his own film. In the event, he did and he didn't. Certainly *The Red and the White* is just about the most unlikely film one could imagine in celebration of anything, being black, ambiguous, anti-heroic, anti-human, anti just about everything. On the other hand, the film is finally not very good: it has very much the air of being made because the chance to make a film was there, rather than because the director had anything he urgently wanted to say or do in it.

Technically, of course, it is remarkable: a Jancsó film could hardly be otherwise. In it he develops a long way further his interest in very long takes, with the camera moving backward and forward, up and down, for minutes at a time without interruption—much more so than in *The Round-Up,* where the camera movements were mostly tight and close, in keeping with the sense of imprisonment required, and hardly ever drew attention to themselves. And undeniably the results are often extraordinary and spectacular. The final suicidal attack of the wandering Hungarians and their allies, lost in the chaos of Revolutionary Russia, for instance, is quite unforgettable. But it is equally true that the camera procedures are often tiresomely arbitrary, and one is often left with the feeling that the camera's movements were decided first and then the action staged to fit, rather than the other way around—which, in fact, Jancsó admits to be the case: he would first map out some very complicated maneuver for the camera, and then arrange the action in relation to it, with people moving in and out of frame, actions being picked up and dropped from view with a casualness which mirrors sometimes all too well the confusion felt by the people within the film itself.

Also, the film's script, if compared with *My Way Home* and *The Round-Up,* is curiously thin in terms of human interest; there is some characterization running through the various episodes of violence and sudden death, but too little to let us feel anything more than a mild, impersonal interest in the mostly unpleasant fates of the characters. The film is divided into a series of episodes, in the course of which are made fully explicit for the first time nearly all the themes and images which from now on are to become obsessive and inescapable in Jancsó's work. The action of the film takes place in 1918, in the confused aftermath of the Russian Revolution, when most of Russia is in a state of civil war. We follow the fate of a group of Hungarian volunteers fighting with the Reds. In the first episode the Whites are in control, and the Reds are rounded up. Many of them escape in the general confusion and rally again in a monastery, under the command of a Hungarian, and promptly (for such is the way of Jancsó's world) start preparing to execute the prisoners they have taken, after first stripping them of their shirts and boots. But suddenly there is another reversal: the Whites surround the monastery and capture the Reds, the Red commander throwing himself from the belfry rather than surrender himself to their tender mercies. The Whites let the Hungarians go, however, telling them to go home and cease meddling in what does not concern them. For the Russian Reds, an elaborate game is played. They are made to remove their shirts and boots, then given fifteen minutes to escape, if they can, before they are hunted and shot down by the surrounding Whites. The sadistic game playing, the pattern of humiliation and counter-humiliation, the endless balancing and rebalancing within the power structure, with no one group seeming morally or humanly preferable to any other, are all going to recur over and over again in Jancsó's films, to the extent that what seemed in *The Round-Up* to be responses to a given, very special situation are now seen to be something like a collection of personal obsessions in embryonic form, now fully grown and openly exposed.

After the Hungarians scatter there are some minor incidents making up the middle of the film, all following much the same pattern of tit for tat, game against game—whoever is on top at any given point finds himself almost instantly overwhelmed, every killer rapidly finds himself killed, everybody dies. The second major episode of the film takes place in and around a military hospital. The area is controlled by the Whites, but the matron takes in the Hungarian Reds and hides them among the wounded. Reds and nurses are united in a silent resistance to the Whites, while the White commander is aware that there are Reds among the hospital's patients and is determined to find them. Down at the river there is a lot of stripping, male and female (another recurring motif in Jancsó's work), and some curious charades take place in the forest, with nurses dressed in pre-Revolutionary clothes acting out a delicate pastoral to distract the White commander. Eventually the Hungarians are betrayed when one of them, the lover of a Polish nurse, is stabbed to death and she thus no longer has any reason to remain silent. A massacre of the Reds is initiated, but before it can get very far a group of Reds surrounds the hospital. The White commander and the Polish nurse are both killed, but the Red commander is content with a mock execution of the Whites, lining them up, stripping them as though for execution, then having a volley shot in the air behind their backs. Then the Reds, armed and jacketless, like those about to be executed, start singing the "Marseillaise" and set out to break through the enemy lines. But it is hopeless, they are completely surrounded and all are shot down: when the next wave of Red victors arrives on the scene, all that remains of them is their guns sticking out of the ground where they died.

Visually the film has some extraordinary moments—most of all, perhaps, the final scenes of confrontation between the thin line of jacketless Reds and the unbreakable ranks of the uniformed Whites drawn up across the bare hillside. But the general impression conveyed by the film is curiously off-center. Though everything in it can be explained in terms of a despairing view of the human condition, in practice it all comes across more like kinky games deriving from a strange private mythology. It has been said by various Hungarian critics that to understand Jancsó's films fully one must have a deeper knowledge of the Hungarian national character, the prevalence of cruel practical jokes, of pride, and of arbitrary, childish humiliations as an important weapon in the breaking of that pride. That, of course, is quite possible, but if it is true one cannot help asking why Jancsó alone should mirror these particular aspects, and with such intensity and persistence. I can think of only one other Hungarian film which comes anywhere near Jancsó in tone, subject matter, and style, András Kovács's *Cold Days,* which concerns a massacre in a similarly confused situation toward the end of the last war. But even that film shows vital differences: to an important extent it analyzes psychologically the events and the motives of the characters we encounter, whereas Jancsó willfully and consistently says nothing, keeps dialogue to a minimum, avoids comment, and just lets things happen, as in a sort of cinematic equivalent of Artaud's Theater of Cruelty.

If we nevertheless need explanations—and often we may feel we do—Jancsó can and will supply them. Many of his recurrent situations, like letting a prisoner loose simply so that he shall be shot in the back (the beginning of *The Round-Up* and of *Silence and Cry*) or in more general terms hunted down (*My Way Home, The Red and the White*), he explains quite realistically—everyone knows that that is the sort of thing which happens in wars. As to the constant stripping of men and women, well, the stripping of the men is very practical—you are not going to waste good clothes and boots when you kill a man—and part of the psychology of war—when does a man feel more vulnerable than when he is naked? The recurrent stripping of women he explains as signifying something different from film to film—defenselessness or (sometimes the best defense) a gesture of defiance, or in *The Round-Up* where a naked girl is at one point paraded in front of some soldiers drawn up in parade order, as a "psychic shock." This is all very well, except that the first thing which strikes one is the recurrence of the motif from film to film, and compared with that immediate consistency the possibility of slight differences of interpretation becomes a minor consideration. *The Red and the White* in particular contains a number of hints that Jancsó may be in danger of being trapped by his own language, imprisoned in his own private vision of a very small, very strange world. But if it was so, his next film, *Csend és Kiáltás* (*Silence and Cry*) (1968) triumphantly escaped from the trap by dramatizing it, by taking the cage in which Jancsó encloses his characters as the subject and the form of the film.

After setting his camera loose in the open spaces of Russia, in *Silence and Cry* Jancsó returns to a chamber drama, very localized, very concentrated, with only six characters who count. The camera moves as constantly as in *The Red and the White*—more constantly, in fact, and with more logical consistency. In the process Jancsó turns upside down one of the most rigidly maintained rules of classic film syntax—that a cut from shot to shot signifies no lapse of time (to show which one needs a dissolve or a fade). Of course, that rule has been broken over and over again by filmmakers of all sorts since the onset of the French New Wave, with its much publicized "jump cuts," which are now, if one sees a film like *A Bout de Souffle* again at this distance of time, absolutely unnoticeable, so habituated have we become to the change. But Jancsó in *Silence and Cry* is the only director I know of to have invented a new rule all his own: in this film each cut represents a lapse of time or change of locale; otherwise each scene is played out in its own time in one unbroken shot (which is somewhat different from Hitchcock's attempt to abolish editing altogether in *Rope*).

The subject of *Silence and Cry* recapitulates in microcosm nearly all Jancsó's themes and images. The story takes place on a lonely farmstead on the Hungarian plains in 1919, just after the first Communist revolution in Hungary. Again, as in all Jancsó's films, things are politically and socially in a state of flux, and in a situation where anyone might prove to be an informer against one or one's own private executioner, there is a great deal of mutual distrust. The remnants of the Red revolution have scattered and hidden, and one of them, István, has holed up on the farm. Not that it provides a very secure or comfortable refuge. It is dominated by two women, the farmer's wife and his sister-in-law. The farmer, a weak man, under interrogation himself, is forced to go through a series of arbitrary, childish humiliations every day, such as standing in his yard and singing, or standing in the field with his arms outstretched. He accepts—he can hardly do otherwise—the evident erotic interest of both women in the fugitive. He also tacitly accepts being slowly poisoned by his wife, who goes through the form of calling the poison "medicine." (This element of the film was apparently suggested by a real case in the 1930's in which the women of a village, under the influence of a mad midwife, indulged in mass murder of their menfolk.) The old mother of the house is also being poisoned, also, it seems, knowingly and acquiescently. The relations among these five characters are economically demonstrated in long scenes of action with very few words, occasionally broken by the visits of the local chief of police, who is protecting István because of their childhood friendship (they may even be brothers—the precise relationship is left unclear). But finally the situation at the farm is too much for István—he must report it to the police, even if he has to give himself up. This he does, and the police chief, no longer able to protect him, gives him a gun and the chance of suicide. But instead, István shoots him—a pointless gesture, perhaps, or the only gesture he can make.

In *Silence and Cry* Jancsó carries his familiar anti-psychological cinema to extremes. Everything is rigorously externalized in event, nothing is ever explained. It is left to us to work out the relationship between István and the police chief, István's situation in relation to the farmer's household, their relations with one another. No explanation is offered of why the farmer should accept his death at the hands of his womenfolk, nor the point and purpose of the ritual humiliations he goes through daily at the behest of the police chief. The political situation and the emotional climate are capsulated right at the beginning in the scene of game-playing execution—the shot in the back as the victim moves away toward the wide-open spaces of the Puszta and the appearance of freedom. Elsewhere in the film we get the impression of a community turned sickly in on itself, caught, police and suspects, hunters and hunted alike, in a savage yet curiously joyless (not even, properly speaking, sadistic) game of humiliation, of psychological destruction. Everything is just what it seems, no more and no less, and the mystery is as complete at the end of the film as at the beginning. *Silence and Cry* is one of Jancsó's masterpieces—perhaps even his best film of all—and totally unlike anything else in the cinema in its cold, myopic concentration on a situation in which the characters seem often reduced to robots, going unemotionally through the actions dictated to them by forces outside them, forces that they themselves hardly comprehend.

After this climax of tightness and precision, a level of intensity which could hardly be improved upon or even sustained, it was inevitable that Jancsó should show some signs of relaxation in his next film. And *Fényes Szelek* (*The Confrontation*) (1969) does in certain respects show such a relaxation, a loosening up, and the introduction of new elements along with the old familiar ones. Though the film is nominally set in 1947, and concerns conflicts in the educational system in the period immediately after the setting up of the Communist government in Hungary, it is obviously an immediate response to the student riots, sit-ins, and general unrest among young people in 1968–69, a celebration which at the same time expresses concern, a "confrontation" in which nothing is decisively resolved—very much as was the case with the series of other, similar confrontations which followed the May riots in Paris in 1968. It is evident that in many respects Jancsó's sympathies, and ours, are directed primarily toward the rebellious students. And yet throughout it is the police chief, a recent student himself and a representative of the people's police (who are, or should be, at one with the students), who represents the voice of sanity, reason (revolutionary reason, that is), and legality.

The film has very little plot. Briefly, it shows a group of students from one of the new people's colleges setting out to teach the staff and pupils of a surviving church school a lesson. In their way, they have a rather jolly encounter with some policemen, whom they throw into a reservoir and then sing and dance with. At the school they begin by trying debate, but find that the students are intimidated and will not answer their questions. They then try to make friends with the students through singing and dancing, but a prospective breakthrough is thwarted when the police arrest some church school pupils for subversive activities. The college students' leader is disillusioned at this, and tries to resign, but instead he is accused of bourgeois deviationism and dismissed; more radical elements take over. Now things start turning nasty—the students try to defrock the clerical staff of the school by force, and change the situation by violence rather than by argument. Before long they are seeking out reactionary books in the school library and piling them in the courtyard, as though to burn them, and answer physical resistance with vandalism, breaking and destroying. At this point their own governors from the people's college arrive to rebuke them and expel the ringleaders—leaving the students disturbed and disoriented, with little or nothing achieved.

Along the way we encounter a number of familiar Jancsó themes, images, and situations: power politics in the state of flux between the old and the new, persuasion versus violence, nudity, humiliation—plus something new, the expression of the tensions and releases of the situation, the shifts of power and attitude, in primarily musical terms. *The Confrontation* is constructed as something very like a revolutionary musical, constantly resolving itself into songs and dances from the repertoire of national folk culture and international revolutionary tradition. In accordance with this, the visual symbolism is often broad and bold—for his first film in color Jancsó cheerfully adopts very obvious, simple devices like the draping of a large crucifix with the red flag of Communism. Also, more disturbingly, the camera is never idle, but always on the move, dancing in intricate choreography among and around the students as they sing and dance, and dispute. There is nothing in the technique adopted which is not absolutely explicable and intellectually justifiable in terms of the subject. The only trouble is that Jancsó seems to have got so carried away with his own virtuosity that the technique has taken over from the subject to the point where one feels that a lot of the vertiginous gliding and craning and swooping is there for its own sake, reflecting perhaps the "celebration" element of this confrontation, the outburst of revolutionary high spirits, but becoming, in its sheer abstract elaboration, self-defeating.

By contrast, *Sirokkó* (*Winter Wind*) (1969), which Jancsó made immediately afterward, is something of a return to functional severity. Made as a Franco-Hungarian co-production, mainly in Yugoslavia, it applies the method of *Silence and Cry* with equal severity to a more externally action-full subject: the story of a Croatian anarchist leader in the 1930's who is eventually destroyed through corruption among those around him, and then, by a historical irony, turned posthumously into a hero, is unrolled in only twelve shots, as against *Silence and Cry*'s sixteen (after an initial photomontage). Again, the film is in color, as are all Jancsó's films subsequent to *The Con-*

frontation, and it glitters in a harsh, cold winter light, a landscape full of violence and foreboding which mirrors the internal problems of the characters with unrelenting sharpness and vividness. Is Jancsó in fact one of the supreme masters of the pathetic fallacy? It is tempting to suppose so, since the landscapes and weather in his films are always so expressive, or seem so, but then we must find ourselves asking whether in letting our understanding of what is going on in the films take color from such elements we are ourselves guilty of the pathetic fallacy in much the same sense as we would be in desiring similar intelligence from nature itself. In other words, is it Jancsó or we who find implications or connections where none essentially exists? A nice question, and one resistant to simple categorical answers. Suffice it to say that everything, visually, aurally, that we can appreciate as objective externals in Jancsó's films seems to be inseparably a part of the world as he sees it, a physical expression or extension of his own private world, a mental construct. From this hermetic, enclosed quality derive most of Jancsó's strengths as a filmmaker—and, necessarily, most of his weaknesses too.

I am myself inclined to see most of the weaknesses and fewest of the strengths in *Égi Bárány* (*Agnus Dei*) (1970), a film which apparently Jancsó himself holds particularly dear, and which many Hungarians regard as the most Hungarian of his films. In many respects it seems like the mixture as before, only more so—a period of civil war on the great plains, with warring factions endlessly alternating, the camera roaming constantly without seeming rhyme or reason as horsemen circle and curvet, drifting in and out of shot. Blood is spilled, people are stripped or strip themselves, are debased and humiliated and sometimes rise again, while for good measure a raving fanatic priest with epileptic tendencies foams, strips, and plunges into a pond every ten minutes or so. The only element of the film which can be appreciated as more than self-repetition is the move in its last third away from a broadly realistic narrative style toward a more free-associating, at times almost surrealistic succession of images without realistic justification or explanation.

At least in the earlier part of the film, right from its almost self-parodying opening, with a naked girl leading a horse out of the water and dressing in a uniform of the Red forces, we know more or less where we are, even if it is hard in this instance to care very much. There are shifts of power as first the Reds and then the Horthy forces (it is 1919, at the end of the short-lived Communist Republic of Councils, about the same period as *Silence and Cry*) take over the scene of the action, the Red officer kills himself, the Horthy-supporting epileptic priest and the priest with the red rosette on his cassock change places, and smoking torches are carried on and off screen in an intricate, hypnotic pattern. But with the mysterious transfer of the epilepsy from the priest to the young Horthy officer (Daniel Olbrychski) the film moves on to a different plane—first the victory of the reactionary forces is celebrated with dance and religious ritual, then the officer leads his people out of history and into myth, a gloomy wasteland of death and destruction where his violin (a deliberate reference to the Pied Piper of Hamelin?) seems all the more sinisterly out of place. It is a weird and impressive transition, as though Jancsó himself is conscious of leaving behind the overfamiliar ground of his earlier films and leading us uncomprehending into the new, overtly symbolic realm of *Red Psalm* and *The Technique and the Rite.*

After *Agnus Dei* Jancsó made a film in Italy, *La Pacifista* (*The Pacifist*) (1970), which seems to represent an interlude in his work, a primarily urban story with many seeming bows in the direction of Antonioni (quite apart from the utilization of Antonioni's once favorite star, Monica Vitti). Monica Vitti plays the pacifist of the title, a worried television reporter in a city full of hostile, not altogether explicable pressures. Jancsó has acknowledged the influence of Antonioni in his earlier work, and here much of the way the film is directed seems suggestive of the final sequence of *L'Eclisse,* in which the characters have given place to the city of objects, impassive and vaguely menacing. It is also, obviously, no coincidence that the cameraman is Antonioni's Carlo di Palma, and many of the compositions and color effects seem to derive from *The Red Desert.* At the same time there are equally striking cross-references to other Jancsó films, not least in the importation of Daniel Olbrychski from *Agnus Dei* to play another epileptic fanatic. There is also Pierre Clementi as a young intruder who dies as part of a mysterious, ritual, suicidal progression similar to that by which so many of Jancsó's Hungarian characters die out there on the plains. The wide, sweeping, wheeling movements of camera and men on the plains are replaced by closer, tighter movements, circumscribed by the cold stone of the city streets, where students rush around chanting slogans (rather less sympathetically observed than in *The Confrontation*) and violent reactionaries plot and act under the impassive gaze of the uninvolved police. Finally the heroine, left to her own devices, her back to the wall, face to face with the students at her gate, ceases to be a pacifist, and takes up a gun. A positive gesture, or a grimly pessimistic conclusion? "My liberty is that of others," says a last title, and interpretation is left to us.

And so to a period of self-renewal, with two of his most remarkable films, which in their different ways take up the researches of the final reels of *Agnus Dei*. The first, also made in Italy, for the RAI television chain, is his least realistic film yet. *La Tècnica ed il Rito* (*The Technique and the Rite*) (1971) professes to outline the early career of Attila, but if it does so at all it is in a fashion far from direct or historical. Rather, we are in the primitive world of the folk ballad and ritual. After the opening sequence, in which the adolescent Attila, an envoy in Ravenna, then the capital of the Western Roman Empire, exacts submission from the other young men of his tribe, all the action takes place in symbolic, quasi-balletic style on the cliffs and rocks of a bare seashore. It is, as we might expect at this stage in our acquaintance with Jancsó and his world, a series of games and tests, token trials of strength and jockeying for position. Like a sort of pagan Christ preoccupied with the mechanics of power, Attila lives in the wilderness with a small group of young male disciples, showing them (rather than telling them) his rules for the conduct of life. The atmosphere is lyrical, fantastic, miraculous—there is a lot of violence, but most of it is mythological and those who die often return mysteriously to life to continue the games. Historical episodes, such as Attila's murder of his brother

Bleda on his ascent to power, are also shown refracted in the same distorting glass, and the film ends with Attila's own symbolic death and the funeral rites performed by his followers, from which he rises to enter the great world of history.

In *The Technique and the Rite,* Jancsó extends his consideration of tyranny and oppression by dealing with it totally in the abstract, in the form of an obviously nonrealistic symbolic drama. Attila is presented as an embodiment of the naked will to power; his road to it takes in all the kinds of terrorization, logical and illogical, brute force and refined psychological subtlety, direct and indirect, which must be used to achieve it. It is all done within the form of a sort of folk tale told in song and dance and mime and words—the words, as usual with Jancsó, coming at the end of the list. The action is not localized in time or place with any noticeable attempt at historical accuracy: rather, as in Pasolini's tangles with myth in *Edipo Re* and *Medea,* a synthetic image of primitive life is presented, using elements of many periods and cultures. Technically, the film differs from Jancsó's earlier films only in its increased concentration on close-ups (perhaps because the film would have a televised showing?). But even in close-up Jancsó's camera is intensely mobile, following characters around and around as they move and change and act out complicated emotions and responses. The film is very curious, closed in on itself, even more secretive about its methods and intentions than *Silence and Cry.* The earlier film approaches a kind of ritual cinema under the guise of realism; this time the ritual is presented directly to us, unexplained, for us to work out to our own satisfaction or, better, just to experience and understand, insofar as we do understand it, through our instincts rather than our intellects.

Much the same is true of *Még Kér a Nép* (*Red Psalm*) (1972). Disturbingly, it comes across at first glance like a combination of two of Jancsó's less successful films, *The Confrontation* and *Agnus Dei.* Again, as in *Agnus Dei,* it is the plains, the rebellious peasants, conflicting factions, constant changes of power and allegiance, horses, humiliation, nudity; as in *The Confrontation,* revolution is a joyful outburst of song and dance, the image of a mass movement going through a cycle of destruction and resurrection in festivity and acceptance. And yet the film, which sounds as though it should be another case of self-repetition almost to the extent of self-parody in Jancsó's work, comes off extraordinarily well. Again it is the spreading plain of the Puszta, again a vaguely defined period of internal unrest (most of Hungary's history, as seen by Jancsó, seems to consist of vaguely defined periods of internal unrest), a time of agrarian rebellion toward the end of the last century. A group of agricultural workers, having made demands for new rights to be accorded them by the landowners, await a reply, and while they wait they sing and dance.

The bailiff of the estate tries to buy them off with a feast and a promise of grain, while the police circle watchfully. When the bribe fails, the grain is set on fire and the bailiff is promptly burned on it by the workers. In consequence the army arrives, but the climate of the action is miraculous. A young cadet is ordered to fire first, and when he hesitates is shot himself. But he is resurrected by a kiss from a wounded girl, while the wound in her palm turns into a flower. In a series of encounters the peasants try to enlist the soldiers as their friends; the count arrives to give the workers a big-brother talk about common national interests, and meets a sudden death; the clergy try to bring the peasants around with all the paraphernalia of organized religion, and have their church burned down for their pains. As the drama moves to its climax the threats become more menacing. Some peasants surrender, but most are confirmed in their resolve, and the meeting turns into a spring festival, with singing and dancing around a maypole, revolutionary songs in the midst of a fertility rite. Soldiers join in for a while, but then are summoned back to their duty, surround the peasants, and shoot them all down. All except one, a girl who remains outside the circle, gun in hand. Faced by her presence the soldiers fall, one by one, and her gun, tied with red ribbon, is lifted high, in a gesture of victory and joy even amid apparent defeat.

The action of the film is not much different in its constituents from that of most other Jancsó films—all his usual motifs come into play, the scene and the political background are the same. And yet in *Red Psalm* Jancsó seems to have achieved a new maturity in his expression of his vision, or perhaps a new conviction. Where in films like *The Confrontation* and *Agnus Dei* his work was hardening into mannerism, the films were more about the technique than the rite, *Red Psalm* is the confirmation of Jancsó's continuing ability to find new creative excitement in old materials: it builds from the concluding sections of *Agnus Dei* and from *The Technique and the Rite* in its unashamed and direct use of symbolic action with no consistent attempt to justify and explain everything in realistic terms. Though the theater of the action on the Hungarian plain is the same, this time we are left in no doubt that it is the setting for a symbolic action, that the precise time and place indicated are merely forms. The localized symbolism is sometimes obvious to the point of naïveté—the gun tied with red, the wound-flower, the revolutionary maidens, naked to the waist, with white doves, the stream running red with blood, death and resurrection. What counts here—what has always counted in Jancsó films for that matter, though often less obviously and effectively—is the total gesture of the work, the celebration of life and vigor, the revolution which will come in joy, with singing and dancing.

The atmosphere is more cheery than in most of Jancsó's other films (even though, as usual, practically everybody dies) —this time he has chosen to examine the mechanics of revolutionary success, or at least the continuance of revolutionary fervor, rather than the mechanics of defeat and oppression. The story is virtually nonexistent, but such as there is, Jancsó points out, is written in a perfectly traditional way. It would in theory be possible to make a perfectly traditional, realistic film out of it. Instead it is broad and simple, difficult to approach only if one tries to appreciate it through the intellect, easy if it is allowed to work on one through the instincts and emotions. It is as though a lot which has been implicit in Jancsó's work since *My Way Home* has become explicit. Curiously enough, Jancsó says he was unusually tense during the shooting of *Red Psalm,* yet the film comes across as one of his most relaxed, one in which he has just let the internal emotional logic of the film carry him along. It is strange, and encouraging, that the progress of the intellectual Jancsó, student of film and of politics, has been toward ever greater flexibility, ever more complete trust in the film as a medium to stand on its own, without need of explanation or paraphrase in any other form. The logic of *The Round-Up* is shattering. But the emotion of *Red Psalm* is like a rising tide, as unstoppable and as irresistible.

Dušan Makavejev

Perhaps all artists in one sense or another keep repeating the same work over and over again in different guises. It is just that some are more obvious about it—and maybe more conscious of what they are doing—than others. Miklós Jancsó is a very obvious, and very aware, example of this; another is Dušan Makavejev, the most interesting and individual of the new wave of Yugoslav filmmakers who emerged in the middle 1960's. At the time of writing he has made five feature films, all of them put together in much the same way, using the same techniques and mirroring in their subject matter the same preoccupations. Of course, this is very much what one would expect in a filmmaker who writes and directs his own original subjects; but Makavejev goes further, to the extent that one can see each of his films as a sort of sketch for the one that comes next, or as part of a continuing research in an unceasing process of definition and redefinition of the director's ideas, particularly on the subjects of Communism and sex.

Given that these are Makavejev's twin preoccupations in his films, it might seem inevitable—in retrospect, at any rate—that he should come sooner or later upon the subject of Wilhelm Reich and his theories, which closely link the two. So *WR: Misterije Organizma* (*WR: Mysteries of the Organism*) (1971), Makavejev's fourth feature, stands as the climax and summary of his work so far, as well as showing his characteristic techniques in their fullest flower. Reich, who managed to get expelled from both Communist Russia and Nazi Germany and died in prison in America, was originally a close associate of Freud and a Marxist who saw full sexual enjoyment as the true point and expression of Communism and, later in America, announced that cancer, among other ailments, could be cured by concentrating, conserving sexual energies in his orgone box.

The film begins, seemingly, as a documentary shot in America: we visit the sites, talk to relatives and disciples of Reich (not to mention his grocer and barber), and get some notion of what he stood for. Then, little by little, fictional scenes are inserted, telling an illustrative tale of a girl, back in Yugoslavia, who preaches Reich's theories and endeavors to carry out in her everyday life those that relate to Communism. The result of this bizarre combination of ideas is riotously funny and at the same time strangely disturbing. The film can be read in at least half a dozen ways: as a political satire (Makavejev's manipulation of film documents, particularly Chinese newsreels and unbelievable extracts from an old Russian fiction film deifying Stalin, is absolutely brilliant), an essay in applied sexology, a subjective autobiography, a Pop Art collage, a story, a documentary, and so on. But whichever way you look at it at any particular moment it imposes itself absolutely, ordering its heterogeneous materials with complete conviction and all the conscious virtuosity of a juggler keeping a twenty-four-piece dinner service flying through the air while he paints a nude with a brush held between his teeth and picks out "The Red Flag" on a piano with his toes.

To give a clearer idea of how Makavejev's films work, the characteristic collage form which originates in his second feature, *Switchboard Operator,* it may be useful to go in more detail into the way *WR* is put together. The constituent parts of the film were gradually assembled from a number of sources, according to Makavejev's progressively modified conception of the whole. The beginning was a straight documentary about Reich, involving the interviews with his relatives, friends, and followers in the United States, Britain, and elsewhere in Europe (the shooting in Europe proving relatively unproductive) and photography of some of the important places in Reich's life. In the course of this research Makavejev acquired various film materials connected with Reich, such as newsreels of him, an early Sexpol film showing lovemaking in a meadow. In connection with this phase of the shooting Makavejev also did some filmed researches in the United States on the development of the sexual revolution advocated by Reich and came thus to shoot material with the poet Tuli Kupferberg and the transvestite Jackie Curtis, and also some material in the office of *Screw* magazine, including a sequence showing one of the editors of *Screw* having his penis molded in plastic, which, to begin with, he had no particular notion of incorporating in the film as he then conceived it.

At the end of this stage, he had enough film for a documentary of ninety minutes or so. But as he began editing the material he came increasingly to feel dissatisfied with it. For one thing, it was exclusively preoccupied with Reich's sexual theories and ignored altogether the sides of Reich represented by his book *The Mass Psychology of Fascism,* in which he traced the causes of Fascism, of both the Right and the Left, to distortions and frustrations of the sexual instincts. Makavejev did not see how to incorporate this in a directly documentary way, so he conceived the idea of a fictional story which would be intercut with the documentary material in some way not at first apparent to him.

This second stage of shooting took place in Yugoslavia. The action is a deliberate play of stereotypes. Each of the four principal characters represents something beyond himself or herself. Milena is the sexual liberationist who preaches Reich's theories and tries to put them into practice. Her roommate, Jagoda, is not so much a liberationist as an already completely, joyously liberated woman. Radmilović, the worker who pursues Milena constantly and without success, is the proletarian natural man. And the Russian ice skater Milena puts the Reichian make on is called Vladimir Ilyich (Lenin's given names) to signify that he represents Lenin as deformed by Stalin. From these constituents the action develops in a broadly nonrealistic fashion, toward the perfectly logical conclusion in which, shattered by the sexual revelation Milena has brought him as her revolutionary message, Vladimir Ilyich kills her and severs her head with one of his skates. With that story shot, Makavejev realized that one more element was needed to reinforce the ironic comment of the fictional story, which he found in the shape of color newsreels of Chinese Communist festivities, a horror documentary about patients in a mental hospital, and a Russian fiction film deifying Stalin, Chiaureli's *The Vow* (1947).

Thus at the start of the final editing of the film Makavejev had in hand material of eight different kinds:

1. Documentary about Reich specially shot
2. Old film footage made by or concerning Reich
3. Marginally connected documentary material commenting on the progress of the sexual revolution
4. Quite unrelated documentary material not intended for the film (the penis-molding episode)
5. The fictional story
6. Chinese newsreels
7. Mental-hospital film
8. Stalinist fiction film

The essence of the finished film, of course, is to be found in the precise way he put this material together—creative editing carrying out what Eisenstein wanted to do with his theory of dialectical montage, through which two and two, if combined in the right way, might not make four but five or six or eight. What Eisenstein *wanted* to do, Makavejev emphasizes, rather than what he did do, which tends in Makavejev's view to suffer from an undue stiffness and coldness, lacking real dynamism and a saving grace of humor. To see just how this is done in *WR* we must look in more detail at the film itself.

The film opens with Tuli Kupferberg, wearing a Castro-type beard, dressing in orange overalls and a Marine helmet, and then, carrying a replica of a Vietnamese rifle, walking down a New York street, to the varying reactions of passers-by, while on the soundtrack he intones one of his revolutionary poems. From this we cut to an egg out of its shell being passed from hand to hand (the hands being those of Milena, Jagoda, and Ljuba, Jagoda's boy friend), until the yolk breaks; this is the background to the credits. Then the theme of Reich is directly approached, by way of a brief statement in Milena's voice (her voice, as commentator, is one of the film's unifying factors) while on screen we see a film made in the early 1920's of Reich sitting with his first wife in a meadow, intercut with a film of young lovers having sex in a similar meadow, tinted and curiously refracted in a six-sided prism. During this sequence statements about Reich's theories alternate on the soundtrack with a Yugoslav folk song in praise of Communism.

It ends with a photograph of Reich holding a baby (Peter Reich, who appears later in the film) and from this we go into the first sequence, in which we are told some more about Reich, see an orgone box (about the size of a telephone booth, with wood on the outside and metal on the inside) in action, and hear some tales about Reich from surviving followers and relatives. Subsequent sequences show us the prison where Reich died, the garbage incinerator where his books were burned, then something of the township of Rangeley, Maine, where he spent his last years and founded the Orgone Research Center. Townspeople recall Reich, his widow speaks of the failure of the American dream, we are given various glimpses of Reich and his associates in old newsreels, and are shown what the Orgonon, his home-*cum*-laboratory, looks like today as a Reich museum.

At this point the pace quickens. In rapid succession we catch glimpses of various Reichian medical procedures currently in use—bioenergetic therapy, vegetotherapy, some sort of breathing exercises, the primal scream—with, in the middle, the first hint of material illustrative of the present-day sexual revolution as envisaged and encouraged by Reich—a woman painter describing how she decided to paint a series of pictures of men and women masturbating, and how each, after initial hesitation, found it a releasing experience to masturbate for her in her studio (therapeutic, by implication, in much the same way as a number of the neo-Reichian tension-releasing techniques). This sequence of shots ends with a further view of Tuli, armed and equipped, walking down Madison Avenue.

From here a transition is effected to the fictional story of Milena, her actions and her ideas. The link is made by beginning with her breaking four eggs (referring back to the background of the credits) and using the same title, "Filme der Sexpol," as was used to introduce the prismatic sex film, only now with the date "Belgrade, May 1, 1971," replacing "Berlin, May 1, 1931." The first scene is a nighttime argument between Milena and her drunken ex-lover Radmilović, who is bent on making a scene. Then, after a brief cut-in encounter with transvestite Jackie Curtis walking around New York and describing a proposal of marriage she once received, we continue with the story in Belgrade. Milena's roommate, Jagoda, is having sex with her soldier boy friend, Ljuba, continuously and obsessively, all over their apartment. Another cut to Betty Dodson, the masturbation painter, talking about masturbation and consciousness raising, and the sad position of women who are totally dependent on men for their orgasms, then back to Jagoda and Ljuba, and Milena in an orgone box.

This gradually leads, through the complaints of a neighbor and the railings of Radmilović outside, into a scene in which Milena harangues an impromptu rally with Reich's early views on the necessity of free love to prevent Fascism, which arises from the diversion and perversion of sexual impulses. At the climax of the scene, with tenants dancing around the balconies of the apartment block in a great chain, we cut to a Chinese newsreel of thousands upon thousands in Peking, a pulsating mass, all waving the Little Red Book of the thoughts of Chairman Mao. This seems like a clear emotional and visual development of what has gone before, but instantly Makavejev cuts away to a cold, formal black-and-white scene (from *The Vow*) in which Stalin, like an animated wax effigy, delivers reverential statements about the legacy of Lenin to a worshipping, frozen audience. And intercut with this, also in black-and-white, some record material of treatment (forced feeding, electroshock) in what appears to be a nightmarishly antiquated mental hospital.

From the electroshock treatment it is a natural-seeming transition back to a scene of orgasmic-release exercises at the Bioenergetic Workshop in New York, and some explanation of unconscious body language. Then back to Belgrade and the fictional story, with Milena, Jagoda, Ljuba, and another soldier watching a pompous Soviet ice ballet. Milena picks out the principal male skater for her special attentions and invites him home. In the apartment they discuss, very theoretically, Communism and sexual freedom, while Jagoda unconcernedly strips as she serves tea and crackers and the unstoppable Radmilović breaks through the wall from the next apartment and shuts the skater in a wardrobe. In the course of this sequence there are a number of inserts—Tuli singing "Kill for Peace" on the streets of New York, Jackie Curtis walking, a couple of shots of American therapy patients screaming, juddering, and regressing—while in the main body of the scene there are several references to graphic material on the walls of Milena's apartment: a photograph of Reich, another of Hitler surrounded by worshipping women, a Russian poster of the 1920's inscribed "Lenin, leader of the International Proletariat," another poster picturing Manhattan and inscribed "Fly to USA."

Suddenly the scene is interrupted (after the shutting up of Vladimir in the wardrobe) by a rapid series of scenes in America—Tuli singing a racist song outside a black bookshop, Al Goldstein talking about *Screw* magazine, which he co-edits, Jackie Curtis describing part of her sexual awakening. These lead to the sequence in which Jim Buckley, the other editor of *Screw,* sits (lies, stands?) for the sculptress Nancy Godfrey while she takes a mold of his erect penis. Into this scene are cut a couple of shots of Milena delivering political rallying cries and one of Jackie Curtis praying before a tinselly altar set up to the Virgin Mary in the corner of her apartment. The sequence rises to a climax as Vladimir is let out of the wardrobe, Stalin is seen from afar by members of the devoted proletariat in *The Vow,* Nancy breaks open the mold to reveal a red plastic cast of Jim Buckley's penis, Stalin (*The Vow,* tinted red) announces: "Comrades, we have successfully completed the first stage of Communism," one of the patients in the mental-hospital footage bangs his head against a doorpost, and Tuli reaches an orgasmic climax masturbating his gun while Reich's futuristic-looking "cloud-buster" machines point mysteriously at the skies.

The stage is set for the consummation of the drama. Milena and Vladimir walk romantically on a snow-clad riverbank while he rapturously describes (in words borrowed from Lenin) the effect that music has on him. Milena meanwhile, rather practically, gropes for his genitals, he hits her, and we cut to more of *The Vow,* with Stalin speaking inspirationally in front of a vast fluttering-flag portrait of Lenin, followed by a mental patient crawling down some stairs on all fours. The Milena/Vladimir sequence then continues with them still fighting and then making up tearfully with passionate kisses. At the very end, in the dark, we hear a scream and see Vladimir with blood on his hands. Next we see an office in the morgue, with Milena's bloody, detached head sitting in a white tray while a doctor and a police inspector discuss in dispassionate clinical terms the circumstances of the killing and the night of extravagant lovemaking which clearly preceded it. Milena's head begins to speak, telling us that Vladimir is "a genuine Red Fascist," and that the orgasmic revelation she brought him proved too much for him. Meanwhile, Vladimir wanders the riverbank, distraught, singing an invocation to God to remember him. At the very end we cut back to the morgue, where Milena's head is smiling contentedly, then dissolve to the last image of the film, the photograph of Reich smiling too.

Even from such a bald description it must be evident with what complexity the film works. Very little in it is directly stated—it is all a subtle, constantly changing pattern of relationships among the various materials brought into play, provoked and directed in the spectator's mind by the cool confidence and precision with which Makavejev combines them, what he chooses to juxtapose with what. Each shot, each scene, takes on color and significance from its context; in the broadest terms the two principal constituents, the Reich documentary and the fictional story, interfused as they are, throw light on each other, representing theory and practice, the static and the dynamic, thought and action. But beyond that the film is constantly aglitter with witty and bizarre juxtapositions implying startling, provocative, and often very funny equations.

The most famous of these is that which equates Stalin with the male sex principle: Jim Buckley's penis, but the penis immobilized, frozen in red plastic, as Stalin himself is tinted red in the next shot, and one of the mental patients seems to comment in despair on the situation by beating his head against a doorpost while Tuli sums it all up by masturbating his gun—the sex impulse transferred completely to the symbol of power through violence. But there are many other occasions in which this cinematic collage works to the same sort of effect, as in the extension of Milena's sex rally to the limitless millions of China or the close relationship between Stalin speaking and forced feeding or the equally close visual comparison between electroshock treatment and voluntary therapy in a Reichian clinic. In Makavejev's work each shot does truly stand by itself, for itself, and yet at the same time, combined with other shots with which at first glance it may seem totally unrelated, can explode into new significance—two and two can unmistakably make five.

Of course, a film of the complexity, sophistication, and technical mastery of *WR: Mysteries of the Organism* did not spring straight from its creator's head without preparation. Makavejev, who was born in Belgrade in 1932, took a diploma in psychology and studied direction in the Academy for Theater, Radio, Film, and Television in Belgrade. He made his first 16-mm. short in 1953, and made three more before he began to work professionally in the cinema in 1958, for Zagreb Films. From then until 1964 he made thirteen documentaries for them. In 1966 he made his first feature film, *Čovek Nije Tica* (*Man Is Not a Bird*), followed immediately by the very similar *Ljubavni Slučaj* (*Switchboard Operator*) in 1967 and his first full-fledged collage film, *Nevinost Bez Zaštite* (*Innocence Unprotected*) in 1968. The next three years were taken up with shooting and editing *WR*. Since then Makavejev has toured extensively and lectured at many universities, and with many incidental difficulties of all kinds has made his first entirely non-Yugoslav film, *Sweet Movie*, a Canadian-French co-production shot in Canada, France, and Holland.

In all this Makavejev's progress has been closely linked to the social and political ferment going on in Yugoslavia today. Yugoslavia, curiously poised between East and West, a Communist society separated from the Russian bloc and allied in various ways with the Western capitalist states, has been constrained for years to tread a tightrope in its cultural products. In certain matters comment is very free—Yugoslavia was, for example, in the forefront of the sexual revolution insofar as it concerned the cinema, with total nudity and very explicit sexual scenes a regular feature of Yugoslav films (by Makavejev and others) some time before they became routine in the West. In other matters, though, particularly political, the situation is more precarious—the implied criticism of Stalinism in *WR* was found offensive by the Russians (rather oddly, unless they were thereby announcing the possibility of a wholesale revision of attitude toward Stalin), and Russian pressure, in the aftermath of the invasion of Czechoslovakia and with military maneuvers going on just over the border, secured the withdrawal of the film within Yugoslavia itself and helped to make professional life difficult for Makavejev.

This odd mixture of sexual freedom and political guardedness in the Yugoslav cinema has an important bearing on Makavejev's work from *Man Is Not a Bird* on. His central theme in *Man Is Not a Bird, Switchboard Operator,* and *WR* is the relationship between sex and politics; in *Innocence Unprotected* it becomes the relationship (or significant lack of a relationship) between private behavior and the working of broader historical forces. Operating within the Serbian cinema (the most important and sophisticated of the various linguistic groups in the various republics of the Yugoslav federation, but still a tiny potential audience by international standards), Makavejev has found himself working with very small resources in terms which his expected home audience might well find puzzlingly obscure. The international success of *Switchboard Operator* assisted his situation by opening a larger than merely local market to his films and helping to assure them the more sophisticated audiences they needed, and *WR* in particular is an obviously international film (partly financed by German television) which breaks out of the limiting context of the usual Yugoslav cinema.

Nevertheless, *WR* contains little that is not implicit already in *Man Is Not a Bird. Man Is Not a Bird* and *Switchboard Operator* are closely allied in subject and technique, so closely that the second could almost be a remake or rather a rethinking of the first. Both work in the characteristic Makavejev fashion, in short, disconnected scenes with some relatively abstract frame of comment. Both keep a lot of details about the characters and their situation from us, leaving it up to us to read as much as we want or need into what we are shown. *Man Is Not a Bird* clings more closely to a conventional narrative form, though—progressively through his films Makavejev has involved himself less and less with the exterior mechanics of storytelling, but *Man Is Not a Bird* comes nearest to telling a fully detailed story including all the ifs and perhapses and buts. The frame of reference this time is provided by the character of the stage hypnotist who appears at the beginning of the film without explanation but eventually appears later to do his theatrical act with some of the characters from the main story in attendance and is given the justification of the film's title in his final manipulation of his helpers from the audience, the hypnotized victims he persuades to see themselves as birds —in dreams man may be a bird, but in reality he is nothing but a man.

There are recurrent images throughout the film—the vast placard with a photograph of upraised hands which is carried through the factory (again eventually "explained" as part of the decor for a concert), the finale of Beethoven's Ninth Symphony, which eventually becomes the central feature of the factory concert and the background to the climactic action—which help to bind together the laconic statements of the story. This concerns two lovers, Raika, a young woman (played by Milena Dravič, Milena in *WR*), and Jan, the older factory worker with whom she lives. We never know precisely what his marital situation is, since he will not talk about it. We see him in the factory, we see vignettes of their lives, together and apart, and we observe the infidelity of Raika with a truck driver, which reaches its (physical) climax at the same time that Jan is attending the long-planned concert and Beethoven's "Ode to Joy" is working toward its triumphant conclusion.

The film is still sufficiently realistic to steer clear of melodrama—Jan does not kill Raika, though he would no doubt like to; at the end he is left alone, walking disconsolately across the mud flats where we have previously seen him with Raika. Is it a gesture of hope (the Choral Symphony recurs on the soundtrack at this moment) or of despair, or both? As usual, Makavejev does not comment, he leaves the reading of the situation to us. The film is, indeed, full of double meanings (it would be misleading to call them ambiguities, since everything is perfectly clear and precise, a concrete statement) or events quite objectively presented which can be read in many different senses.

The most obvious example of this is the big sequence near the end in which Raika's lovemaking with her truck driver in his truck is intercut with the prize-day preliminaries (during which Jan gets a medal for doing good work and makes a speech) and the performance of the finale from Beethoven's Ninth. The relationship between the two happenings can be seen as purely arbitrary and coincidental (though in that case we might well wonder why that piece of music specifically) or as instinct with all sorts of ironies. Is the music, in its context of socialist aspirations—prize day at the factory and all that—to be understood as an oblique comment on Raika and her private animal pleasure in sex? Possibly, but then again the synchronization of the music's climax with the point of orgasm leaves us free to understand also that these are both legitimate, worthwhile expressions of "joy"—perhaps the sex act constitutes a comment on the music as much as the reverse, the musical performance takes on the coloring of a communal sex experience, and as though to remind us of this possibility, as well as to amuse us with an instant joke, Makavejev cuts away (in a fashion frequently used in *WR*) from the lovers' orgasm to Jan and the concert audience bursting with applause, as though the one is a comment on and response to the other.

The elements which still seem a little diffuse and unfocused in *Man Is Not a Bird* are selected and sharpened in *Switchboard Operator* to produce a completely personal form of expression. The film is very short and concise, running a bare sixty-nine minutes (not that any of Makavejev's films can be called expansive), and much the same subject as that of *Man Is Not a Bird* turns up again, in an even more concentrated form, without the earlier film's subplot, outlined in a succession of brief, disconnected episodes. The central couple this time are a blonde switchboard operator and her lover, a husky, timid young rat catcher. In both films the affair concludes with an infidelity by the woman, carried further in *Switchboard Operator* in that it results in the death of the girl, not, as we at first suspect, murdered by her lover, but accidental, as she tries to prevent him from killing himself.

In *Man Is Not a Bird* the episodes are kept in an explicable chronological order, even if the connections between the episodes are often suppressed—even the preliminary appearance of the hypnotist is eventually tied in to the plot. In *Switchboard Operator,* on the other hand, the episodes are somewhat shuffled, so that, for instance, the first meeting of Isabela, the switchboard operator, with Ahmed, the rat catcher, is immediately followed by the (at the time) totally unexplained fishing of Isabela's body out of a manhole. From then on episodes of the investigation and a lecture by a criminologist about police methods of investigation in murder cases are shuffled in with other episodes showing Isabela's seduction of Ahmed and the development of their relationship. The very fact that the body is Isabela's remains obscure for a while, until a catalogue of the corpse's possessions, including a pendant, is juxtaposed with Isabela's search in her bed for the same pendant. There are in fact two elements of abstract framework reflecting on our understanding of the central situation though only peripherally if at all connected with it—the criminologist's lecture already mentioned, and another lecture, with which the film starts, delivered by a sexologist who discourses learnedly about the history of open sexual expression in other cultures and the comparative degree of concealment and hypocrisy prevalent in modern Western society.

Nevertheless, a significant structure can be distinguished, working upon us and coloring our understanding of the various episodes and their relation to the whole by a cunning manipulation of the film's syntax. Again, a brief summary of the episodes and how they fit together may be revealing. The film starts with a series of captions asking general questions about the future of man, most of them with some sort of faintly sexual connotation ("Will Future Man Preserve Certain Old Organs?"). This is followed by the sexologist's lecture, very cool and clinical, though obviously advocating greater freedom and the throwing off of mankind's present artificial and harmful constraints. The credits come next, interspersed with photographs of erotic works of art.

In the first sequence of the film proper we meet the two switchboard operators, Isabela and Rusa, at work in their drab office, and the telegraph boy, Mica, who will eventually precipitate the tragedy. From their reactions to his sexy chatter, in the office and on the way home, we divine that Isabela and Rusa stand in relation to each other rather as Jagoda and Milena do in *WR*—Rusa is not only open-minded about sex and readily responsive, but she clearly believes in practice before preaching; Isabela, though seemingly not upset by anything said or done, keeps her own counsel. A couple of brief sequences follow in which we see a poster of Mao and one of Lenin, the latter being unrolled in a city square, then advertising floats for soap powder and toothpaste moving slowly along a street where Isabela walks alone. From this we cut directly to a similar scene in which Rusa is walking with Isabela and they meet Ahmed, who gets into conversation with them crossing a road and takes them to a café for a drink while all around old buildings are being reduced to rubble in the midst of a redevelopment program.

It is at this point that the first significant break in what we assume to be chronological order appears. We cut to a girl's body being pulled out of a dark hole which connects with the sewer system. First a flare is dropped down the hole by a mysterious smiling boy, garlanded like a Greek god, and then as the body is drawn up, we hear on the soundtrack the beginning of a lecture on murder. From this sequence we go into the lecture itself, illustrated with various gruesome materials, which concludes that a perfect crime is rapidly becoming impossible owing to the ever greater degree of scientific perfection in police methods. At this point, still unaware of the body's identity or the relevance of the criminologist's lecture, we go back to Isabela and Ahmed, now shyly alone together in her room. She gives him brandy (which he is unused to), then makes some coffee and turns on the television set. This action leads to Isabela's seduction of Ahmed, overcoming his timidity and moral scruples, while on the television the theme of demolition is taken up again in a documentary of the Russian Revolution showing a demonstration against religion and the destruction of churches. At least, we assume this is on the television, though the two kinds of material, the acted scene and the newsreel, are directly intercut without any establishing shot showing the television set in action.

At the conclusion of the newsreel Ahmed and Isabela are in bed naked together, talking rather tenderly, until the soundtrack conversation is interrupted by a sound which, in the next shot, we identify as that of the elevator at the morgue carrying the girl's body; the sequence follows the various stages of the autopsy, which reveals among other things that she was three months pregnant, and ends with a listing of her effects, among them a pendant. At once we cut back to Isabela rummaging in the bedclothes for that same pendant, so now we know for sure that she is the dead girl. The scene develops into a particularly tender, charming picture of morning domesticity, with Isabela taking in the milk and feeding her cat while Ahmed wanders naked around the apartment.

Then comes another cut-away of a quite different kind—to a little documentary on rats and the sanitation service, "explained" by a shot of a group of rat catchers which includes Ahmed, but otherwise completely arbitrary-seeming in its introduction at this point. The tone of the commentary is one of self-congratulation at the fine work the sanitation department is doing in its ceaseless fight against rats, the enemy of health. Immediately afterward we get the opposite view, presented in a poem printed as a caption on screen, in which the poet Dušan Radovic identifies with the rat in his agony at being hunted and poisoned, thereby using the rat's situation as a parallel to the human condition. Back with Ahmed and Isabela, we see him taking her up to his apartment, a curious structure on the roof of a large, old, undefined building; this is followed by a fantasizing love scene, at the end of which Isabela claims that it is too cramped at his place. In the next sequence they both move into her apartment block. Here we have another brief nude scene for Isabela (the famous shot with the black cat resting by her buttocks), then another "documentary" interlude, the equivalent of the rat-catching sequence in relation to Ahmed, showing Isabela in her housewife role making a cranberry strudel to the accompaniment of the Triumphal March from *Aïda*.

Another complete cut-away follows: we see the sexologist again, this time in a snow-covered chicken coop, lecturing us about hens and eggs and the development of living beings from embryo. Then follow a series of six brief scenes reflective of the kind of "married" life Ahmed and Isabela enjoy together, with its mixture of tiresome work (Isabela hangs out the washing while Ahmed plays a record of a revolutionary song by Hans Eisler to words of Mayakovsky) and simple play (they eat a gooey dessert made of honey and nuts with their hands). Isabela sings Ahmed a seductive Hungarian folk song (she has been established as Hungarian rather than Yugoslav); Ahmed and a friend bring in a shower as a surprise for Isabela; Isabela takes a shower with Ahmed's aid; Isabela lies naked on the bed. Then the sexologist reappears, advocating complete freedom and lack of concealment in sexual matters; he tells us about a painting in which the parents make love in a kitchen while unconcerned children play naturally around them. The stage is being set for the final act of the drama now, which of course has already been prefigured in what we know or guess about Isabela's death. We see Isabela at the switchboard, talking rather discontentedly with Rusa; then, in another scene, Mica, the telegraph boy, selling his own sexual irresistibility to Isabela. A brief interlude at home with the visit of a mattress cleaner to Isabela's apartment. At the switchboard Mica continues to wear down her resistance, at home her life is seen as an increasingly tedious round of domesticities, and finally, in Ahmed's absence on business, she succumbs to Mica's attentions at the switchboard.

Another interlude shows us five naked tableaux of sexual situations—Adam and Eve, the Rape of the Sabines, Theseus and Ariadne, etc.—set on a revolving stage. Then we see Isabela working out her period times, Isabela and Ahmed visiting a doctor (with a voice-over from the first morgue sequence about the embryo in her womb) and Ahmed's puzzlement at Isabela's hostile reaction to the news of her pregnancy. The final showdown between them is omitted: we jump from this minor quarrel straight to Ahmed's drunken reaction to the big break-up, roaming the night streets while Isabela searches desperately for him. Inserted at this point is a still photograph of Ahmed and Isabela together, with a square being drawn decisively around Ahmed's head and a voice on the soundtrack stating that he is wanted for Isabela's murder. Back to the last night, we see Isabela, apparently contrite, catching up with Ahmed, his fighting her off, his ineffectual attempt at drowning himself in shallow water, then his more serious attempt at the pit-like entrance to the sewers, where Isabela's struggles to intervene end in her accidental fall and death. After a brief insert of a street parade the police move in to look for Ahmed at his old apartment, then find him drunkenly asleep in a flowerbed and carry him off under arrest, while the Mayakovsky revolutionary song is heard again on the soundtrack. It continues through the final shot, which shows Ahmed and Isabela walking together arm in arm down the steps of her apartment block.

Looked at from one point of view, the film can be seen as a dossier, a bundle of materials for the story of Ahmed and Isabela, shuffled in a sometimes rather curious order—one cannot help being reminded of other films which have explicitly defined themselves as such—Don Owen's *Notes for a Film on Donna and Gail* or Godard's *Une Femme Mariée,* which is subtitled "Fragments of a Film Made in 1964." But, as in both those cases, the film is evidently very *soigné,* very carefully put together so that the disconnected fragments balance one another, playing with or against their context, and thereby taking on new, strange, and unexpected significances. Frequently, significances which defy precise verbalization—the placing of the first sequence of the discovery of Isabela's body, and our gradual realization that it might be she, and finally that it is she, colors all our responses to the scenes of her burgeoning romance with Ahmed which are intertwined with the deliberately clinical scenes of the autopsy and the criminologist's lecture.

This shuffling of the time scheme gives us a new perspective on what is happening, and not one which is very easy to define. One might suppose that the advance information that this seemingly fairly lighthearted romance is doomed to an unfortunate ending would cast a gloom over the proceedings, but instead the removal of suspense, or a large part of it (we know Isabela will die; we do not know exactly how), enables us to evaluate the relationship in terms other than the strictly linear, which would lead us to a negative view because everything ends badly—by implication, every moment is as valid as every other, the final image of the two of them happy together is just as true, enduring, and valuable as the death and separation which chronologically (but not in the film's ordering of events) follow it. Similarly, the documentary, objective episodes—the lectures of the sexologist and the criminologist, the treatment of the rat catcher's ethos, the depiction of Isabela making strudel—all offer an abstract framework which, without stating any comment on the principal action, constantly changes our appreciation of it.

Take, for instance, the scene in which Isabela's seduction of Ahmed is intercut with the Russian newsreel about the destruction of churches. The collocation seems at a glance quite arbitrary, but the choice is obviously deliberate, referring back to the landscape of debris in which Isabela and Rusa first met Ahmed, and raising the question of the exact value we should place on the constituent elements—as with the use of the "Ode to Joy" in *Man Is Not a Bird,* so here each element reflects on the other, backward and forward. The newsreel depicts the replacement of the old by the new in generally triumphant terms, and it is tempting to equate Ahmed's crumbling old-fashioned morality with the outmoded religion which is being swept away. And yet the film as a whole suggests an enduring nostalgia for old ways, for old buildings as compared with the drab utility structures against which much of the action takes place, for the settled values of domesticity exemplified by the unhappy Isabela—after all, her achievement of the strudel is accompanied by the triumphant march from *Aïda* (irony or endorsement, who can be sure?).

Seen in this context, even the sexologist's opening pronouncement about sexual freedom takes on a slightly old-fashioned, hollow tone, and though one may suspect, especially in the light of *WR,* that much of what the sexologist says mirrors Makavejev's own views, it is still possible to see the ironic context in which his statements are presented, which in turn throws doubt on their reliability as an index to the filmmaker's intentions. As always in Makavejev, the effects are complex, unpredictable; two and two seldom simply make four, and indeed the film takes on different shapes with each viewing, as one's interpretation of the balance of sympathies inclines now one way, now another, as another cross-reference becomes evident and demands evaluation.

The ambiguous attitude toward the past versus the present, visible in parts of *Switchboard Operator,* becomes a leading theme in *Innocence Unprotected,* Makavejev's following film. The ambiguity starts with the subtitle: "The new edition of a good old movie, prepared, ornamented, and annotated by Dušan Makavejev." Is the observation ironic or to be taken straight? As usual with Makavejev, a bit of both no doubt. To explain the nature and purpose of the film, it is necessary to go back a while in Yugoslav film history. In 1942, under conditions of considerable difficulty and at times in semi-secrecy, the noted acrobat and strong man Dragoljub Aleksić made a film (the first Serbian talkie, apparently) written, directed by, and starring himself. It was a fiction film, about a pretty orphan, Nada, whose stepmother is trying to force her to marry a rich but repulsive suitor when all the time she hankers after an honest acrobat (none other than . . .), who manages at last to carry her off after many a daredevil feat. The film opened to considerable local success, and was promptly suppressed by the Germans, because for all its crudities it was doing better at the local box office than the top German product. Aleksić himself was, ironically, accused of collaboration after the war, because no one could believe that the film could really have been made without authorization, but he managed to clear himself. The film was forgotten.

Until, that is, Makavejev rediscovered it and set about chasing up the surviving actors to find out all he could about it. Having done so, he conceived the weird idea of "preparing, ornamenting, and annotating" this new edition of the good old movie. The annotation consists of a series of confrontations between the actors as they were, in grimy black-and-white, with themselves as they are today, in color, talking about their lives, reminiscing about the film and its making, and in one case still singing spiritedly, in another, the indomitable Aleksić himself, still cheerfully bending iron bars in his teeth. The ornamentation includes the cutting in of newsreel material showing the contemporary state of Yugoslavia as this naïve dream fantasy was actually being spun: outside in the streets, the Resistance is being shot down while, within, the characters of Aleksić's fiction continue their private intrigues, sublimely unaware or unwilling to take note.

The result is, in its responses, a very complex and sophisticated film, though not at all difficult or hard to take. On the contrary, it has an enormous nostalgic charm; what it finally demonstrates is the power of a dream, however simple, to win out over the most pressing realities. And it is not as though Aleksić's original film is a neglected masterpiece. Far from it: it is the height of tattiness, amateurish in the extreme. It is rather as though Lindsay Anderson, say, had taken it into his head to produce a new edition of *Old Mother Riley Joins Up,* confronting it with the war as it really was, and the people concerned as they are now. And yet, for all that, the original is curiously touching. It has some of the unshakable conviction of all truly primitive art. We may start by laughing, a little unkindly, at the film and the people in it, and yet so patent is their own belief in what they are doing, their mission to produce a native Serbian cinema, that respect for them sneaks up on one. And affection. Makavejev so obviously loves them all, and enjoys his raw material so unaffectedly in its own terms, that one cannot help warming to the whole odd enterprise. And after all, the cinema, though we keep saying what a young art it is, is already old enough to have its primitives as well as its sophisticates, its artless amateurs as well as its tired professional. There is an undeniable charm about the ultimate in tattiness, the most shamelessly simple-minded. Makavejev's film is a tribute to simpler days, and a pleasure we can all share.

But, needless to say, it is more than that. If the "decorations" suggest an element of nostalgia camp, with flickering hand-applied color on the heroine's black-and-white lips and some quaint tinting to suffuse a rosy blush through certain scenes, the "comments" look like something far more serious. There is one point where Makavejev pulls his familiar trick of faking a reaction by intercutting two different things in such a way that one seems to comment on the other—as the suffering orphan gazes out the window in histrionic despair at her idiot plight, Makavejev cuts in newsreel material of burning buildings and all the horrors of war as though this is what she is looking out at, which puts the sentimental-naïve drama of Aleksić's original *Innocence Unprotected* in a different context, one justified, after all, by its historical situation, and, moreover, suggests a sort of broad allegorical extension of the action as an exemplar of the eternal battle between good and evil, a notion further developed when the wicked Petrović's molestation of Nada is paralleled by animated maps of the Nazi invasion of Russia. But of course this too imposes its own level of irony, since obviously no one, and least of all Makavejev, could really expect something as silly as the original film to carry any serious weight of allegory. More seriously serious, however, are the images of Aleksić today, still indomitably doing the same tricks, undergoing the same trials of strength. Idiotic, certainly, but at the same time touching in its naïve conviction, and therefore in spite of everything acceptable as a true tribute to the simple, heroic virtues, the "innocence" of the "good old movie" and its dedicated maker.

Makavejev's latest film, *Sweet Movie* (1974), is a disappointment and in some respects the weakest of all his films. No doubt the circumstances under which it was made have something to do with this. It is a Canadian-French co-production, and it seems that he had troubles in setting it up, heavy pressures that it be a commercial as well as an artistic success; most damaging of all, lengthy disagreements with his Canadian leading lady, who became increasingly alarmed at what she was required to do and finally, after a two-month layoff, had to leave the film altogether, making necessary a frantic rewriting and restructuring of the whole film. The structure of the finished work seems characteristic of Makavejev (to the point of self-parody), with its parallel stories: the first of a certified-virgin bride for one of the richest men in the world, who begins her traumatic experiences by being urinated on from a golden penis on her wedding night and then raped by a black muscle man (mentally if not physically), shut into a suitcase and taken to Paris, involved in a brief affair with a macho singing star, traumatized in a commune where planned regression leads to an orgy of urination and defecation at the dinner table, and ends smothered in a bath of chocolate while making a sexy chocolate commercial; the other story concerning a Marxist whore who roams the canals of Amsterdam in her boat, the *Survival,* servicing all and sundry, even very little boys, and becoming involved with a sailor from the battleship *Potemkin,* whom she eventually (rather puzzlingly) stabs to death in a bed of sugar.

It is easy enough to see in general outline that the virgin bride is woman as object in capitalist society and the Marxist whore is woman as free agent in a Reichian-Communist world of liberation through a good orgasm. (Why, one might inquire, does satisfactory, liberated sex, like all such in Makavejev's films, end in violent death? Makavejev's curious explanation is that this female character, Anna Planeta, has gone mad, which is also a response to life.) But apparently the original intention was for the film's structure to be simple and linear: the two stories, now intercut, should be of one woman, who is brought out of her trauma by the commune instead of, as now appears, pushed deeper into it, and who then leads a new life as a dispenser of satisfactory orgasm.

Maybe the film would have worked better this way, or at least been clearer in its meaning. But as it is, it seems too much like an arbitrary rerun of familiar Makavejev themes and images (the good ship *Survival,* with its gigantic Karl Marx figurehead; the intercutting of fiction with documentaries and newsreels, particularly in this case material relating to the Katyn massacre; the references to Reich's ideas, sexual liberation, and the primal scream; the concentration on the consumption and elimination of food) exaggerated into sheer self-indulgence and strung out loosely, with little or none of the electric tension which holds the disparate elements of *WR* so marvelously, teasingly together. Some have seen the exaggeration of the sheer shock value of some of the images as sensationalism purposely designed to ensure the film's commercial success. That I doubt. Makavejev is certainly well aware of commercial values, but the images of joyful excretion are more likely to turn spectators off, and will certainly get him into a lot of trouble with the censors of the world. In any case, they are hardly titillating, except, I suppose, to a tiny coprophilic minority; for the rest of us, they are more likely to be an endurance test.

Sweet Movie must, I think, be regarded as a failure, but not such a dishonorable failure. Its techniques are (perhaps in this case *faute de mieux*) much the same as those of his earlier films: the ultimate effect of the film, as of all the others, is built on paradox, contradiction, the seeming comparison or equation of obvious unlikes, so that meanings echo and re-echo, perspectives shake and dissolve and re-form. The dislocations thus produced can be categorized in various ways—as Brechtian devices to produce alienation in an audience, an assumption of a critical distance at which judgments are made, discriminations are enforced; as effects of surrealist gratuity; as chop-logic pattern making; or as free association. Not that any of these categorizations help very much—at most they give a faint notion of how Makavejev's films *may* work on us, not necessarily how they do work on us. There is an important sense in which Makavejev is an intellectual filmmaker, so many of his effects being based on the manipulation of film syntax and the ingenious contrivances of dialectical montage. And yet such a term at once suggests something cold and calculating and humorless, which is the very last effect Makavejev's films ever give. Despite all their constructive intelligence, they give the impression of having somehow just happened.

Makavejev's own outline of how *WR* evolved over a period of months, as the pieces gradually fell into place in a way totally unpredictable even to him, is wholly believable—Makavejev's art is the art of seeing connections rather than making them. His films carry a unique charge, often like depth charges, dropping unobtrusively into our consciousness and then exploding into meaning after the event. And they are genuinely funny, with an expansive, sometimes Rabelaisian, jollity. Makavejev's view of the world is comic and it is compassionate—but he feels no necessity to set his intelligence aside just because of that. Few if any other modern filmmakers manage to appeal, in equal degrees, to the head, the heart, and the funny bone at the same time. It sounds like, and it is, one of the most desirable combinations in contemporary cinema.

Filmographies

CLAUDE CHABROL

1958 *Le Beau Serge*

Production Company: AJYM/CGCF
Director: Claude Chabrol
Assistant Directors: Philippe de Broca, Charles Bitsch, Claude de Givray
Script and Dialogue: Claude Chabrol
Director of Photography: Henri Decae
Technical Adviser: Jean-Paul Sassy
Editor: Jacques Gaillard
Music: Emile Delpierre
Cast: Gérard Blain (Serge), Jean-Claude Brialy (François), Bernadette Lafont (Marie), Michèle Meritz (Yvonne), Claude Cerval (the Priest), Jeanne Perez (Mme. Chaunier), Edmond Beauchamp (Glomaud), André Dino (Michel, the Doctor), Claude Chabrol (la Truffe), Philippe de Broca (Jacques Rivette de la Chasuble)
Running Time: 97 minutes

Les Cousins

Production Company: AJYM
Producer: Claude Chabrol
Director: Claude Chabrol
Assistant Directors: Philippe de Broca, Hedjie Ben Califa, Olga Varen
Script: Claude Chabrol
Dialogue: Paul Gégauff
Director of Photography: Henri Decae
Art Directors: Jacques Saulnier, Bernard Evein
Editor: Jacques Gaillard
Music: Paul Misraki, Mozart, Wagner
Cast: Gérard Blain (Charles), Jean-Claude Brialy

(Paul), Juliette Mayniel (Florence), Claude Cerval (Clovis), Guy Decomble (Bookseller), Corrado Guarducci (Italian Count), Geneviève Cluny (Geneviève), Michèle Meritz (Vonvon), Stéphane Audran (Françoise), Françoise Vatel (Ernestine), Paul Bisciglia (Marc), Jeanne Perez, Jean-Pierre Moulin, Jean-Louis Maury, André Jocelyn.
Running Time: 103 minutes

1959 *A Double Tour* (*Web of Passion*) (*Léda*)
Production Company: Paris Film/Titanus (Rome)
Producers: Robert and Raymond Hakim
Director: Claude Chabrol
Assistant Directors: Philippe de Broca, Charles Bitsch
Script: Paul Gégauff, from the novel *The Key to Nicholas Street,* by Stanley Ellin
Director of Photography (Eastmancolor): Henri Decae
Art Directors: Jacques Saulnier, Bernard Evein
Editor: Jacques Gaillard
Music: Paul Misraki, Berlioz, Mozart
Cast: Madeleine Robinson (Thérèse Marcoux), Jacques Dacqmine (Henri Marcoux), Jean-Paul Belmondo (Laszlo Kovacs), Bernadette Lafont (Julie), Antonella Lualdi (Léda), André Jocelyn (Richard), Jeanne Valérie (Elisabeth), Mario David (Roger, the Milkman), Laszlo Szabo (Laszlo's Friend), Raymond Pélissier, André Dino.
Running Time: 110 minutes

1960 *Les Bonnes Femmes*
Production Company: Hakim/Panitalia
Producers: Robert and Raymond Hakim
Director: Claude Chabrol
Script: Paul Gégauff
Director of Photography: Henri Decae
Art Director: Jacques Mély
Editor: Jacques Gaillard
Music: Paul Misraki, Pierre Jansen
Cast: Bernadette Lafont (Jane), Lucile Saint-Simon

(Rita), Clotilde Joano (Jacqueline), Stéphane Audran (Ginette), Mario David (André, the Motorcyclist), Pierre Bertin (M. Belin), Ave Ninchi (Mme. Louise), Jean-Louis Maury (Marcel), Albert Dinan (Albert), Sacha Briquet (Henri), Claude Berri (Jane's Fiancé), Serge Bento (Deliveryman), Karen Blanguernon (Girl in Dance Hall)
Running Time: 104 minutes

Les Godelureaux
Production Company: International Production/Cocinor/SPA Cinematografica
Director: Claude Chabrol
Script: Claude Chabrol, Paul Gégauff, adapted from the novel by Eric Ollivier
Dialogue: Paul Gégauff
Director of Photography: Jean Rabier
Art Directors: Georges Glon and Mercojel
Editor: James Cuenet
Music: Pierre Jansen
Cast: Jean-Claude Brialy (Ronald), Charles Belmont (Arthur), Bernadette Lafont (Ambroisine), Jean Tissler (President), Jean Galland (Uncle), Sacha Briquet (Henri), Sophie Grimaldi, André Jocelyn, Stéphane Audran, Jean-Louis Maury, Albert Dinan, Serge Bento, Juliette Mayniel
Running Time: 99 minutes

1961 *Les Sept Péchés Capitaux* (*The Seven Deadly Sins*)
"Avarice" episode
(Other episodes directed by Edouard Molinaro, Jean-Luc Godard, Jacques Demy, Roger Vadim, Philippe de Broca, Sylvain Dhomme)
Production Company: Gibe/Franco-London/Titanus
Director: Claude Chabrol
Director of Photography (Dyaliscope): Jean Rabier
Script: Félicien Marceau
Art Director: Bernard Evein

Editor: Jacques Gaillard
Music: Pierre Jansen
Cast: Danièle Barraud (Suzan), Jacques Charrier (Antoine), Jean-Claude Brialy (Arthur), Jean-Pierre Cassel (Raymond), Claude Rich (Armand), Sacha Briquet, Jean-Claude Masseulier, André Jocelyn, Claude Berri, Michel Benoist, Serge Bento, André Chanel
Running Time: 18 minutes (of 115 minutes)

1962 *L'Oeil du Malin*
Production Company: Rome-Paris Film/Lux Film
Producers: Georges de Beauregard, Carlo Ponti
Director: Claude Chabrol
Script: Claude Chabrol
Director of Photography: Jean Rabier
Editor: Jacques Gaillard
Music: Pierre Jansen
Cast: Jacques Charrier (Albin Mercier), Stéphane Audran (Hélène), Walter Reyer (Andreas Hartman), Daniel Boulanger and Badri (Policemen)
Running Time: 80 minutes

Ophélia
Production Company: Boréal
Director: Claude Chabrol
Script: Paul Gégauff, adapted by Paul Gégauff, Claude Chabrol
Director of Photography: Jean Rabier
Editor: Jacques Gaillard
Music: Pierre Jansen
Cast: Alida Valli (Claudia), André Jocelyn (Yvan Lesurf), Juliette Mayniel (Lucie), Claude Cerval (Adrien Lesurf), Robert Burnier (André Lagrange), Jean-Louis Maury (Sparkos), Sacha Briquet (Gravedigger), Serge Bento (François), Liliane David (Ginette), Pierre Vernier (Paul), Laszlo Szabo, Henri Attal, Dominique Zardi, Roger Carel, Jean-Marie Arnoux
Running Time: 109 minutes

Landru (*Bluebeard*)
Production Company: Rome-Paris Films (Paris)/Compagnia Cinematografica Champion (Rome)
Producers: Georges de Beauregard, Carlo Ponti
Director: Claude Chabrol
Assistant Directors: Francis Cognany, Jean Grouet
Script: Françoise Sagan
Director of Photography (Eastmancolor): Jean Rabier
Art Director: Jacques Saulnier
Costumes: Maurice Albray
Editor: Jacques Gaillard
Music: Pierre Jansen
Cast: Michèle Morgan (Célestine Buisson), Danielle Darrieux (Berthe Héon), Charles Denner (Henri-Désiré Landru), Hildegarde Neff (Mme. Ixe), Juliette Mayniel (Anna Colomb), Stéphane Audran (Fernande Segret), Mary Marquet (Mme. Guillin), Catherine Rouvel (Andrée Babelet), Denise Provence (Mme. Laporte), Françoise Lugagne (Mme. Landru), Robert Burnier (Presiding Judge), Huguette Forge (Mme. Vidal), Giselle Sandré (Georgette), Jean-Louis Maury (Commissaire Belin), Mario David (Prosecutor), Claude Mansard (Defense Attorney), Sacha Briquet (Assistant Prosecutor), Serge Bento (Maurice Landru), Denise Lenvrier (Catherine Landru), Raymond Queneau (Clemenceau), Jean-Pierre Melville (Georges Mandel)
Running Time: 115 minutes

1963 *Les Plus Belles Escroqueries du Monde*
"L'Homme Qui Vendit la Tour Eiffel" episode
(Other episodes directed by Iromichi Horikawa, Ugo Gregoretti, Roman Polanski)
Production Company: Ulysse Productions (Paris)/UNITEC/Vides Cinematografica/Toho/Cesar Film (Holland)
Director: Claude Chabrol
Script: Paul Gégauff
Director of Photography (Franscope): Jean Rabier
Editor: Jacques Gaillard

Music: Pierre Jansen
Cast: Jean-Pierre Cassel (the Crook), Catherine Deneuve, Francis Blanche (the Buyer), Jean-Louis Maury
Running Time: 18 minutes (of 90 minutes)

1965 *Le Tigre Aime le Chair Fraiche* (*The Tiger Likes Fresh Blood*)
Production Company: Progéfi
Producer: Christine Gouze-Renal
Director: Claude Chabrol
Assistant Directors: Pierre Gauchet, José Dagnant
Script: Jean Halain, from a story by Antoine Flachot (Roger Hanin)
Director of Photography: Jean Rabier
Editor: Jacques Gaillard
Music: Pierre Jensen
Cast: Roger Hanin (Louis Rapière, the Tiger), Maria Mauban (Mme. Baskine), Daniela Bianchi (Mehlica), Roger Dumas (Duvet), Mario David (Dobrovsky), Albert Dagnant (General Condé), Sauveur Sasportes (Baskine), Pierre-François Moro (Ghislain), Antonio Passalia (Koubassi), Roger Rudel (Benita), Carlo Nell (Theater Assassin), Henri Attal (Airport Gunman), Dominique Zardi (Airport Gunman), Jimmy Karoubi (Jean-Luc, the Midget), Christa Lang (Dobrovsky's Girl), Guy d'Avout (French Minister), Stéphane Audran (Soprano), Charles Audisio (Tenor), Maurice Besson, Michel Charrel, Marcel Maurice Gassouk and François Terzion (Inspectors)
Running Time: 85 minutes

Marie-Chantal Contre le Docteur Kha
Production Company: Rome-Paris Films/Productions Georges de Beauregard (Paris)/Producciones DIA (Madrid)/Mega Films (Rome)/Maghreb Uni Films (Casablanca)
Producer: René Demoulin
Director: Claude Chabrol
Assistant Directors: Philippe Fourastie, Alexis Poliakoff, Mohammed Osfour

Script: Claude Chabrol, Christian-Yve; the character of Marie-Chantal from Jacques Chazot's creation
Dialogue: Daniel Boulanger
Director of Photography (Eastmancolor): Jean Rabier
Editor: Jacques Gaillard
Music: Pierre Jansen
Cast: Marie Laforêt (Marie-Chantal), Francisco Rabal (Paco Castillo), Serge Reggiani (Ivanov), Charles Denner (Johnson), Roger Hanin (Bruno Kerrien), Akim Tamiroff (Doctor Kha), Stéphane Audran (Olga), Pierre-François Moro (Hubert), Gilles Chusseau (Gregor, Ivanov's Son), Antonio Passalia (Sparafucile), Robert Burnier (the Old Swiss), Gerard Tichy (Maître d'Hotel), Claude Chabrol (Bartender), Serge Bento
Running Time: 110 minutes

Le Tigre se Parfume à la Dynamite (*An Orchid for the Tiger*)
Production Company: Progéfi (Paris) / Producciones Balcazar (Barcelona) / Dino De Laurentiis (Rome)
Producer: Christine Gouze-Renal
Director: Claude Chabrol
Script: Antoine Flachot (Roger Hanin)
Director of Photography (Eastmancolor): Jean Rabier
Editor: Jacques Gaillard
Music: Pierre Jansen
Cast: Roger Hanin (Louis Rapière, the Tiger), Margaret Lee (Pamela Mitchum), Roger Dumas (Duvet), Michel Bouquet (Jacques Vermorel), J.-M. Caffarel (Colonel Pontarlier), Georges Rigaud (Commander Damerec), Assad Bahador (Hans von Wunchendorf), Carlos Casaravilla (Ricardo Sanchez), Michaela Cendali (Sarita Sanchez), Michel Etcheverry, Claude Chabrol
Running Time: 110 minutes

1966 *La Ligne de Démarcation*
Production Company: Rome-Paris Films/Georges de Beauregard Productions/SNC Production
Director: Claude Chabrol

Script: Colonel Remy and Claude Chabrol
Director of Photography: Jean Rabier
Editor: Jacques Gaillard
Music: Pierre Jansen
Cast: Jean Seberg (Mary, Comtesse de Grandville), Maurice Ronet (Pierre, Comte de Grandville), Daniel Gélin (Dr. Lafaye), Stéphane Audran (Wife), Jacques Perrin (Michel), Mario David (Urbain), Roger Dumas (Passer), Noël Roquevert (Innkeeper), Jean Yanne, Claude Leveillée, Jean-Louis Maury, René Koldehoff, Serge Bento
Running Time: 120 minutes

Paris Vu Par . . .
"La Muette" episode
(Other episodes directed by Jean Douchet, Jean-Luc Godard, Jean-Daniel Pollet, Eric Rohmer, Jean Rouch)
Production Company: Films du Losange
Director: Claude Chabrol
Script: Claude Chabrol
Director of Photography (Eastmancolor, 16 mm.): Jean Rabier
Editor: Jacqueline Raynal
Cast: Stéphane Audran (the Wife), Claude Chabrol (the Husband), Gilles Chusseau (the Son), Dany Saryl (the Maid)
Running Time: 22 minutes (of 98 minutes)

1967 *Le Scandale* (*The Champagne Murders*)
Production Company: Universal
Producer: Raymond Eger
Director: Claude Chabrol
Assistant Director: Pierre Gauchet
Script: Claude Brûlé, Derek Prouse, from an idea by William Benjamin
Dialogue: Paul Gégauff
Director of Photography (Technicolor, Techniscope): Jean Rabier
Art Director: Rino Mondellino
Costumes: Maurice Albray

Editor: Jacques Gaillard
Music: Pierre Jansen
Cast: Anthony Perkins (Christopher), Maurice Ronet (Paul), Stéphane Audran (Jacqueline), Yvonne Furneaux (Christine), Suzanne Lloyd (Evelyn), Catherine Sola (Denise), Christa Lang (Paula), Henry Jones (Mr. Clarke), George Skaff (Mr. Ffeiffer), Marie-Ange Agnès
Running Time: French version, 105 minutes; English version, 98 minutes

La Route de Corinthe (*The Road to Corinth*)
Production Company: Les Films la Boétie (Paris)/Compagnia Generale Finanzaria Cinematografica (Rome)/Orion Films (Athens)
Producer: André Génovès
Director: Claude Chabrol
Assistant Directors: Pierre Gauchet, Michel Gregoriou
Script: Claude Brûlé, Daniel Boulanger, from the novel by Claude Rank
Dialogue: Daniel Boulanger
Director of Photography (Eastmancolor): Jean Rabier
Art Director: Aravantino
Editors: Jacques Gaillard, Monique Fardoulis
Music: Pierre Jansen
Cast: Jean Seberg (Shanny), Maurice Ronet (Dex), Christian Marquand (Robert Ford), Michel Bouquet (Sharps), Saro Urzi (Kalhides), Antonio Passalia (the Killer), Paulo Justi (Josio), Claude Chabrol (Alcibiades)
Running Time: 90 minutes

1968 *Les Biches*
Production Company: Les Films la Boétie (Paris)/Alexandra (Rome)
Producer: André Génovès
Director: Claude Chabrol
Script: Paul Gégauff, Claude Chabrol
Director of Photography (Eastmancolor): Jean Rabier
Art Director: Marc Berthier
Editor: Jacques Gaillard
Music: Pierre Jansen

Cast: Stéphane Audran (Frédérique), Jacqueline Sassard (Why), Jean-Louis Trintignant (Paul Thomas), Nane Germon (Violetta), Henri Attal (Robègue), Dominique Zardi (Riais), Serge Bento (Bookseller), Henri Frances
Running Time: 99 minutes

La Femme Infidèle
Production Company: Les Films la Boétie (Paris) /Cinegai (Rome)
Producer: André Génovès
Director: Claude Chabrol
Assistant Directors: Jacques Fansten, Jean-François Detré
Script: Claude Chabrol
Director of Photography (Eastmancolor): Jean Rabier
Art Director: Guy Littaye
Editor: Jacques Gaillard
Music: Pierre Jansen
Singer: Dominique Zardi
Cast: Stéphane Audran (Hélène Desvallées), Michel Bouquet (Charles Desvallées), Maurice Ronet (Victor Pégala), Serge Bento (Bignon), Michel Duchaussoy (Police Officer Duval), Guy Marly (Police Officer Gobet), Stéphane di Napoli (Michel), Louise Chevalier (the Maid), Louise Rioton (Charles's Mother), Henri Marteau (Paul), François Moro-Giafferi (Frédéric), Dominique Zardi (the Truck Driver), Michel Charrel (Policeman), Henri Attal (Man in Café), Jean-Marie Arnoux (False Witness), Donatella Turri (Brigitte)
Running Time: 98 minutes

1969 *Que le Bête Meure* (*Killer!*)
Production Company: Les Films la Boétie (Paris) /Rizzoli Films (Rome)
Producer: André Génovès
Director: Claude Chabrol
Assistant Director: Jacques Fansten
Script: Paul Gégauff, from the novel *The Beast Must Die,* by Nicholas Blake (C. Day Lewis)
Director of Photography (Eastmancolor): Jean Rabier

Art Director: Guy Littaye
Music: Pierre Jansen
Songs: "Vier Ernste Gesänge," Brahms, sung by Kathleen Ferrier
Cast: Michel Duchaussoy (Charles Thenier), Caroline Cellier (Hélène Lanson), Jean Yanne (Paul Decourt), Anouk Ferjac (Jeanne), Marc di Napoli (Philippe), Maurice Pialat (Police Inspector), Guy Marly (Jacques Ferrand), Lorraine Rainer (Anna Ferrand), Louise Chevalier (Mme. Levenès), Dominique Zardi (Police Officer), Stéphane di Napoli (Michel), Raymone, Michel Charrel, Franco Girard, Bernard Papineau, Robert Rondo, Jacques Masson, Georges Charrier, Jean-Louis Maury
Running Time: 110 minutes

1970 *Le Boucher* (*The Butcher*)
Production Company: Les Films la Boétie (Paris) /Euro International (Rome)
Producer: André Génovès
Director: Claude Chabrol
Script: Claude Chabrol
Director of Photography (Eastmancolor) : Jean Rabier
Art Director: Guy Littaye
Editor: Jacques Gaillard
Music: Pierre Jansen
Cast: Stéphane Audran (Mlle. Hélène), Jean Yanne (Popaul), Roger Rudel (Grumbach, the Police Inspector), Mario Beccari (Léon Hamel), Antonio Passalia (Angelo), William Guerault (Charles)
Running Time: 90 minutes

La Rupture
Production Company: Les Films la Boétie (Paris) /Euro International (Rome) /Cinévog-Films (Brussels)
Producer: André Génovès
Director: Claude Chabrol
Assistant Director: Pierre Gauchet
Script: Claude Chabrol, based on the novel by Charlotte

Armstrong, *Le Jour des Parques*
Director of Photography (Eastmancolor): Jean Rabier
Art Director: Guy Littaye
Editor: Jacques Gaillard
Music: Pierre Jansen
Cast: Stéphane Audran (Hèlène Regnier), Jean-Pierre Cassel (Paul Thomas), Jean-Claude Drouot (Charles Regnier), Michel Bouquet (Ludovic Regnier), Marguerite Cassan (Emilie Regnier), Annie Cordy (Mme. Pinelli), Jean Carmet (M. Pinelli), Michel Duchaussoy (Maître Jourdan), Catherine Rouvel (Sonia), Mario David (Gerard Mostelle), Katia Romanoff (Elise), Margo Lion (Parque 1), Louise Chevalier (Parque 2), Maria Michi (Parque 3), Angelo Infanti (Dr. Blanchard), Laurent Brunschwick (Michel, l'Enfant), Dominique Zardi (Balloon Seller), Claude Chabrol (Passenger on the Train)
Running Time: 124 minutes

1971 *Juste Avant la Nuit* (*Just Before Nightfall*)
Production Company: Les Films la Boétie (Paris)/Cinemar (Rome)
Producer: André Génovès
Director: Claude Chabrol
Assistant Directors: Patrick Saglio, Michel Dupuy
Script: Claude Chabrol, based on the novel *The Thin Line,* by Edward Atiyah
Director of Photography (Eastmancolor): Jean Rabier
Art Director: Guy Littaye
Editor: Jacques Gaillard
Music: Pierre Jansen
Cast: Michel Bouquet (Charles Masson), Stéphane Audran (Hélène Masson), François Périer (François Tellier), Jean Carmet (Jeannot), Dominique Zardi (Prince), Henri Attal (Inspector Cavanna), Paul Temps (Bardin), Daniel Lecourtois (Dorfmann), Celia (Jacqueline), Patrick Gillot (Auguste Masson), Brigitte Perin (Joséphine Masson), Marcel Gassouk (the Bartender), Clelia Matania (Mme. Masson), Anna Douking

(Laura), Roger Leumon (Commissioner Delfeil), Marina Ninchi (Gina), J. M. Arnoux (an Agent), Dominique Marcas (Mme. Ortiz), Gilbert Servien (Policeman)
Running Time: 106 minutes

1972 *La Décade Prodigieuse* (*Ten Days' Wonder*)
Production Company: Les Films la Boétie
Producer: André Génovès
Director: Claude Chabrol
Assistant Directors: Patrick Saglio, Michael Rupoy
Script: Paul Gégauff, Paul Gardner, Eugene Archer, based on the novel *Ten Days' Wonder,* by Ellery Queen
Director of Photography (Eastmancolor): Jean Rabier
Editor: Jacques Gaillard
Art Director: Guy Littaye
Music: Pierre Jansen
Song (in French version only): Dominique Zardi
Cast: Orson Welles (Theo Van Horn), Marlène Jobert (Hélène), Anthony Perkins (Charles Van Horn), Michel Piccoli (Paul Régis), Guido Alberti (Ludovic), Giovanni Sciuto (Moneylender), Ermano Casanova (Old Man with Eye Patch), Sylvana Blasi (Woman), Tsilla Chelton (Charles's Mother), Eric Frisdal (Charles as a Boy), Aline Montovani (Hélène as a Girl), Vittorio Sanipoli (Police Inspector), Mathilde Ceccarelli, Corrine Koeningswarter, Fabienne Gauglof
Running Time: 108 minutes

1973 *Les Noces Rouges*
Production Company: Les Films la Boétie/Canaria Films
Producer: André Génovès
Director: Claude Chabrol
Assistant Directors: Michel Dupuy, Alain Wermus
Script: Claude Chabrol
Director of Photography (Eastmancolor): Jean Rabier
Editors: Jacques Gaillard, Monique Gaillard
Art Director: Guy Littaye
Music: Pierre Jansen

Cast: Michel Piccoli (Pierre Maury), Stéphane Audran (Lucienne Delamare), Claude Pieplu (Paul Delamare), Eliana de Santis (Hélène), Clotilde Joano (Clotilde Maury), François Robert (Inspector Auriol), Daniel Lecourtois (Prefect), Pipo Merisi (Berthier), Ermano Casanova (Town Council Member), Maurice Fourre (Dr. Bon), Philippe Fourre (Prefect's Assistant), Mme. Pelle (Clarisse), M. Mailley (Director of C.E.G.), Gilbert Servien (Football Coach), Henri Berger (Billiard Player), M. Torot (Postman), Mme. Meunier (Librarian)
Running Time: 90 minutes

Le Banc de Désolation
De Grey
Production Company: Technisonor
Producer: Philippe Baraduc
Director: Claude Chabrol
Script: Roger Grenier, based on the short stories by Henry James
Director of Photography (color): Jean Rabier
Editor: Jacques Gaillard
Art Director: Guy Littaye
Music: Pierre Jansen
Cast, *Le Banc de Désolation:* Catherine Samie (Kate Cookham), Michel Duchaussoy (Herbert Dodd), Michel Piccoli (Captain Roper)
Cast, *De Grey:* Catherine Jourdan (Margaret), Yves Lefebvre (Father Herbert), Hélène Perdrière (Mrs. De Grey)
Running Time: 52 minutes each

1974 *NADA* (*The NADA Gang*)
Production Company: Les Films la Boétie/Verona Films
Producer: André Génovès
Director: Claude Chabrol
Assistant Directors: Michel Dupuy, Alain Wermus
Script: Jean-Patrick Manchette, based on his own novel
Director of Photography (Eastmancolor): Jean Rabier

Editor: Jacques Gaillard
Art Director: Guy Littaye
Music: Pierre Jansen
Cast: Fabio Testi (Buenaventura Diaz), Michel Duchaussoy (Marcel Treuffais), Maurice Garrel (André Epaulard), Michel Aumont (Goémond), Lou Castel (D'Arey), Didier Kaminka (Meyer), Lyle Joyce (Ambassador Richard Poindexter), André Falcon (the Minister), Viviane Romance (Mme. Gabrielle), Mariangela Melato (Véronique Cash), Katia Romanoff (Anna Meyer), Francis Lax (Edouard Longuevache), Jean-Louis Maury (Minister's Private Secretary), Rudy Lenoir (M. Bouillon), Daniel Lecourtois (Prefect), Jacques Préboist (Motorist), Dominique Zardi, Henri Attal (Goémond's Men), Henri Poirier (Treuffais's Fellow Teacher)
Running Time: 134 minutes

PIER PAOLO PASOLINI

AS A WRITER

1954 *La Donna del Fiume*
Director: Mario Soldati
Script: Basilio Franchina, Giorgio Bassani, Pier Paolo Pasolini, Florestano Vancini, Antonio Altovitti, Mario Soldati

1955 *Il Prigioniero della Montagna*
Director: Luis Trenker
Script: Luis Trenker, Giorgio Bassani, Pier Paolo Pasolini, from the novel by C. G. Bienek

1956 *Notti di Cabiria*
Director: Federico Fellini
Subject and Script: Federico Fellini, Ennio Flaiano, Tullo Pinelli
Adviser/Collaborator on the script: Pier Paolo Pasolini

1957 *Marisa la Civetta*
Director-Scenarist: Mauro Bolognini
Script: Mauro Bolognini, Pier Paolo Pasolini, Titina Demby

1958 *Giovani Mariti*
Director: Mauro Bolognini
Subject: Massimo Franciosa, Pasquale Festa Campanile
Script: Enzo Curreli, Luciano Martino, Mauro Bolognini, Pier Paolo Pasolini

1959 *La Notte Brava*
Director: Mauro Bolognini
Subject: from *Ragazzi di Vita,* by Pier Paolo Pasolini
Script: Pier Paolo Pasolini, Laurence Bost

1960 *Morte di un Amico*
Director: Franco Rossi
Subject: Giuseppe Berto, Oreste Biancoli, Pier Paolo Pasolini, Franco Riganti
Script: Franco Riganti, Ugo Guerra, Franco Rossi

Il Bel Antonio
Director: Mauro Bolognini
Subject: from the novel by Vitaliano Brancati
Script: Pier Paolo Pasolini, Gino Visentini, Mauro Bolognini

La Canta delle Marane
Director: Cecilia Mangini
Story: from a chapter in *Ragazzi di Vita,* by Pier Paolo Pasolini
Commentary by Pier Palo Pasolini

La Giornata Balorda
Director: Mauro Bolognini
Subject: Pier Paolo Pasolini and Alberto Moravia from *Racconti Romani* and *Nuovi Racconti Romani,* by Alberto Moravia

Script: Pier Paolo Pasolini, Alberto Moravia, Mario Visconti

La Lunga Notte del '43
Director: Florestano Vancini
Subject: from the story "Una Notte del '43" (part of the cycle *Le Storie Ferraresi*), by Giorgio Bassani
Script: Ennio de Concini, Pier Paolo Pasolini, Florestano Vancini

Il Carro Armato dell'8 Settembre
Director: Gianni Puccini
Subject: Rodolfo Sonego, Tonino Guerra, Elio Petri
Script: Gianni Puccini Baratti, Elio Bartolini, Pier Paolo Pasolini, Giulio Questi

1961 *La Ragazza in Vetrina*
Director: Luciano Emmer
Subject: Emanuele Cassuto, Luciano Emmer, Rodolfo Sonego
Script: Luciano Emmer, Pier Paolo Pasolini, Luciano Martino, Vincio Marinucci

1962 *Una Vita Violenta*
Directors: Paolo Heusch, Brunello Rondi
Subject: from the novel *Una Vita Violenta,* by Pier Paolo Pasolini
Treatment: Ennio de Concini, Franco Brusati
Script: Paolo Heusch, Brunello Rondi, Franco Solinas

La Commare Secca
Director: Bernardo Bertolucci
Subject: from a story by Pier Paolo Pasolini
Script: Bernardo Bertolucci, Sergio Citti

AS AN ACTOR

1960 *Il Gobbo*
Director: Carlo Lizzani

1966 *Requiescant*
Director: Carlo Lizzani

Il Cinema di Pasolini (documentary short)
Director: Maurizio Ponzi

AS DIRECTOR

1961 *Accattone*
Production Company: Arco Film-Cino del Duca
Producer: Alfredo Bini
Director: Pier Paolo Pasolini
Script: Pier Paolo Pasolini
Assistant Directors: Bernardo Bertolucci, Leopoldo Savona
Assistant for Script: Sergio Citti
Director of Photography: Tonino delli Colli
Editor: Nino Baragli
Music: Bach, coordinated by Carlo Rustichelli
Cast: Franco Citti (Accattone), Franca Pasut (Stella), Silvana Corsini (Maddalena), Paola Guidi (Ascenza), Adriana Asti (Amore)
Accattone's voice: Paolo Ferrari
Running Time: 120 minutes

1962 *Mamma Roma*
Production Company: Arco Film-Cineriz
Producer: Alfredo Bini
Director: Pier Paolo Pasolini
Script: Pier Paolo Pasolini
Assistant for Script: Sergio Citti
Director of Photography: Tonino delli Colli
Editor: Nino Baragli
Music: Vivaldi, coordinated by Carlo Rustichelli
Cast: Anna Magnani (Mamma Roma), Ettore Garofolo (Ettore), Franco Citti (Carmine), Silvana Corsini (Bruna), Luisa Loiano (Biancofiore), Paolo Volponi (Priest), Luciano Gonnini (Zacaria), Vittorio La Paglia

(Signore Pellissier), Piero Morgia (Piero)
Running Time: 110 minutes

Rogopag, or *Laviamoci il Cervello*
"La Ricotta" episode
(Other episodes directed by Roberto Rossellini, Jean-Luc Godard, Ugo Gregoretti)
Production Company: Arco Film-Cineriz (Rome) /Lyre (Paris)
Director: Pier Paolo Pasolini
Subject and Script: Pier Paolo Pasolini
Director of Photography: Tonino delli Colli
Costumes: Danilo Donati
Musical Coordinator: Carlo Rustichelli
Cast: Orson Welles (the Director), Mario Cipriani (Stracci), Laura Betti (the Star), Edmonda Aldini (another Star), Vittorio La Paglia (the Journalist), Ettore Garofolo (an Extra), Maria Bernardini (Extra who does Striptease)
The Director's voice: Giorgio Bassani
Running Time: 40 minutes

La Rabbia (First Part)
(Second Part by Giovanni Guareschi)
Producer: Gastone Ferrante
Production Company: Opus Film
Director: Pier Paolo Pasolini
Script: Pier Paolo Pasolini
Commentary spoken by Giorgio Bassani, Renato Guttuso
Editor: Nino Baragli
Running Time: 50 minutes
The film was withdrawn because of controversy over the Guareschi episode and has never been shown commercially.

1964 *Sopraluoghi in Palestina per "Il Vangelo Secondo Matteo"*
Production Company: Arco Film

Cameraman: Aldo Pennelli
Speakers: Pier Paolo Pasolini, Don Andrea Carraro
Commentary: Pier Paolo Pasolini
Running Time: 50 minutes
The film was put together hurriedly without Pasolini's supervision from materials shot by a cameraman working for the company producing *Il Vangelo Secondo Matteo;* it was never intended for commercial distribution.

Comizi d'Amore
Production Company: Arco Film
Producer: Alfredo Bini
Director: Pier Paolo Pasolini
Commentary: Pier Paolo Pasolini
Commentary spoken by Lello Bersani, Pier Paolo Pasolini
Directors of Photography: Mario Bernardo, Tonino delli Colli
Editor: Nino Baragli
Participants: Pier Paolo Pasolini, Cesare Musatti, Giuseppe Ungaretti, Susanna Pasolini, Camilla Cederna, Adele Cambria, Oriana Fallaci, Antonella Lualdi, Graziella Granata (and, suppressed in the editing, Giuseppe Ravegnani and Eugenio Montale)
Running Time: 90 minutes

Il Vangelo Secondo Matteo (*The Gospel According to St. Matthew*)
Production Company: Arco Film (Rome)/Lux Cie Cinematographique de France (Paris)
Producer: Alfredo Bini
Director: Pier Paolo Pasolini
Costumes: Danilo Donati
Editor: Nino Baragli
Music: Bach, Mozart, Prokofiev, Webern, Luis E. Bacalov
Sound: Mario del Pezzo
Cast: Enrique Irazoqui (Christ), Margherita Caruso (the Young Mary), Susanna Pasolini (the Old Mary), Mar-

cello Morante (Joseph), Mario Socrate (John the Baptist), Settimio di Porto (Peter), Otello Sestili (Judas), Ferruccio Nuzzo (Matthew), Giacomo Morante (John), Alfonso Gatto (Andrew), Enzo Siciliano (Simon), Giorgio Agamben (Philip), Guido Cerretani (Bartholomew), Luigi Barbini (James, the Son of Alphaeus), Marcello Galdini (James, the Son of Zebedee), Elio Spaziani (Thaddeus), Rosario Migale (Thomas), Rodolfo Wilcock (Caiphas), Alessandro Clerici (Pontius Pilate), Amerigo Bevilacqua (Herod I), Francesco Leonetti (Herod II), Paola Tedesco (Salome), Rossana di Rocco (Angel), Eliseo Boschi (Joseph of Aramathea), Natalia Ginzburg (Mary of Bethany), Ninetto Davoli (Shepherd Boy)
Christ's voice: Enrico Maria Salerno
Running Time: 140 minutes

1966 *Uccellacci e Uccellini* (*Hawks and Sparrows*)
Production Company: Arco Film
Producer: Alfredo Bini
Director: Pier Paolo Pasolini
Assistant Director: Sergio Citti
Script: Pier Paolo Pasolini
Directors of Photography: Mario Bernardo, Tonino delli Colli
Costumes: Danilo Donati
Editor: Nino Baragli
Music: Ennio Morricone
Sound: Pietro Ortolani
Cast: Toto (Innocenti Toto and Brother Ciccillo), Ninetto Davoli (Innocenti Ninetto and Brother Ninetto), Femi Benussi (Luna), Rossana di Rocco (Friend of Ninetto), Lena Lin Solaro (Urganda La Sconosciuta), Rosina Moroni (Peasant Woman), Renato Capogna and Pietro Davoli (Medieval Louts), Gabriele Baldini (Dante's Dentist), Riccardo Redi (Ingegnere)
The Crow's voice: Francesco Leonetti
Running Time: 86 minutes

Le Streghe (*The Witches*)
"La Terra Vista dalla Luna" episode
(Other episodes by Luchino Visconti, Mauro Bolognini, Franco Rossi, Vittorio de Sica)
Production Company: Dino De Laurentiis Cinematografica
Director: Pier Paolo Pasolini
Assistant Director: Sergio Citti
Script: Pier Paolo Pasolini
Director of Photography (Technicolor): Giuseppe Rotunno
Costumes: Piero Tosi
Sculptures: Pino Zac
Editor: Piero Piccioni
Cast: Toto (Ciancicato Miao), Ninetto Davoli (Basciu Miao), Silvana Mangano (Assurdina Cai), Laura Betti (Tourist), Luigi Leone (Tourist), Mario Cipriani (Priest)

Capriccio all'Italiana
"Che Cosa Sono le Nuvole?" episode
(Other episodes by Steno, Mauro Bolognini [2], Pino Zac, Mario Monicelli)
Production Company: Dino De Laurentiis Cinematografica
Producer: Dino De Laurentiis
Director: Pier Paolo Pasolini
Script: Pier Paolo Pasolini
Director of Photography (Technicolor): Tonino delli Colli
Editor: Nino Baragli
Song: "Cosi Sono le Nuvole," by Domenico Modugno, Pier Paolo Pasolini
Cast: Toto (Iago), Franco Franchi (Cassio), Ciccio Ingrassia (Roderigo), Domenico Modugno (Dustman), Ninetto Davoli (Othello), Laura Betti (Desdemona), Adriana Asti (Bianca), Carlo Pisacane (Brabantio), Francesco Leonetti (Puppeteer)

1967 *Edipo Re* (*Oedipus Rex*)
Production Company: Arco Film
Producer: Alfredo Bini
Director: Pier Paolo Pasolini
Assistant Director: Jean-Claude Biette
Script: Pier Paolo Pasolini, inspired by *Oedipus Rex* and *Oedipus at Colonus,* by Sophocles
Director of Photography (Technicolor): Giuseppe Ruzzolini
Cameraman: Otello Spila
Costumes: Danilo Donati
Editor: Nino Baragli
Music: Rumanian and Japanese folk music, plus original music coordinated by Pier Paolo Pasolini
Cast: Franco Citti (Oedipus), Silvana Mangano (Jocasta), Alida Valli (Merope) Carmelo Bene (Creon), Julian Beck (Tiresias), Luciano Bartoli (Laius), Francesco Leonetti (Servant), Ahmed Bellashmi (Polybus), Giandomenico Davoli (Shepherd of Polybus), Ninetto Davoli (Messenger), Pier Paolo Pasolini (High Priest), Jean-Claude Biette (Priest)
Running Time: 110 minutes

Amore e Rabbia
"La Fiore di Campo" episode
(Other episodes directed by Carlo Lizzani, Bernardo Bertolucci, Jean-Luc Godard, Marco Bellocchio)
Production Company: Castoro Film (Rome)/Anouchka Film (Paris)
Director: Pier Paolo Pasolini
Director of Photography (Technicolor): Giuseppe Ruzzolini
Music: Giovanni Fusco; St. Matthew Passion, by Bach
Cast: Ninetto Davoli
Running Time: 12 minutes
The film was originally conceived as *Vangelo '70,* and Pasolini's episode was then called "Il Fico Innocente."

1968 *Teorema* (*Theorem*)
Production Company: Aetos Film
Producers: Franco Rossellini, Manolo Bolognini
Director: Pier Paolo Pasolini
Assistant Director: Sergio Citti
Script: Pier Paolo Pasolini, based on his own novel
Director of Photography (Eastmancolor): Giuseppe Ruzzolini
Editor: Nino Baragli
Music: Ennio Morricone
Sound: Dario Fronzetti
Cast: Terence Stamp (the Visitor), Silvana Mangano (Lucia), Massimo Girotti (Paolo), Anne Wiazemsky (Odetta), Laura Betti (Emilia), Andrés José Cruz (Pietro), Ninetto Davoli (Angelino), Alfonso Gatto, Carlo de Mejo, Adele Cambria
Running Time: 98 minutes

Appunti per un Film Indiano
Director: Pier Paolo Pasolini
Short television reportage made of materials shot on a location-scouting trip to India.

1969 *Porcile* (*Pigsty*)
Production Company: Film dell'Orso
Producer: Gian Vittorio Baldi
Director: Pier Paolo Pasolini
Assistant Directors: Sergio Citti, Fabio Garriba
Script: Pier Paolo Pasolini
Directors of Photography: Tonino delli Colli, Armando Nanuzzi, Giuseppe Ruzzolini
Costumes: Danilo Donati
Editor: Nino Baragli
Music: Benedetto Ghiglia
Sound: Alberto Salvatori
Cast: Pierre Clementi (the Man), Jean-Pierre Léaud (Julian), Alberto Lionello (Klotz), Ugo Tognazzi (Herthitze), Anne Wiazemsky (His Daughter), Margherita Lozano (the Mother), Mario Ferresi (Hans Gunzther),

Franco Citti (a Companion), Ninetto Davoli (Marachione)
Running Time: 100 minutes

Medea
Production Company: San Marco
Producer: Franco Rossellini
Director: Pier Paolo Pasolini
Script: Pier Paolo Pasolini, from the *Medea* of Euripides
Director of Photography (Eastmancolor): Ennio Guarnieri
Costumes: Piero Tosi
Editor: Nino Baragli
Music: Supervised by Pier Paolo Pasolini, Elsa Morante
Cast: Maria Callas (Medea), Giuseppe Gentile (Jason), Laurent Terzieff (the Centaur) Massimo Girotti, Margaret Clementi (Glancia), Ninetto Davoli, Luigi Barbini
Running Time: 118 minutes

1970 *Ostia*
Production Company: Mancori-Chretien
Producer: Salvatore Gerbino
Artistic and Technical Supervision: Pier Paolo Pasolini
Director: Sergio Citti
Assistant Director: Claudio Duccini
Script: Pier Paolo Pasolini, Sergio Citti
Director of Photography: Mario Mancini
Costumes: Mario Ambrosino
Editor: Nino Baragli, Carlo Reali
Music: Franco de Masi
Sound: Angelo Spadone
Cast: Laurent Terzieff (Bandicra), Franco Citti (Rabbino), Anita Sanders (the Girl), Ninetto Davoli (Fiorino), Lambert Maggiorani, Celessino Compagnoni, Luisa Tirinnanzi
Running Time: 105 minutes

Appunti per un Orestiade Africana
Director: Pier Paolo Pasolini

Director of Photography: Giorgio Pelloni
Short based on material shot on a location-scouting trip

Appunti per un Romanzo nell'Immondismi
Director: Pier Paolo Pasolini
Short documentary on a strike of street cleaners

1971 *Il Decamerone* (*The Decameron*)
Production Company: REA
Producer: Alberto Grimaldi
Director: Pier Paolo Pasolini
Associate Director: Sergio Citti
Assistant Director: Umberto Angelucci
Script: Pier Paolo Pasolini, based on Boccaccio's *Il Decamerone*
Director of Photography (Technicolor): Tonino delli Colli
Production Design: Dante Ferretti
Costumes: Danilo Donati
Editor: Enzo Ocone
Music: Ennio Morricone, historical selections coordinated by Pier Paolo Pasolini
Sound: Pietro Spadone
Cast: Franco Citti (Ciappelletto), Ninetto Davoli (Andreuccio), Pier Paolo Pasolini (Giotto), Silvana Mangano (the Madonna), Angela Ince (Personella), Patrizia Capparelli (Alibech), Jovan Jovanić (Rustico), Giani Rizzo (Chief Friar)
Running Time: 111 minutes

1972 *The Canterbury Tales*
Production Company: PEA Produzione
Producer: Alberto Grimaldi
Director: Pier Paolo Pasolini
Assistant Directors: Sergio Citti, Umberto Angelucci, Peter Shepherd
Script: Pier Paolo Pasolini, based an Chaucer's *Canterbury Tales*
Director of Photography: Tonino delli Colli

Costumes: Dante Ferretti
Editor: Nino Baragli
Music: Ennio Morricone, historical selections coordinated by Pier Paolo Pasolini
Sound: Danilo Donati
Cast: Hugh Griffith (January), Josephine Chaplin (May), Laura Betti (the Wife of Bath), Ninetto Davoli (the Cook's Apprentice), Franco Citti (the Devil), Pier Paolo Pasolini (Chaucer), Alan Webb (the Host)
Running Time: 109 minutes

1973 *Storie Scellerate*
Production Company: PEA/United Artists
Producer: Alberto Grimaldi
Director: Sergio Citti
Script: Pier Paolo Pasolini, Sergio Citti
Director of Photography (Technicolor): Tonino delli Colli
Art Director: Dante Ferretti
Editors: Enzo Ocone, Nino Baragli
Music: Francesco de Masi
Cast: Ninetto Davoli (Bernardino), Franco Citti (Mammone), Nicoletta Machiavelli (Duchess Catarina), Elizabeth Genovesi (Bertolina), Oscar Fochetti (Agostino), Giacomo Rizzo (Don Leopoldo), Silvano Gatti, Roberto Simmi, Sebastiano Soldati, Gianni Rizzo, Enzo Patriglia, Ennio Panosetti, Fabrizio Mennoni
Running Time: 105 minutes

1974 *Il Fiore delle Mille e Una Notte* (*The Arabian Nights*)
Production Company: PEA/United Artists
Producer: Alberto Grimaldi
Director: Pier Paolo Pasolini
Script: Pier Paolo Pasolini
Director of Photography (Technicolor): Giuseppe Ruzzolini
Art Director: Dante Ferretti
Editors: Enzo Ocone, Nino Baragli, Tatiana Casini
Music: Ennio Morricone

Cast: Ninetto Davoli (Aziz), Franco Citti (Prince Tagi), Ines Pellegrini (Zumurrud), Franco Merli (Mur-el-Din), Luigina Rocchi, Francesco Paolo Governale, Zeudi Biasolo, Tessa Bouche, Margaret Clementi, Alberto Argentino
Running Time: 155 minutes

LINDSAY ANDERSON

AS ACTOR, EDITOR, PRODUCER

1952 *The Pleasure Garden*
Director: James Broughton
Producer/Actor: Lindsay Anderson

1956 *Together*
Director: Lorenza Mazzetti
Supervising Editor: Lindsay Anderson

The Parachute
Director: Anthony Page
Lindsay Anderson plays the Gestapo lawyer.

1969 *Inadmissible Evidence*
Director: Anthony Page
Lindsay Anderson plays a barrister.

AS DIRECTOR

1948 *Meet the Pioneers*
Production Company: Richard Sutcliffe Ltd.
Producers: Desmond and Lois Sutcliffe
Director: Lindsay Anderson
Directors of Photography: John Jones, Edward Brendon
Editors: Lindsay Anderson, Edward Brendon
Art Adviser: Eric Westbrook
Music: Len Scott
Commentary spoken by Lindsay Anderson
Running Time: 33 minutes

1949 *Idlers That Work*
Production Company: Richard Sutcliffe Ltd.
Producer: Richard O'Brien
Director: Lindsay Anderson
Director of Photography: George Levy
Music: from Ralph Vaughan Williams, Aaron Copland
Continuity: Lois Sutcliffe
Unit Assistants: Bill Longley, Geoff Oakes, Ernest Singer, George Wilby
Commentary spoken by Lindsay Anderson
Running Time: 17 minutes

1952 *Three Installations*
Production Company: Richard Sutcliffe Ltd.
Producer: Dermod Sutcliffe
Director: Lindsay Anderson
Director of Photography: Walter Lassally
Additional Photography: John Jones
Assistant Cameraman: Desmond Davis
Editor: Derek York
Music: from Aaron Copland, Don Gillis, Aram Khatchaturian; "Conveyor Boogie" by Alan Clare (piano) and Johnny Flanagan (drums)
Sound: Charles Green
Commentary spoken by Lindsay Anderson
Running Time: 28 minutes

Wakefield Express
Production Company: The Wakefield Express Series Ltd.
Producer: Michael Robinson
Director: Lindsay Anderson
Director of Photography: Walter Lassally
Songs: Snapethorpe and Horbury Secondary Modern Schools
Band Music: Horbury Victoria Prize Band
Production Assistant: John Fletcher
Commentary spoken by George Potts
Running Time: 33 minutes

1953 *Thursday's Children*
Production Company: World Wide Pictures
Directors: Guy Brenton, Lindsay Anderson
Script: Guy Brenton, Lindsay Anderson
Photographed by Walter Lassally
Music: Geoffrey Wright
Commentary spoken by Richard Burton
With children from the Royal School for the Deaf, Margate
Running Time: 20 minutes

O Dreamland
Production Company: Sequence
Director: Lindsay Anderson
Camera and Assistance: John Fletcher
Running Time: 12 minutes

1954 *Trunk Conveyor*
Production Company: Richard Sutcliffe Ltd./National Coal Board
Producer: Dermod Sutcliffe
Director: Lindsay Anderson
Director of Photography: John Reid
Editor: Bill Megarry
Songs by Herr Lloyd; Alf Edwards (concertina), Fitzroy Coleman (guitar)
Commentary spoken by Lindsay Anderson
Running Time: 38 minutes

1955 *Green and Pleasant Land*
Henry
The Children Upstairs
A Hundred Thousand Children
Production Company: Basic Films
Producer: Leon Clore
Director: Lindsay Anderson
Script: Lindsay Anderson
Director of Photography: Walter Lassally

Running Time: *Henry,* 5½ minutes; the others, each 4 minutes

£20 a Ton
Energy First
Production Company: Basic Films
Producer: Leon Clore
Director: Lindsay Anderson
Director of Photography: Larry Pizer
Running Time: About 5 minutes each

Foot and Mouth
Production Company: Basic Films
Producer: Leon Clore
Director: Lindsay Anderson
Script: Lindsay Anderson
Director of Photography: Walter Lassally
Editor: Bill Megarry
Technical Adviser: J. C. Davidson
Commentary spoken by Lindsay Anderson
Running Time: 20 minutes

1955–56 *The Adventures of Robin Hood*
Episodes in the television series
Production Company: Incorporated Television (Weinstein Productions for Sapphire Films)
Executive Producer: Hannah Weinstein
Associate Producer: Sidney Cole
Director: Lindsay Anderson
Assistant Director: Christopher Noble
Script Supervisor: Albert G. Ruben
Director of Photography: Ken Hodges
Supervising Editor: Thelma Connell
Art Supervisor: William Kellner
Sound: H. C. Pearson
Running Time: Each 25 minutes

1955 "Secret Mission"
Script: Ralph Smart

Music: Edwin Astley
Cast: Richard Greene (Robin Hood), Patrick Barr (Peregrinus), Alan Wheatley (Sheriff), Alexander Guage (Friar Tuck), Archie Duncan (Little John), John Longden (Wulfric), Charles Stapley (Will), Paul Connell (Innkeeper), Victor Woolf (Derwent)

1956 "The Imposters"
Script: Norman Best
Music: Edwin Astley
Cast: Richard Greene (Robin Hood), Alexander Guage (Friar Tuck), Bernadette O'Farrell (Maid Marian), Archie Duncan (Little John), Brenda de Banzie (Lady Pomfret), Nigel Green (Prival), Jack Melford (Lord Pomfret), Edward Mulhare (Le Blond), Victor Woolf (Notarius), Paul Hansard (Rolf), Shaun O'Riordan (Quentin), Martin Lane (Tom)

1956 "Ambush"
Script: Ernest Borneman, Ralph Smart
Music: Albert Elms
Cast: Richard Greene (Robin Hood), Alexander Guage (Friar Tuck), Bernadette O'Farrell (Maid Marian), Archie Duncan (Little John), Alan Wheatley (Sheriff), Donald Pleasance (Prince John), Peter Asher (Prince Arthur), Dorothy Alison (Constance), Victor Woolf (Derwent), Peter Bennett (Edwin), Shaun O'Riordan (Prince John's Captain), Edward Mulhare (Courtier), Martin Lane (Spy)

"The Haunted Mill"
Script: Paul Symonds
Music: Edwin Astley
Cast: Richard Greene (Robin Hood), Alexander Guage (Friar Tuck), Bernadette O'Farrell (Maid Marian), Alan Wheatley (Sheriff), Archie Duncan (Little John), James Hayter (Tom the Miller), Laurence Hardy (Sir William), John Schlesinger (Hale), Victor Woolf (Abbot of Whitby), Edward Mulhare (Baron Mornay),

Peter Bennett (Edward), Shaun O'Riordan (Seneschal), Martin Lane (Page)

"Isabella"
Script: Neil R. Collins
Music: Edwin Astley
Cast: Richard Greene (Robin Hood), Bernadette O'Farrell (Maid Marian), Archie Duncan (Little John), Zena Walker (Isabella), Helen Cherry (Avice), Donald Pleasance (Prince John), Alan Edwards (Pembroke), Martin Lane (Sir Damon), Howard Lang (Landlord), Shaun O'Riordan (Page), Peter Bennett (Tavernkeeper), Noel Hood (Old Woman), Lynette Mills (Chambermaid), Nicholas Brady (Will), Isobel Greig (Maid-in-Waiting)

1957 *Every Day Except Christmas*
Production Company: Ford of Britain (A Graphic Production)
Producers: Leon Clore, Karel Reisz
Director: Lindsay Anderson
Director of Photography: Walter Lassally
Music: Daniel Paris
Sound: John Fletcher
Assistants: Alex Jacobs, Brian Probyn, Maurice Ammar
Commentary spoken by Alun Owen
Running Time: 40 minutes

1958 *March to Aldermaston*
Producer: Derrick Knight
Directors: Lindsay Anderson, Karel Reisz, Stephen Peet, Derek York, Kurt Lewnhack, Derrick Knight
Script: Lindsay Anderson, Christopher Logue
Photography: Brian Probyn, Lewis McLeod, Wolfgang Suschinsky, Peter Jessop, Bill Smeaton-Russell, Allen Forbes, Derek York
Editors: Lindsay Anderson, Mary Beale
Commentary spoken by Richard Burton
Running Time: 33 minutes

1963 *This Sporting Life*

Production Company: Independent Artists (A Julian Wintle/Leslie Parkyn Production)
Producer: Karel Reisz
Director: Lindsay Anderson
Assistant Director: Ted Sturgis
Script: David Storey, based on his novel *This Sporting Life*
Director of Photography: Denys Coop
Art Director: Alan Withy
Set Dresser: Peter Lamont
Costumes: Sophie Devine
Editor: Peter Taylor
Assistant Editor: Tom Priestley
Music: Roberto Gerhard
Sound Editor: Chris Greenham
Sound: John W. Mitchell, Gordon K. McCallum
Cast: Richard Harris (Frank Machin), Rachel Roberts (Mrs. Hammond), Alan Badel (Weaver), William Hartnell (Johnson), Colin Blakely (Maurice Braithwaite), Vanda Godsell (Mrs. Weaver), Arthur Lowe (Slomer), Anne Cunningham (Judith), Jack Watson (Len Miller), Harry Markham (Wade), George Sewell (Jeff), Leonard Rossiter (Phillips), Frank Windsor (Dentist), Peter Dugold (Doctor), Wallas Eaton (Waiter), Anthony Woodruff (Headwaiter), Katherine Parr (Mrs. Farrer), Bernadette Benson (Lynda), Andrew Nolan (Ian), Michael Logan (Riley), Murray Evans (Hooker), Tom Clegg (Gower), John Gill (Cameron), Ken Traill (Trainer)
Running Time: 134 minutes

1966 *The White Bus*

Production Company: Woodfall Films
Executive Producer: Michael Deeley
Director: Lindsay Anderson
Assistant Director: Kip Gowans
Script: Shelagh Delaney

Director of Photography (in color and black-and-white): Miroslav Ondricek
Editor: Kevin Brownlow
Art Director: David Marshall
Music: Misha Donat
Sound Editor: John Fletcher
Sound Recording: Peter Handford
Cast: Patricia Healey (the Girl), Arthur Lowe (the Mayor), John Sharp (the Macebearer), Julie Perry (Bus Conductress), Victor Henry ("Transistorite"), Stephen Moore (Smart Young Man), Fanny Carby (Football Supporter), Anthony Hopkins (Brechtian Singer), Jeanne Watts (Fish-and-Chip Shop Woman), Alaba Peters, Ronald Lacey, Margaret Barron
Running Time: 46 minutes

1967 *Raz Dwa Trzy* (*The Singing Lesson*)
Production Company: Warsaw Documentary Studios
Chief of Production: Miroslaw Podolski
Director: Lindsay Anderson
Assistant Director: Joanna Nawrocka
Director of Photography: Zygmunt Samosiuk
Editor: Barbara Kosidowska
Arrangement of Songs: Ludwik Sempolinski
Piano Accompaniment: Irena Klukowna
Sound Editor: Henryk Kuzniak
Sound Recording: Malgorzata Jaworska
Singers: Piotr Fronczewski ("The Coat"), Anita Przysiecka and Marian Ginka ("Big Beat"), Aniceta Raczek ("A Lullaby—for Those Who Wait"), Waldemar Walisiak ("Sunshine Street"), Andrzej Nardelli ("Sweet Peas"), Joanna Sobieska and Andrzej Seweryn ("Oh, Miss Sabina!")
Running Time: 20 minutes

1968 *If . . .*
Production Company: Memorial
Producers: Michael Medwin, Lindsay Anderson

Director: Lindsay Anderson
Assistant Directors: John Stoneham, Stephen Frears, Stuart Baird
Script: David Sherwin, from the original script *Crusaders,* by David Sherwin and John Howlett
Director of Photography (in color and black-and-white): Miroslav Ondricek
Production Designer: Jocelyn Herbert
Costumes: Shura Cohen
Editor: David Gladwell
Music: Marc Wilkinson; "Sanctus" from the *Missa Luba*
Dubbing Editor: Alan Ball
Sound Recordist: Christian Wangler
Crusaders: Malcolm McDowell (Mick), David Wood (Johnny), Richard Warwick (Wallace), Christine Noonan (the Girl), Rupert Webster (Bobby Philips); *Whips:* Robert Swann (Rowntree), Hugh Thomas (Denson), Michael Cadman (Fortinbras), Peter Sproule (Barnes); *Staff:* Peter Jeffrey (Headmaster), Arthur Lowe (Mr. Kemp), Mona Washbourne (Matron), Mary MacLeod (Mrs. Kemp), Geoffrey Chater (Chaplain), Ben Aris (John Thomas), Graham Crowden (History Master), Charles Lloyd Pack (Classics Master), Anthony Nicholls (General Denson), Tommy Godfrey (Finchley); *Seniors:* Guy Ross (Stephans), Robin Askwith (Keating), Richard Everett (Pussy Graves), Philip Bagenal (Peanuts), Nicholas Page (Cox), Robert Yetzes (Fisher), David Griffin (Willens), Graham Sharman (Van Eyssen), Richard Tombleson (Baird); *Juniors:* Richard Davis (Machin), Brian Pettifer (Biles), Michael Newport (Brunning), Charles Sturridge (Markland), Sean Bury (Jute), Martin Beaumont (Hunter)
Running Time: 112 minutes

1973 *O Lucky Man!*
Production Company: Warners
Producers: Michael Medwin, Lindsay Anderson
Director: Lindsay Anderson
Assistant Director: Derek Cracknell

Script: David Sherwin, based on an idea by Malcolm McDowell
Director of Photography: Miroslav Ondricek
Supervising Film Editor: Tom Priestley
Film Editor: David Gladwell
Production Designer: Jocelyn Herbert
Music and Songs: Allan Price
Sound: Christian Wangler, Doug Turner
Art Director: Alan Withy
Cast: Malcolm McDowell (Mick), Ralph Richardson (Monty, Sir James), Rachel Roberts (Gloria Rowe, Madame Paillard), Arthur Lowe (Mr. Duff, Charlie Johnson, Dr. Munda), Helen Mirren (Patricia), Dandy Nichols (Tea Lady), Mona Washbourne (Shopkeeper, Sister Hallett, Usher), Graham Crowden (Professor Miller, Professor Stewart, Meths Drinker), Peter Jeffrey (Factory Chairman, Prison Governor), Philip Stone (Interrogator, Jenkins), Mary MacLeod (Mary Ball, Vicar's Wife), Wallas Eaton (John Stone, Colonel Steiger, Warer, Meths Drinker, Film Executive), Vivian Pickles (Good Lady), Michael Medwin (Army Captain, Power Station Technician, Duke of Belminster), Michael Bangerter (Interrogator, William, Released Prisoner, Assistant), Jeremy Bulloch (Young Man, Pig Boy), Warren Clarke (Master of Ceremonies, Male Nurse, Warner), Bill Owen (Superintendent Barlow, Inspector Carding), Edward Judd (Oswald), Pearl Numez (Mrs. Naida), Geoffrey Palmer (Doctor, Basil Keyes), Geoffrey Chater (Vicar, Bishop), Anthony Nicholls (General, Judge), Brian Glover (Foreman, Power Station Guard), Pat Healey (Receptionist), Alan Price (Alan), Colin Green (Colin, guitar), Ian Leake (Roadie), Clive Thacker (Clive, drums), Dave Maskee (Dave, bass guitar), Lindsay Anderson (Director)
Running Time: 176 minutes

1974 *In Celebration*
Production Company: Ely Landau Organization/American Film Theatre

Producer: Ely Landau
Director: Lindsay Anderson
Script: David Storey, based on his play
Director of Photography (Eastmancolor): Dick Rush
Art Director: Alan Withy
Editor: Russell Lloyd
Sound: Bruce White
Cast: Alan Bates (Andrew), Bill Owen (Mr. Shaw), Brian Cox (Stephen), James Bolam (Colin), Constance Chapman (Mrs. Shaw), Gabrielle Daye (Mrs. Burnett)
Running Time: 131 minutes

STANLEY KUBRICK

1951 *Day of the Fight* (U.S.A.)
Director, Photography, Editor, Sound: Stanley Kubrick
Commentary: Douglas Edwards
Documentary short on Walter Cartier, middleweight prizefighter.
Running Time: 16 minutes

Flying Padre (U.S.A.)
Director, Photography, Editor, Sound: Stanley Kubrick
Documentary short on the Reverend Fred Stadtmueller, Roman Catholic missionary of a New Mexican parish of four hundred square miles.
Running Time: 9 minutes

1953 *Fear and Desire* (U.S.A.)
Production Company: Stanley Kubrick Productions
Producer: Stanley Kubrick
Director, Photography, Editor: Stanley Kubrick
Script: Howard O. Sackler
Cast: Frank Silvera (Mac), Kenneth Harp (Corby), Virginia Leith (the Girl), Paul Mazursky (Sidney), Steve Colt (Fletcher)

1955 *Killer's Kiss* (U.S.A.)
Production Company: Minotaur
Producers: Stanley Kubrick, Morris Bousel
Director, Photography, Editor: Stanley Kubrick
Script: Stanley Kubrick, Howard O. Sackler
Music: Gerald Fried
Choreography: David Vaughan
Cast: Frank Silvera (Vincent Rapallo), Jamie Smith (Davy Gordon), Irene Kane (Gloria Price), Jerry Jarret (Albert), Iris (Ruth Sobotka), Mike Dana, Felice Orlandi, Ralph Roberts, Phil Stevenson (Hoodlums), Julius Adelman (Mannequin-Factory Owner), David Vaughan, Alec Rubin (Conventioneers)
Running Time: 64 minutes

1956 *The Killing* (U.S.A.)
Production Company: Harris-Kubrick Productions
Producer: James B. Harris
Director: Stanley Kubrick
Script: Stanley Kubrick, based on the novel *Clean Break,* by Lionel White
Additional Dialogue: Jim Thompson
Director of Photography: Lucien Ballard
Art Director: Ruth Sobotka Kubrick
Editor: Betty Steinberg
Music: Gerald Fried
Sound: Earl Snyder
Cast: Sterling Hayden (Johnny Clay), Jay C. Flippen (Marvin Unger), Marie Windsor (Sherry Peatty), Elisha Cook (George Peatty), Coleen Gray (Fay), Vince Edwards (Val Cannon), Ted de Corsia (Randy Kennan), Joe Sawyer (Mike O'Reilly), Tim Carey (Nikki), Kola Kwariani (Maurice), James Edwards (Parking-Lot Attendant)
Running Time: 83 minutes

1956 *Paths of Glory* (U.S.A.)
Production Company: Harris-Kubrick Productions

Producer: James B. Harris
Director: Stanley Kubrick
Script: Stanley Kubrick, Calder Willingham, Jim Thompson, based on the novel by Humphrey Cobb
Director of Photography: George Krause
Art Director: Ludwig Reiber
Editor: Eva Kroll
Music: Gerald Fried
Sound: Martin Muller
Cast: Kirk Douglas (Colonel Dax), Ralph Meeker (Corporal Paris), Adolphe Menjou (General Broulard), George Macready (General Mireau), Wayne Morris (Lieutenant Roget), Richard Anderson (Major Saint-Auban), Joseph Turkel (Private Arnaud), Timothy Carey (Private Ferol), Peter Capell (Colonel Judge), Susanne Christian (German Girl), Bert Freed (Sergeant Boulanger), Emile Meyer (Priest), John Stein (Captain Rousseau)
Running Time: 86 minutes

1960 *Spartacus* (U.S.A.)
Production Company: Bryna
Executive Producer: Kirk Douglas
Producer: Edward Lewis
Director: Stanley Kubrick
Script: Dalton Trumbo, based on the book by Howard Fast
Director of Photography (Technicolor, Super Technirama-70): Russell Metty
Additional Photography: Clifford Stine
Production Designer: Alexander Golitzen
Art Director: Eric Orbom
Set Decoration: Russell A. Gausman, Julia Heron
Costumes: Peruzzi, Valles, Bill Thomas
Editors: Robert Lawrence, Robert Schultz, Fred Chulack
Titles: Saul Bass
Technical Adviser: Vittorio Nino Novarese
Music: Alex North
Music Director: Joseph Gershenson

Sound: Waldon O. Watson, Joe Lapis, Murray Spivack, Ronald Pierce
Cast: Kirk Douglas (Spartacus), Laurence Olivier (Marcus Crassus), Jean Simmons (Varinia), Charles Laughton (Gracchus), Peter Ustinov (Batiatus), John Gavin (Julius Caesar), Tony Curtis (Antoninus), Nina Foch (Helena), Herbert Lom (Tigrantes), John Ireland (Crixus), John Dall (Gabrus), Charles McGraw (Marcellus), Joanna Barnes (Claudia), Harold J. Stone (David), Woody Strode (Draba), Peter Brocco (Ramon), Paul Lambert (Gannicus), Robert J. Wilke (Captain of Guard), Nicholas Dennis (Dionysius), John Hoyt (Roman Officer), Fred Worlock (Laelius), Dayton Lummis (Symmachus)
Running Time: 196 minutes (193 minutes in Great Britain)

1962 *Lolita* (Great Britain)
Production Company: Seven Arts/Anya/Transworld
Producer: James B. Harris
Director: Stanley Kubrick
Script: Vladimir Nabokov, based on his own novel
Director of Photography: Oswald Morris
Art Director: William Andrews
Set Design: Andrew Low
Editor: Anthony Harvey
Music: Nelson Riddle
Theme Music: Bob Harris
Sound: H. L. Bird, Len Shilton
Cast: James Mason (Humbert Humbert), Sue Lyon (Lolita Haze), Shelley Winters (Charlotte Haze), Peter Sellers (Clare Quilty), Diana Decker (Jean Farlow), Jerry Stovin (John Farlow), Suzanne Gibbs (Mona Farlow), Gary Cockrell (Dick), Marianna Stone (Vivian Darkbloom), Cec Linder (Physician), Lois Maxwell (Nurse Mary Lore), William Greene (Swine), C. Denier Warren (Potts), Isobel Lucas (Louise), Maxine Holden (Receptionist), James Dyrenforth (Beale), Roberta Shore (Lorna), Eric Lane (Roy), Shirley Douglas (Mrs.

Starch), Roland Brand (Bill), Colin Maitland (Charlie), Irvin Allen (Hospital Attendant), Marion Mathie (Miss Lebone), Craig Sams (Rex), John Harrison (Tom)
Running Time: 153 minutes

1964 *Dr. Strangelove, or How I Learned to Stop Worrying and Love the Bomb* (Great Britain)
Production Company: Hawk Films
Producer: Stanley Kubrick
Associate Producer: Victor Lyndon
Director: Stanley Kubrick
Script: Stanley Kubrick, Terry Southern, Peter George, based on the novel *Red Alert,* by Peter George
Director of Photography: Gilbert Taylor
Production Designer: Ken Adam
Art Director: Peter Murton
Editor: Anthony Harvey
Special Effects: Wally Veevers
Music: Laurie Johnson
Aviation Adviser: Captain John Crewdson
Sound: John Cox
Cast: Peter Sellers (Group Captain Lionel Mandrake, President Muffley, Dr. Strangelove), George C. Scott (General "Buck" Turgidson), Sterling Hayden (General Jack D. Ripper), Keenan Wynn (Colonel "Bat" Guano), Slim Pickens (Major T. J. "King" Kong), Peter Bull (Ambassador de Sadesky), Tracy Reed (Miss Scott), James Earl Jones (Lieutenant Lothar Zogg, Bombardier), Jack Creley (Mr. Staines), Frank Berry (Lieutenant H. R. Dietrich, D.S.O.), Glenn Beck (Lieutenant W. D. Kivel, Navigator), Shane Rimmer (Captain G. A. "Ace" Owens, Copilot), Paul Tamarin (Lieutenant B. Goldberg, Radio Operator), Gordon Tanner (General Faceman), Robert O'Neil (Admiral Randolph), Roy Stephens (Frank), Laurence Herder, John McCarthy, Hal Galili (Members of Burpelson Base Defense Corps)
Running Time: 94 minutes

1968 *2001: A Space Odyssey* (Great Britain)
Production Company: Metro-Goldwyn-Mayer
Producer: Stanley Kubrick
Director: Stanley Kubrick
Script: Stanley Kubrick, Arthur C. Clarke, based on Clarke's short story "The Sentinel"
Director of Photography (Super Panavision, Metrocolor): Geoffrey Unsworth
Additional Photography: John Alcott
Special Photographic Effects Designer and Director: Stanley Kubrick
Special Photographic Effects Supervisors: Wally Veevers, Douglas Trumbull, Con Pederson, Tom Howard
Production Designers: Tony Masters, Harry Lange, Ernie Archer
Art Director: John Hoesli
Costumes: Hardy Amies
Editor: Ray Lovejoy
Music: from Richard Strauss, Johann Strauss, Aram Khachaturian, György Ligeti
Sound: Winston Ryder
Cast: Keir Dullea (David Bowman), Garry Lockwood (Frank Poole), William Sylvester (Dr. Heywood Floyd), Daniel Richter (Moonwatcher), Douglas Rain (Voice of HAL 9000), Leonard Rossiter (Smyslov), Margaret Tyzack (Elena), Robert Beatty (Halvorsen), Sean Sullivan (Michaels), Frank Miller (Mission Control), Penny Brahms (Stewardess), Alan Gifford (Poole's Father), Edward Bishop, Glenn Beck, Edwina Carroll, Mike Lovell, Peter Delman, Dany Grover, Brian Hawley
Running Time: 141 minutes

1971 *A Clockwork Orange* (Great Britain)
Production Company: Polaris Productions
Producer: Stanley Kubrick
Executive Producers: Max L. Raab, Si Litvinoff
Director: Stanley Kubrick

Script: Stanley Kubrick, based on the novel by Anthony Burgess
Director of Photography (color): John Alcott
Production Designer: John Barry
Art Directors: Russell Hagg, Peter Shields
Editor: Bill Butter
Music: Walter Carlos, Ludwig Van Beethoven, Giacomo Rossini, Edward Elgar, Terry Tucker
Songs: "Singin' in the Rain," Arthur Freed, Nacio Herb Brown; "I Want to Marry a Lighthouse Keeper," Erika Eigen
Sound: John Jordan
Cast: Malcolm McDowell (Alex), Patrick Magee (Mr. Alexander), Michael Bates (Chief Guard), Warren Clarke (Dim), John Clive (Stage Actor), Adrienne Corri (Mrs. Alexander), Carl Duering (Dr. Brodsky), Paul Farrell (Tramp), Clive Francis (Lodger), Michael Gover (Prison Governor), Miriam Karlin (Cat Lady), James Marcus (Georgie), Aubrey Morris (Deltoid), Godfrey Quigley (Prison Chaplain), Shela Raynor (Mum), Madge Ryan (Dr. Branom), John Savident (Conspirator), Anthony Sharp (Minister), Phillip Stone (Dad), Pauline Taylor (Psychiatrist), Margaret Tyzack (Conspirator); also Steven Berkoff, Lindsay Campbell, Michael Tarn, David Prowse, Barrie Cookson, Jan Adair, Gaye Brown, Peter Burton, John J. Carney, Vivienne Chandler, Richard Connaught, Prudence Drage, Carol Drinkwater, Lee Fox, Cheryl Grunwald, Gillian Hills, Craig Hunter, Shirley Jaffe, Barbara Scott, Virginia Weatherell, Neil Wilson, Katya Wyeth
Running Time: 137 minutes

ANDY WARHOL/PAUL MORRISSEY

Necessarily tentative and full of holes, since many of the films were abandoned, never shown, or combined and divided in various ways, while few before 1970 have any credits.

1963 *Tarzan and Jane Regained, Sort of . . .* (2 hours) (silent)
Cast: Taylor Mead (Tarzan), Naomi Levine (Jane), Dennis Hopper, Claes and Pat Oldenburg, Wally Berman

Eat (40 minutes)
Robert Anderson eats a mushroom.

Sleep (6 hours) (silent)

Kiss (*Andy Warhol Serial*) (50 minutes) (silent)
Cast: Naomi Levine with Ed Sanders, Rufus Collins, Gerard Malanga; Baby Jane Holzer with John Palmer, Gerard Malanga; John Palmer with Andrew Meyer; Freddie Herko, Johnny Dodd, Charlotte Gilbertson, Philip van Rensselaet, Pierre Restaney, Marisol

Andy Warhol Films Jack Smith Filming "Normal Love" (silent)

Dance Movie (*Roller Skate*) (45 minutes) (silent)
Freddie Herko roller skating.

Haircut (33 minutes) (silent)
Billy Linich having his hair cut.

1964 *Blow Job* (30 minutes) (silent)

Batman Dracula (2 hours) (silent)
Cast: Jack Smith (Dracula), Baby Jane Holzer, Beverly Grant, Ivy Nicholson

Empire (8 hours) (silent)
Directed by Andy Warhol and John Palmer

Harry Geldzahler (100 minutes) (silent)
Harry Geldzahler smoking a cigar.

Salome and Delilah (30 minutes) (silent)
Cast: Freddie Herko, Debbie Lee

Soap Opera (*The Lester Persky Story*) (70 minutes) (silent)
Directed by Andy Warhol and Jerry Benjamin
Cast: Baby Jane Holzer

Couch (40 minutes) (silent)
Cast: Gerard Malanga, Piero Heliczer, Naomi Levine, Gregory Corso, Allen Ginsberg, John Palmer, Baby Jane Holzer, Ivy Nicholson, Amy Taubin, Ondine, Peter Orlovski, Jack Kerouac, Taylor Mead, Kate Heliczer, Rufus Collins, Joseph Le Seuer, Bingingham Birdie, Mark Lancaster, Gloria Wood, Billy Linich

Shoulder (4 minutes) (silent)
Lucinda Childs's shoulder.

Mario Banana (4 minutes) (silent)
Mario Montez eats a banana.

Harlot (70 minutes)
Cast: Mario Montez, Gerard Malanga, Philip Fagan, Carol Koshinskie
Voices of: Ronald Tavel, Harry Fainlight, Billy Linich

13 Most Beautiful Women (40 minutes) (silent)
Cast: Baby Jane Holzer, Anne Buchanan, Sally Kirkland, Barbare Rose, Beverly Grant, Nancy Worthington Fish, Ivy Nicholson, Ethel Scull, Esabel Eberstadt, Jane Wilson, Imu, Marisol, Lucinda Childs, Olga Kluever

13 Most Beautiful Boys (40 minutes) (silent)
Cast: Freddie Herko, Gerard Malanga, Dennis Deegan, Kelly Eddy, Bruce Rudo, Existiert nur im Original

50 Fantastics and 50 Personalities (1964–66) (silent)
Cast: Allen Ginsberg, Ed Sanders, Jim Rosenquist,

Zachary Scott, Peter Orlovski, Henry Rago, Ted Berrigan, Roy Lichtenstein, Gregory Battcock, Barbara Rubin, Daniel Cassidy, Harry Fainlight

Taylor Mead's Ass (70 minutes) (silent)
Cast: Taylor Mead

1965 *Ivy and John* (35 minutes)

Suicide (70 minutes) (color)

Screen Test No. 1 (70 minutes)
Script: Ronald Tavel
Cast: Philip Fagan

Screen Test No. 2 (70 minutes)
Script: Ronald Tavel
Cast: Mario Montez

The Life of Juanita Castro (70 minutes)
Script: Ronald Tavel
Cast: Marie Menken (Juanita), Elektrah (Raoul), Waldo Diaz Bahart, Mercedes and Marina Ospina, Ronald Tavel

Drunk (70 minutes)
Emile de Antonio drinks whisky.

Horse (105 minutes)
Script: Ronald Tavel
Cameraman: Buddy Wirtschafter
Cast: Larry Lattrae, Gregory Battcock, Daniel Cassidy, Tosh Carillo

Poor Little Rich Girl (70 minutes)
Assistant Director: Chuck Wein
Cast: Edie Sedgwick

Vinyl (70 minutes)
Script: Ronald Tavel
Cast: Gerard Malanga, Victor and Edie Sedgwick, Ondine, Tosh Carillo, Larry Lattrae, Jacques Potin, John MacDermott

Bitch (70 minutes)
Cast: Marie Menken, Willard Maas, Edie Sedgwick, Gerard Malanga

Restaurant (35 minutes)
Assistant: Chuck Wein
Cast: Edie Sedgwick, Ondine

Kitchen (70 minutes)
Script: Ronald Tavel
Cast: Edie Sedgwick, Roger Trudeau, Donald Lyons, Elektrah, David McCabe, Reni Ricard

Prison (70 minutes)
Script: Ronald Tavel
Cameraman: Buddy Wirtschafter
Cast: Edie Sedgwick, Bibie Hansen, Marie Menken

Face (70 minutes)
Cast: Edie Sedgwick

Afternoon (105 minutes)
Cast: Edie Sedgwick, Ondine, Arthur Loeb, Donald Lyons, Dorothy Dean

Beauty No. 2 (70 minutes)
Script/Assistant: Chuck Wein
Cast: Edie Sedgwick, Gino Pesichio

Space (70 minutes)
Cast: Edie Sedgwick, Eric Anderson

Outer and Inner Space (70 minutes)
Cast: Edie Sedgwick

My Hustler (70 minutes)
Director: Chuck Wein
Cast: Paul America, Ed Hood, John MacDermott, Geneviève Charbon, Joseph Campbell, Dorothy Dean

Camp (70 minutes)
Cast: Paul Swan, Baby Jane Holzer, Mar-Mar Donyle, Jodie Babs, Tally Brown, Jack Smith, Fu-Fu Smith, Tosh Carillo, Mario Montez, Gerard Malanga

Paul Swan (70 minutes) (color)
Cast: Paul Swan

Hedy (*Hedy the Shoplifter*) (*The 14 Year Old Girl*) (*The Shopper*) (70 minutes)
Script: Ronald Tavel
Music and Sound: John Cale, Louis Reed
Cast: Mario Montez (Hedy), Mary Woronov, Harvey Tavel, Ingrid Superstar, Ronald Tavel, Gerard Malanga, Rich Lockwood, James Claire, Randy Borscheidt, David Meyers, Jack Smith, Arnold Rockwood

The Closet (70 minutes)
Based on an idea by Barbara Rubin
Cast: Nico and Randy Borscheidt

More Milk Yvette (*Lana Turner*) (70 minutes)
Script: Ronald Tavel
Cast: Mario Montez, Paul Caruso, Richard Schmidt

Lupe (70 minutes)
Cast: Edie Sedgwick, Billy Linich

1966 *Bufferin* (*Gerard Malanga Reads Poetry*) (35 minutes) (color)
Cast: Gerard Malanga, Rouna

Eating Too Fast (70 minutes)
Cast: Gregory Battcock
A sound version of *Blow Job*.

The Velvet Underground and Nico (70 minutes)

The Chelsea Girls (3 hours 15 minutes) (color and black-and-white, two screens)
"The Gerard Malanga Story"—Marie Menken, Mary Woronov, Gerard Malanga
"Hanoi Hanna (Queen of China)"—Script: Ronald Tavel; with Mary Woronov, "International Velvet," Ingrid Superstar, Angelina "Pepper" Davis
"The Pope Ondine Story"—Bob "Ondine" Olivio, Angelina "Pepper" Davis, "International Velvet," Mary Woronov, Gerard Malanga, René Ricard, Ingrid Superstar
"Their Town"—Eric Emerson; strobe lighting by Billy Linich

1967 **** (*Four Stars*) (25 hours) (color)
Dismembered after one showing into:
- *International Velvet* (30 minutes)
- *Alan and Dickin* (2 hours)
  Alan Midgette, Dickin
- *Imitation of Christ* (8 hours; shorter version, 100 minutes)
  Photographed by Paul Morrissey
  Patrick Tilden, Nico, Ondine, Tom Baker, Taylor Mead, Brigid Polk
- *Courtroom* (30 minutes)
  Ondine, Ivy, Ultra Violet, René Ricard
- *Gerard Has His Hair Removed with Nair* (30 minutes)
- *Katrina Dead* (30 minutes)
- *Sansolito* (30 minutes)
- *Alan and Apple* (30 minutes)
  Alan Midgette
- *Group One* (30 minutes)

Ingrid Superstar
Sunset Beach on Long Island (30 minutes)
High Ashbury (30 minutes)
Ultra Violet, Ondine, Nico
Tiger Morse (20 minutes)
Tiger Morse
Other reels (each 20 minutes) entitled:
Ondine and Ingrid, Ivy and Susan, Sunset in California, Ondine in Yellow Hair, Philadelphia Story, Katrina, Barbara and Ivy, Ondine and Edie, Susan and David, Orion, Emanuel, Rolando, Easthampton Beach, Swimming Pool, Nico-Katrina, Tally and Ondine, Ondine in Bathroom, Susan Screen Test, Susan Bottomly

I, a Man (100 minutes)
Cast: Tom Baker, Ivy Nicholson, Ingrid Superstar, Valerie Solanis, Cynthia May, Betina Coffin, Ultra Violet, Nico

Bike Boy (96 minutes) (color)
Script: Andy Warhol
Cameraman: Paul Morrissey
Cast: Joe Spencer (Bike Boy), Viva (Girl on Couch), Brigid Polk (Girl with Husband), Ingrid Superstar (Girl in Kitchen), Ed Hood (Florist), George Ann, Bruce Ann (Sales Assistants)

Nude Restaurant (96 minutes) (color)
Cameraman: Paul Morrissey
Cast: Viva, Taylor Mead, Louis Waldon, Alan Midgette, Brigid Polk, Ingrid Superstar, Julian Burroughs, Julian Davis

The Loves of Ondine (another derivative from ****) (86 minutes)
Cameraman: Paul Morrissey
Cast: Ondine, Viva, Joe Dallesandro, Angelina Davis, Ivy Nicholson, Brigid Polk

1968 *Lonesome Cowboys* (100 minutes) (color)
Cameraman: Paul Morrissey
Cast: Taylor Mead, Louis Waldon, Viva, Eric Emerson, Francis Francine, Alan Midgette, Julian Burroughs, Tom Hompertz, Joe Dallesandro

Fuck (*Blue Movie*) (90 minutes) (color)
Produced, directed, and photographed by Andy Warhol
Associate Producer: Paul Morrissey
Sound: Jed Johnson
Cast: Viva, Louis Waldon

San Diego Surf (*Surfing Movie*) (90 minutes) (color)
Cameraman: Paul Morrissey
Cast: Viva, Taylor Mead, Louis Waldon, Ingrid Superstar, Eric Emerson, Tom Hompertz, Joe Dallesandro

1969 *Flesh* (105 minutes)
Directed, written, and photographed (Eastmancolor) by Paul Morrissey
Producer: Andy Warhol
Cast: Joe Dallesandro (Joe), Geraldine Smith (Joe's Wife), Maurice Bradell (the Artist), Louis Waldon (the Gymnast), Geri Miller (Geri), Candy Darling and Jackie Curtis (the Transvestites), Patti d'Urbanville (Wife's Girl Friend)

1970 *Trash* (103 minutes)
Directed, written, and photographed (Eastmancolor) by Paul Morrissey
Producer: Andy Warhol
Editor: Jed Johnson
Song: "Mama Look at Me Now," by Joe Saggarino; sung by Geri Miller
Sound: Jed Johnson
Cast: Joe Dallesandro (Joe), Holly Woodlawn (Holly), Jane Forth (Jane), Michael Sklar (Welfare Investigator), Geri Miller (Go-Go Dancer), Andrea Feldman (Rich Girl), Johnny Putnam (Boy from Yonkers), Bruce

Pecheur (Jane's Husband), Diane Podlewski (Holly's Sister), Bob Dallesandro (Boy on the Street)

1972 *Heat* (100 minutes)
Written, photographed, and directed by Paul Morrissey
Script based on an original idea by John Hallowell
Cast: Joe Dallesandro (Joe), Sylvia Miles (Sally), Andrea Feldman (Jessica), Pat Ast (Motel Owner), Ray Vestal (Movie Producer), P. J. Lester (Sally's Former Husband), Harold Child (His Roommate), Eric Emerson (Mute), Gary Koznocha (Mute's Brother), John Hallowell (Hollywood Columnist), Bonnie Glick (Jessica's Girl Friend), Pat Parlemon (Girl by the Pool)

Women in Revolt (*Sex*) (85 minutes)
Produced and photographed by Andy Warhol
Executive Producer: Paul Morrissey
Associate Producer: Jed Johnson
Cast: Candy Darling, Jackie Curtis, Holly Woodlawn, Jane Forth

L'Amour (90 minutes)
Directors: Andy Warhol, Paul Morrissey
Cameraman: Jed Johnson
Music: Ben Weisman
Lyrics: Michael Sklar
Cast: Michael Sklar, Donna Jordon, Jane Forth, Max Delys

1974 *Frankenstein* (*Flesh for Frankenstein*) (95 minutes)
Presented by Andy Warhol
Production Company: Carlo Ponti/Jean Yanne/Jean-Pierre Rassem
Producer: Andrew Braunsberg
Director: Paul Morrissey
Script: Paul Morrissey
Director of Photography (Eastmancolor, 3-D): Luigi Kueveillier
Editor: Jed Johnson

Music: Carlo Gizzi
Cast: Joe Dallesandro (Nicholas), Udo Kier (Frankenstein), Monique Van Vooren (Katrin), Arno Juerging (Otto), Srdjan Zelenović (Man Monster), Dalila di Lazzaro (Girl Monster)

Dracula (*Blood for Dracula*) (90 minutes)
Presented by Andy Warhol
Production Company: Carlo Ponti/Jean Yanne/Jean-Pierre Rassem
Producer: Andrew Braunsberg
Director: Paul Morrissey
Script: Paul Morrissey
Director of Photography (Eastmancolor): Luigi Kueveillier
Editor: Jed Johnson
Music: Carlo Gizzi
Cast: Joe Dallesandro (Mario), Udo Kier (Dracula), Vittorio de Sica (Marquis), Maxime McKendry (Marquisa), Arno Juerging (Anton), Milena Vukotić (Esmerelda), Dominique Darel (Saphiria), Stefania Casini (Rubinia), Silvia Dionisic (Perla), Roman Polanski (Man at Inn)

SATYAJIT RAY

1955 *Pather Panchali* (*Song of the Little Road*)
Production Company: Government of West Bengal
Director: Satyajit Ray
Script: Satyajit Ray, based on the novel by Bibhuti Bhushan Bannerjee
Director of Photography: Subrata Mitra
Editor: Dulal Dutta
Art Director: Bansi Chandragupta
Music: Ravi Shankar
Cast: Karuna Bannerjee (Sarbojaya), Kanu Bannerjee (Harihar), Chunnibala (Auntie), Subir Chatterjee

(Apu), Uma Das Gupta (Durga)
Running Time: 115 minutes

1956 *Aparajito* (*The Unvanquished*)
Production Company: Epic Films
Director: Satyajit Ray
Script: Satyajit Ray, based on the novel by Bibhuti Bhushan Bannerjee
Director of Photography: Subrata Mitra
Editor: Dulal Dutta
Art Director: Bansi Chandragupta
Music: Ravi Shankar
Cast: Karuna Bannerjee (Sarbojaya), Kanu Bannerjee (Harihar), Pinaki Sen Gupta (Apu as a Child), Sumuran Ghoshal (Apu as an Adolescent), Subodh Ganguli (Headmaster), Ramani Sen Gupta (Uncle)
Running Time: 113 minutes

1957 *Paras Pathar* (*The Philosopher's Stone*)
Production Company: L. B. Films International
Director: Satyajit Ray
Script: Satyajit Ray, based on a story by Parasuram
Director of Photography: Subrata Mitra
Editor: Dulal Dutta
Art Director: Bansi Chandragupta
Music: Ravi Shankar
Cast: Tulsi Chakravarty (Paresh Dutta), Ranibala (Mrs. Dutta)
Running Time: 90 minutes

1958 *Jalsaghar* (*The Music Room*)
Production Company: Satyajit Ray Productions
Director: Satyajit Ray
Script: Satyajit Ray, based on a story by Tara Shanker Bannerjee
Director of Photography: Subrata Mitra
Editor: Dulal Dutta
Art Director: Bansi Chandragupta

Music: Ustad Vilayat Khan
Cast: Chabbi Biswas (Bishamber Rai), Ganga Pada Basu, Kali Sarkar, Padma Devi, Tulsi Lahari, Pinaki Sen Gupta
Running Time: 100 minutes

1959 *Apur Sansar* (*The World of Apu*)
Production Company: Satyajit Ray Productions
Director: Satyajit Ray
Script: Satyajit Ray, based on the novel by Bibhuti Bhushan Bannerjee
Director of Photography: Subrata Mitra
Editor: Dulal Dutta
Art Director: Bansi Chandragupta
Music: Ravi Shankar
Cast: Soumitra Chatterjee (Apu), Sharmila Tagore (Aparna), Shapan Mukherjee (Pulu), Aloke Chakravarty (Kajole)
Running Time: 106 minutes

1960 *Devi* (*The Goddess*)
Production Company: Satyajit Ray Productions
Director: Satyajit Ray
Script: Satyajit Ray, based on a story by Prabhat Kumar Mukherjee
Director of Photography: Subrata Mitra
Editor: Dulal Dutta
Art Director: Bansi Chandragupta
Music: Ali Akbar Khan
Cast: Chabbi Biswas (Kalikanker), Sharmila Tagore (Doyamoyee), Soumitra Chatterjee (Uma Prased), Purnendu Mukherjee (Taraprasad), Karuna Bannerjee (Harasundari), Arpan Choudhury (Khoka)
Running Time: 93 minutes

1961 *Rabindranath Tagore*
Production Company: Indian Government Films Division
Director: Satyajit Ray

Script and commentary: Satyajit Ray
Director of Photography: Soumendu Roy
Editor: Dulal Dutta
Art Director: Bansi Chandragupta
Music: Jyotirindra Moitra
Cast: Raya Chatterjee (Tagore as a Child), Sumuran Ghoshal (Tagore as a Youth)
Running Time: 55 minutes

Teen Kanya (*Three Daughters*)
Production Company: Satyajit Ray Productions
Director: Satyajit Ray
Script: Satyajit Ray, based on stories by Rabindranath Tagore
Director of Photography: Soumendu Roy
Editor: Dulal Dutta
Art Director: Bansi Chandragupta
Music: Satyajit Ray
Cast:
"The Postmaster"–Anil Chatterjee (Nandal), Chandana Bannerjee (Ratan)
"Monihara"–Kali Bannerjee (Phani Bhushan), Kanika Mozumdar (Monimalika)
"Samapti"–Aparna Dasgupta (Mrinmoyee), Soumitra Chatterjee (Amulya)
Running Time: 171 minutes

1962 *Kanchenjunga*
Production Company: N.C.A. Productions
Director: Satyajit Ray
Script: Satyajit Ray
Director of Photography (Eastmancolor): Subrata Mitra
Editor: Dulal Dutta
Music: Satyajit Ray
Cast: Chabbi Biswas (Rai Bahadur Indranath), Alakananda Ray (Monisha), Anubha Gupta (Anima), Karuna Bannerjee (Labanya)
Running Time: 100 minutes

Abhijan
Production Company: Abhijatrik
Director: Satyajit Ray
Script: Satyajit Ray, based on the novel by Tara Shanker Bannerjee
Director of Photography: Soumendu Roy
Editor: Dulal Dutta
Art Director: Bansi Chandragupta
Music: Satyajit Ray
Cast: Soumitra Chatterjee (Narsingh), Waheeda Rehman (Gulabi), Ruma Guha Thakurta (Neelma)
Running Time: 135 minutes (approximately)

1963 *Mahanagar* (*The Big City*)
Production Company: R. D. Bansal
Director: Satyajit Ray
Script: Satyajit Ray
Director of Photography: Subrata Mitra
Editor: Dulal Dutta
Art Director: Bansi Chandragupta
Music: Satyajit Ray
Cast: Anil Chatterjee (Subrata Mozumdar), Madhabi Mukherjee (Arati Mozumdar), Vicky Redwood (Edith), Haradhan Bannerjee (Mr. Mukherjee), Haren Chatterjee (Father), Jaya Badhuri (Sister)
Running Time: 131 minutes

1964 *Charulata*
Production Company: R. D. Bansal
Director: Satyajit Ray
Script: Satyajit Ray, based on a novel by Rabindranath Tagore
Director of Photography: Subrata Mitra
Editor: Dulal Dutta
Art Director: Bansi Chandragupta
Music: Satyajit Ray
Cast: Madhabi Mukherjee (Charulata), Soumitra Chatterjee (Amal), Sailen Mukherjee (Bhupati)
Running Time: 117 minutes

1965 *Two* (short story)
Production Company: Esso
Director: Satyajit Ray
Script: Satyajit Ray
Music: Satyajit Ray
Running Time: 14 minutes

Kapurush-o-Mahapurush (*The Coward and the Holy Man*)
Production Company: R. D. Bansal
Director: Satyajit Ray
Script: Satyajit Ray, based on stories by Premendra Mitra ("Kapurush") and Parasuram ("Mahapurush")
Director of Photography: Soumendu Roy
Editor: Dulal Dutta
Art Director: Bansi Chandragupta
Music: Satyajit Ray
Cast: "Kapurush"–Soumitra Chatterjee (Amitabha); "Mahapurush"–Charuprakash Gosh (Birinchibaba)
Running Time: 140 minutes

1966 *Nayak* (*The Hero*)
Production Company: R. D. Bansal
Director: Satyajit Ray
Script: Satyajit Ray
Director of Photography: Subrata Mitra
Editor: Dulal Dutta
Art Director: Bansi Chandragupta
Music: Satyajit Ray
Cast: Uttam Kumar (Arindam), Sharmila Tagore (Aditi), Ranjit Sen (Haren Bose)
Running Time: 120 minutes

1967 *Chidiakhana* (*The Zoo*)
Production Company: Star Productions
Director: Satyajit Ray
Script: Satyajit Ray, based on the novel by Saradindu Bandopadkaya
Director of Photography: Soumendu Roy

Editor: Dulal Dutta
Art Director: Bansi Chandragupta
Music: Satyajit Ray
Cast: Uttam Kumar (Byom Kesh), Sailen Mukherjee (Byom Kesh's Assistant), Sushil Majumdar, Jahar Ganguly, Kanika Majumdar
Running Time: 120 minutes (approximately)

1968 *Goopy Gyne Bagha Byne* (*The Adventures of Goopy and Bagha*)
Production Company: Purnima Pictures
Director: Satyajit Ray
Script: Satyajit Ray, based on the story by Upendrakishore Ray Choudhury
Director of Photography (part in color): Soumendu Roy
Editor: Dulal Dutta
Art Director: Bansi Chandragupta
Music: Satyajit Ray; Goopy's songs sung by Anup Kumar Ghosal
Costumes: Satyajit Ray
Choreography: Shambhunath Bhattacherji
Cast: Tapan Chatterjee (Goopy), Robi Ghose (Bagha), Santosh Dutt (King of Halla, King of Shundi), Jahar Roy (Prime Minister of Halla), Harindranath Chatterjee (Magician Borfi)
Running Time: 132 minutes

1969 *Aranyer Din Ratri* (*Day and Nights in the Forest*)
Production Company: Priya Films
Director: Satyajit Ray
Script: Satyajit Ray, based on the novel by Sunil Ganguly
Director of Photography: Soumendu Roy
Editor: Dulal Dutta
Art Director: Bansi Chandragupta
Music: Satyajit Ray
Cast: Soumitra Chatterjee (Ashim), Subhendu Chatterjee (Sanjoy), Samit Bhanja (Harinath), Robi Ghose (Sekhar), Pahari Sanyal (Sadashiv Tripathy), Sharmila

Tagore (Aparna), Kaberi Bose (Jaya), Simi Garewal (Duli), Aparna Sen (Atasi)
Running Time: 115 minutes

1970 *Pratidwandi* (*The Adversary*)
Production Company: Priya Films
Director: Satyajit Ray
Script: Satyajit Ray, based on a story by Sunil Ganguly
Directors of Photography: Soumendu Roy, Purnedu Bose
Editor: Dulal Dutta
Art Director: Bansi Chandragupta
Music: Satyajit Ray
Cast: Dhritiman Chatterjee (Siddhartha Choudhury), Indira Devi (Sarojini) Debraj Roy (Tunu), Krishna Bose (Sutapa), Joyshree Roy (Keya)
Running Time: 110 minutes

1971 *Seemabadha* (*Company Limited*)
Production Company: Chitranjali (Calcutta)
Director: Satyajit Ray
Script: Satyajit Ray, from a story by Shankar
Director of Photography: Soumendu Roy
Editor: Dulal Dutta
Art Director: Ashoke Bose
Music: Satyajit Ray
Cast: Barun Chanda, Sharmila Tagore, Paromita Choudhury
Running Time: 112 minutes

Sikkim (documentary)
Producer: The Chogyal of Sikkim
Director: Satyajit Ray
Script: Satyajit Ray
Director of Photography (Eastmancolor): Soumendu Roy
Editor: Dulal Dutta
Music: Satyajit Ray
Running Time: 55 minutes

1973 *Ashani Sanket* (*Distant Thunder*)
Production Company: Mrs. Sarbani Bhattacharya
Director: Satyajit Ray
Script: Satyajit Ray, based on a novel by Bibhuti Bhushan Bannerjee
Director of Photography (Eastmancolor): Soumendu Roy
Editor: Dulal Dutta
Art Director: Ashoke Bose
Music: Satyajit Ray
Cast: Soumitra Chatterjee (Gangacharan), Babita (Ananga), Sandhya Roy (Chhutki), Gobinda Chakravarty (Dinabandhu), Ramesh Mukherjee (Biswas), Nony Ganguly (Jadu), Chitra Bannerjee (Moti)
Running Time: 100 minutes

The Inner Eye (short)
Director: Satyajit Ray
Script: Satyajit Ray
Director of Photography: Soumendu Roy
Editor: Dulal Dutta
Running Time: 10 minutes

MIKLÓS JANCSÓ

1954 *Ósz Badaczonyban* (*Autumn in Badacsony*) (documentary)
Éltető Tiszavis (*Life-Bringing Water*) (documentary)
Emberek, ne Engedjétek (*Don't Allow It!*) (documentary)
Egy Kiállitás Képei (*Pictures at an Exhibition*) (documentary)

1955 *Emlékezz, Ifjuság* (*Young People, Remember*) (documentary)

1956 *Móricz Zsigmond* (*Zsigmond Moricz*) (short)

1957 *A Város Peremén* (*In the Outskirts of the City*) (short)
Dél-Kina Tájain (*The Landscapes of Southern China*) (documentary)
Szinfoltok Kinából (*Colorful China*) (documentary)
Pekingi Paloták (*Palaces of Peking*) (documentary)

1958 *Derkovits* (*Derkovits*) (short)

A Harangok Rómába Mentek (*The Bells Have Gone to Rome*)
Director: Miklós Jancsó
Script: Lajos Szilvásy, Lajos Galambos
Director of Photography: Tamás Somló
Art Director: Ferenc Ruttka
Editor: Zoltán Farkas
Music: Iván Patachich
Cast: Miklós Gábor, Vilmos Mendelényi, Ferenc B. Deák, Sándor Pécsi, Gabi Magda, Ferenc Ladányi, István Holl, József Fonyó

1959 *Halhatatlanság* (*Immortality*) (short)

1960 *Három Csillag* (*Three Stars*)
First episode
(Other episodes directed by Zoltán Várkonyi, Károly Wiedermann)
Production Company: Budapest Filmstúdió
Director: Miklós Jancsó
Script: Lajos Galambos
Director of Photography: István Hildebrand
Art Director: Tivadar Bertalan
Editor: Zoltán Farkas
Music: Ferenc Farkas
Cast: Eva Ruttkai, Miklós Gábor, Lajos Básti, István Velenczei

1961 *Az Idó Kereke* (*The Wheels of Time*) (documentary)
Alkonyok és Hajnalok (*Dusks and Dawns*) (documentary)
Indian Történet (*Indian Story*) (short)

1963 *Oldás és Kötés* (*Cantata*)
Production Company: Budapest Filmstúdió
Director: Miklós Jancsó
Script: Miklós Jancsó, from József Lengyel's short story
Director of Photography: Tamás Somló
Art Director: Ferenc Ruttka
Editor: Zoltán Farkas
Music: Bálint Sárosi
Cast: Zoltán Latinovits, Miklós Szakáts, Andor Ajtay, Béla Barsi, Edit Domján, Gyula Bodrogi, Mária Medgyesi, István Avar
Running Time: 100 minutes

Hej, te Eleven Fa . . . (*Living Tree . . .*) (documentary)

1964 *Így Jöttem* (*My Way Home*)
Production Company: Mafilm IV
Director: Miklós Jancsó
Script: Gyula Hernádi, from Imre Vadász's short story
Director of Photography: Tamás Somló
Editor: Zoltán Farkas
Music: Zoltán Jeney
Cast: András Kozák, Sergey Nyikonyenko
Running Time: 109 minutes (originally); cut by Jancsó to 82 minutes

1965 *Szegénylegények* (*The Round-Up*)
Production Company: Mafilm IV
Director: Miklós Jancsó
Script: Gyula Hernádi
Director of Photography: Tamás Somló
Art Director: Tamás Banovich
Editor: Zoltán Farkas
Cast: János Görbe, Tibor Molnár, András Kozák, Gábor Agárdy, Zoltán Latinovits
Running Time: 94 minutes

1967 *Csillagosok, Katonák* (*The Red and the White*)
Production Company: Mafilm IV/Mosfilm
Director: Miklós Jancsó
Script: Georgij Mdivani, Gyula Hernádi, Miklós Jancsó
Director of Photography (Agascope) : Tomás Somló
Art Director: Boris Tchebotariov
Costumes: Maia Abar-Baranovskaia
Cast: Tatyana Konyukova (Yelizaveta), Krystyna Mikolaiewska (Olga), Mikhail Kozakov (Nestor), Viktor Avdiushko (Sailor), Bolot Beisenalyev (Tschingiz), Sergei Nyikonyenko (Cossack Officer), Anatoli Yabbarov (Tshelpanov), József Madaras (the Commander), Tibor Molnár (András), András Kozák (László), Jácint Juhász (István)
Running Time: 92 minutes

1968 *Csend és Kiáltás* (*Silence and Cry*)
Production Company: Mafilm IV
Director: Miklós Jancsó
Script: Gyula Hernádi, Miklós Jancsó
Director of Photography (Ultrascope): János Kende
Art Director: Tamás Banovich
Editor: Zoltán Farkas
Cast: András Kozák (István), Zoltán Latinovits (Kémeri), József Madaras (Farmer), Mari Törócsik (His Wife), Andrea Drahota (His Sister-in-Law)
Running Time: 79 minutes

1969 *Fényes Szelek* (*The Confrontation*)
Production Company: Mafilm I
Director: Miklós Jancsó
Script: Gyula Hernádi
Director of Photography (Agascope, Eastmancolor): Tamás Somló
Song, "March of the International Brigade," by Paul Anma (music) and Aladar Komjath (words)
Editor: Zoltán Farkas
Cast: Andrea Drahota (Judit), Kati Kovács (Terez),

Lajos Balázsovits (Laci), Benedek Tóth (Delegate of the Central Board), András Bálint (András), András Kozák (Police Officer)
Running Time: 86 minutes

Sirokkó (*Winter Wind*)
Production Company: Marquise Films/Mafilm I
Director: Miklós Jancsó
Script: Gyula Hernádi
Director of Photography (CinemaScope, Eastmancolor): János Kende
Art Director: Tamás Banovich
Editor: Zoltán Farkas
Cast: Marina Vlady (Maria), Jacques Charrier (Marko Lazar), Eva Swann (Ilona), József Madaras (Markovics), István Bujtor (Tarro), György Bánffy (Ante), Philippe March (Captain Kovács), András Kozák (Farkas)

1970 *Égi Bárány* (*Agnus Dei*)
Production Company: Mafilm I
Director: Miklós Jancsó
Script: Gyula Hernádi, Miklós Jancsó
Director of Photography (Eastmancolor): János Kende
Art Director: Tamás Banovich
Art Adviser: Yvette Biro
Editor: Zoltán Farkas
Cast: József Madaras (Father Varga), Mark Zala (Priest), Lajos Balázsovits (Canon), Anna Szeles (Maria), Jaroslava Schallerova (Magdalena), Daniel Olbrychski (Daniel), András Kozák, István Bujtor
Running Time: 91 minutes

La Pacifista (*The Pacifist*)
Production Company: Cinematografica Lombarda/O.C.F./Neue Emelka
Director: Miklós Jancsó
Script: Gyula Hernádi, Giovanna Gagliardo, Miklós Jancsó, from a story by Giovanna Gagliardo
Director of Photography (Technicolor): Carlo di Palma

Editor: Alberto Moro
Music: Giorgio Gaslini
Cast: Monica Vitti (Angela), Pierre Clementi (the Boy), Daniel Olbrychski, Peter Pasetti, Piero Faggioni, Gino Lavagetto, Sergio Tramonti
Running Time: 87 minutes

1971 *La Tècnica ed il Rito* (*The Technique and the Rite*)
Production Company: RAI
Executive Producer: Beppe Dell'Angelo
Script: Giovanna Gagliardo, Gyula Hernádi, Miklós Jancsó; scenario by Giovanna Gagliardo
Director of Photography (Eastmancolor) : János Kende
Costumes: Francesca Saitto
Editor: Giulano Mattioli
Music: Francesco di Masi
Cast: József Madaras (Attila), Adalberto Maria Merli (Massimo), Marco Guglielmi (Old Soldier), Piero Faggioni (Centurion), Luigi Montini (Hun Philosopher), Sergio Enria (Bleda), Anna Zinneman (Bleda's Wife)
Running Time: 80 minutes

1972 *Még Kér a Nép* (*Red Psalm*)
Production Company: Mafilm I
Director: Miklós Jancsó
Script: Gyula Hernádi
Director of Photography (Eastmancolor) : János Kende
Art Director: Tamás Banovich
Editor: Zoltán Farkas
Choreography: Ferenc Pesovár
Music: Ferenc Sebo
Cast: Andrea Drahota (Militant Girl), Lajos Balázsovits (Officer Cadet), András Bálint (Count), Gyöngyi Bürös (Young Peasant Woman), József Madaras, Tibor Molnár, Tibor Orbán, Bertalan Solti
Running Time: 88 minutes

1974 *Roma Rivuole Cesare* (*Rome Wants Another Caesar*)
Production Company: RAI/Films S.P.A.

Director: Miklós Jancsó
Script: Miklós Jancsó, Giovanna Gagliardo
Director of Photography (Eastmancolor): János Kende
Editor: Giulano Mattioli
Costumes: Uberta Bertacca
Music: Gianni Ferrio
Sound: Alberto Bartolomei
Cast: Daniel Olbrychski (Claudius), Hiram Keller (Octavius), Lino Troisi (Proconsul), Gino Lavagetto (First Republican), Luigi Montini (Second Republican), Guido Lollobrigida (Blue Tunic), José de Vega (Oxyntas), Renato Baldini (Old Senator)
Running Time: 100 minutes

DUŠAN MAKAVEJEV

1953 *Jatagan Mala* (short, unreleased)

1955 *Pečat* (*The Seal*) (short, unreleased)

1957 *Antonijevo Razbijeno Ogledalo* (*Anthony's Broken Mirror*) (short, unreleased)

1958 *Spomenicima Ne Treba Verovati* (*Don't Believe in Monuments*) (short)
Slikovnica Pčelara (*Beekeeper's Scrapbook*) (documentary)
Prokleti Praznik (*Damned Holiday*) (documentary)
Boje Sanjaju (*Colors Are Dreaming*) (documentary)

1959 *Što Je Radnički Savjet?* (*What Is a Workers' Council?*) (documentary)

1961 *Eci, Pec, Pec* (*One Potato, Two Potato . . .*) (documentary)
Pedagoška Bajka (*Educational Fairy Tale*) (documentary)
Osmjeh 61 (*Smile 61*) (documentary)

1962 *Parada* (*Parade*) (documentary)
Dole Plotovi (*Down with the Fences*) (documentary)
Ljepotica 62 (*Miss Yugoslavia 62*) (documentary)
Film o Knjizi A.B.C. (*Film about the Book*) (documentary)

1964 *Nova Igračka* (*New Toy*) (documentary)
Nova Domaća Životinja (*New Domestic Animal*) (documentary)

1966 *Čovek Nije Tica* (*Man Is Not a Bird*)
Production Company: Avala Film
Director: Dušan Makavejev
Script: Dušan Makavejev
Director of Photography: Aleksandar Petković
Art Director: Dragoljub Ivkov
Editor: Lujbica Nešić
Music: Petar Bergamo
Cast: Milena Dravić (Hairdresser), Janez Vrhovec (Engineer Rudinski), Eva Ras (Barbulovitch's Wife), Stojan Arandjelović (Barbulovitch), Boris Dvornik (Truck Driver), Roko (Hypnotist)
Running Time: 80 minutes

1967 *Ljubavni Slučaj, Tragedija Sluzbenice PTT* (*Switchboard Operator*) (*An Affair of the Heart*)
Production Company: Avala Film
Director: Dušan Makavejev
Script: Dušan Makavejev
Director of Photography: Aleksandar Petković
Art Director: Vladislav Lašić
Editor: Katarina Stojanović
Music: Dušan Aleksić
Cast: Eva Ras (Isabela), Ružica Sokić (Isabela's Friend), Slobodan Aligrudić (Ahmed), Miodrag Andrić (Mica), Dr. Aleksandar Kostić (Sexologist), Dr. Zivojin Aleksić (Criminologist)
Running Time: 69 minutes

1968 *Nevinost Bez Zaštite* (*Innocence Unprotected*)
"A new edition of a good old movie"
Production Company: Avala Film
Director: Dušan Makavejev
Script: Dušan Makavejev
Original film directed by Dragoljub Aleksić
Director of Photography (Eastmancolor): Branko Perak
Additional Photography: Stevan Mišković
Editor: Ivanka Vukasović
Music: Vojislav Kostić
Song: Vojislav Kostić, Aleksandar Popović
Cast: Dragoljub Aleksić (Himself), Ana Milosavljević (the Orphan), Vera Jovanović (the Wicked Stepmother), Bratoljub Gligorijevi (the Rich and Ugly Mr. Petrović), Ivan Zivković (the Acrobat's Brother), Pera Milosavljević (Servant)
Running Time: 78 minutes

1971 *WR: Misterije Organizma* (*WR: Mysteries of the Organism*)
Production Company: Neoplanta Film
Producer: Svetozar Udovički
Director: Dušan Makavejev
Script: Dušan Makavejev
Directors of Photography: Pega Popović, Aleksandar Petković
Art Director: Dragoljub Ivkov
Research: Gary Burstein
Editor: Ivanka Vukasović
Sound: Sarlo, Ludwig Probst, Dušan Aleksić
Music: Bojana Makavejev
Villon ballad written, composed, and performed by Bulat Okudzava
Cast: Milena Dravić (Milena), Jagoda Kaloper (Jagoda), Ivica Vidović (Vladimir Ilyich), Zoran Radmilović (Radmilović), Miodrag Andrić, Tuli Kupferberg, Jackie Curtis, the ghost of J. V. Stalin, Zivka Matić, Nikola Milić, Dragoljub Ivkov, Milan Jelić
Running Time: 86 minutes

1974 *Sweet Movie*
Production Company: V. M. Production/Mojack Films/Maran Films
Director: Dušan Makavejev
Script: Dušan Makavejev, Joël Santoni
Director of Photography (Eastmancolor): Pierre Lhomme
Editor: Yanne Dedet
Music: Manos Hadjidakis
Cast: Carole Laure (Miss Monde 1984), Pierre Clementi (*Potemkin* Sailor), Anna Prucnal (Anna Planeta), Sami Frey (El Macho), Jane Mallet (PDG), Otto Mühl Commune (Themselves), Marpessa Dawn (Mama Communa), John Vernon (Mr. Kapital), Roy Callender (Jeremian Muscle)
Running Time: 99 minutes

Bibliography

CLAUDE CHABROL

Scripts

La Femme Infidèle and "La Muette." Paris: *L'Avant-Scène du Cinéma,* No. 42, 1969.
Les Noces Rouges. Paris: Seghers, 1973.

Writings

Eric Rohmer and Claude Chabrol: *Hitchcock.* Paris: Editions Universitaires, Classiques du Cinéma, 1957.

Critical and Biographical

Robin Wood and Michael Walker: *Claude Chabrol.* London: Studio Vista, Movie Paperbacks; New York: Praeger, 1970.
Guy Brancourt: *Claude Chabrol.* Paris: Seghers-Cinéma d'Aujourd-hui, 1971.

PIER PAOLO PASOLINI

Scripts

Accattone. Rome: Edizioni FN, 1961.
La Commare Secca (with Bernardo Bertolucci). Milan: Zibetti, 1962.
Mamma Roma. Milan: Rizzoli, 1962.
Il Vangelo Secondo Matteo. Milan: Garzani, 1964.
Ali dagli Occhi Azzurri. Milan: Garzani, 1965. (Includes *Accattone,* "La Ricotta," *La Notte Brava.*)
Uccellacci e Uccellini. Milan: Garzani, 1966.
Il Padre Selvaggio. In *Cinema e Film,* Nos. 3 and 4, 1967.
Edipo Re. Milan: Garzani, 1967.

Ostia (with Sergio Citti). Milan: Garzani, 1970.
Medea. Milan: Garzani, 1970.
Oedipus Rex (in English). London: Lorrimer, 1971.

Critical and Biographical

Jean Duflor: *Entretiens avec Pier Paolo Pasolini*. Paris: Pierre Belfond, 1970.
Marc Gervais: *Pier Paolo Pasolini*. Paris: Seghers-Cinéma d'Aujourd'hui, 1973.
Oswald Stack: *Pasolini*. London: Thames and Hudson; Bloomington: Indiana University Press, 1969.

LINDSAY ANDERSON

Scripts

If . . . (with David Sherwin). London: Lorrimer, 1969.
O Lucky Man! (with David Sherwin). London: Lorrimer, 1973.

Critical and Biographical

Elizabeth Sussex: *Lindsay Anderson*. London: Studio Vista, Movie Paperbacks; New York: Praeger, 1969.

STANLEY KUBRICK

Scripts

A Clockwork Orange. New York: Ballantine Books, 1972.

Critical and Biographical

Jerome Agel (ed.): *The Making of Kubrick's 2001*. New York: Signet Books, 1970.
Arthur C. Clarke: *The Lost Worlds of 2001*. New York: New American Library, 1972.

Carolyn Geduld: *Filmguide to 2001: A Space Odyssey.* Bloomington and London: Indiana University Press, 1973.

Norman Kagan: *The Cinema of Stanley Kubrick.* New York: Holt, Rinehart and Winston, 1972.

Alexander Walker: *Stanley Kubrick Directs.* New York: Harcourt Brace Jovanovich, 1971; London: Davis-Poynter, 1972.

ANDY WARHOL / PAUL MORRISSEY

Scripts

Harlot. In Ronald Tavel: "The Banana Diary," *Film Culture,* No. 40, 1966.

Blue Movie. New York: Grove Press, 1970.

Critical and Biographical

Adriano Apra and Enzo Ungari: *Il Cinema di Andy Warhol.* Rome: Arcana Editrice, 1972.

Andreas Brown: *Andy Warhol: His Early Works, 1947–1959.* New York: Gotham Book Mart, 1971.

John Coplans: *Andy Warhol.* New York: New York Graphic Society, 1970.

Rainer Crone: *Andy Warhol.* New York: Praeger, 1970.

Peter Gidal: *Andy Warhol: Films and Paintings.* London: Studio Vista; New York: Dutton, 1971.

Enno Patalas: *Andy Warhol und Sein Filme.* Munich: Wilhelm Heyne Verlag, 1971.

John Wilcock: *The Autobiography and Sex Life of Andy Warhol.* New York: Other Scenes, 1970.

SATYAJIT RAY

Scripts

Nayak. In *Montage,* below.

Critical and Biographical

Montage. Special Satyajit Ray Issue, Bombay, July 1966.
Marie Seton: *Satyajit Ray*. London: Dennis Dobson, 1971.
Robin Wood: *The Apu Trilogy*. London: Studio Vista, Movie Paperbacks; New York: Praeger, 1972.

DUŠAN MAKAVEJEV

Scripts

Nevinost Bez Zaśtite (*Innocence Unprotected*). Zagreb: Avala Films, 1968.
WR: Mysteries of the Organism. New York: Bard Books, 1972.

Critical and Biographical

Robin Wood: "Dušan Makavejev." In *Second Wave*. London: Studio Vista, Movie Paperbacks; New York: Praeger, 1970.

GENERAL

In addition to the monographs listed above there are, of course, a number of more general books that provide background, either as critical/historical studies of national schools or groups or by recording, through interviews, the comments of the film-makers themselves.

Jacques Belmans: *Jeune Cinéma Anglais*. Paris: Premier Plan, 1967.
Background on Anderson, Free Cinema, etc., from an unusual standpoint.
Joseph Gelmis: *The Film Director as Superstar*. New York: Doubleday, 1970.
Contains interviews with Andy Warhol, Lindsay Anderson, and Stanley Kubrick.

Claude B. Levenson: *Jeune Cinéma Hongrois.* Paris: Premier Plan, 1966.

Background on Jancsó.

G. Roy Levin: *Documentary Explorations.* New York: Doubleday, 1971.

Includes an interview with Lindsay Anderson.

Jonas Mekas: *Movie Journal: The Rise of the New American Cinema, 1959–1971.* New York: Macmillan, 1972.

Idiosyncratic diary of American underground happenings.

Sheldon Renan. *An Introduction to the American Underground Film.* New York: Dutton, 1967.

Background on Warhol and associates.